Casenote® Legal Briefs

WILLS, TRUSTS AND ESTATES

Keyed to Courses Using

Dukeminier and Sitkoff
Wills, Trusts, and Estates

Ninth Edition

Wolters Kluwer

Law & Business

Copyright © 2014 CCH Incorporated. All Rights Reserved.

Published by Wolters Kluwer Law & Business in New York.

Wolters Kluwer Law & Business serves customers worldwide with CCH, Aspen Publishers, and Kluwer Law International products. (www.wolterskluwerlb.com)

No part of this publication may be reproduced or transmitted in any form or by any means, electronic or mechanical, including photocopy, recording, or utilized by any information storage and retrieval system, without written permission from the publisher. For information about permissions or to request permission online, visit us at wolterskluwerlb.com or a written request may be faxed to our permissions department at 212-771-0803.

To contact Customer Service, e-mail customer.service@wolterskluwer.com, call 1-800-234-1660, fax 1-800-901-9075, or mail correspondence to:

Wolters Kluwer Law & Business
Attn: Order Department
P.O. Box 990
Frederick, MD 21705

Printed in the United States of America.

1 2 3 4 5 6 7 8 9 0

ISBN 978-1-4548-1988-2

About Wolters Kluwer Law & Business

Wolters Kluwer Law & Business is a leading global provider of intelligent information and digital solutions for legal and business professionals in key specialty areas, and respected educational resources for professors and law students. Wolters Kluwer Law & Business connects legal and business professionals as well as those in the education market with timely, specialized authoritative content and information-enabled solutions to support success through productivity, accuracy and mobility.

Serving customers worldwide, Wolters Kluwer Law & Business products include those under the Aspen Publishers, CCH, Kluwer Law International, Loislaw, ftwilliam.com and MediRegs family of products.

CCH products have been a trusted resource since 1913, and are highly regarded resources for legal, securities, antitrust and trade regulation, government contracting, banking, pension, payroll, employment and labor, and healthcare reimbursement and compliance professionals.

Aspen Publishers products provide essential information to attorneys, business professionals and law students. Written by preeminent authorities, the product line offers analytical and practical information in a range of specialty practice areas from securities law and intellectual property to mergers and acquisitions and pension/benefits. Aspen's trusted legal education resources provide professors and students with high-quality, up-to-date and effective resources for successful instruction and study in all areas of the law.

Kluwer Law International products provide the global business community with reliable international legal information in English. Legal practitioners, corporate counsel and business executives around the world rely on Kluwer Law journals, looseleafs, books, and electronic products for comprehensive information in many areas of international legal practice.

Loislaw is a comprehensive online legal research product providing legal content to law firm practitioners of various specializations. Loislaw provides attorneys with the ability to quickly and efficiently find the necessary legal information they need, when and where they need it, by facilitating access to primary law as well as state-specific law, records, forms and treatises.

ftwilliam.com offers employee benefits professionals the highest quality plan documents (retirement, welfare and non-qualified) and government forms (5500/PBGC, 1099 and IRS) software at highly competitive prices.

MediRegs products provide integrated health care compliance content and software solutions for professionals in healthcare, higher education and life sciences, including professionals in accounting, law and consulting.

Wolters Kluwer Law & Business, a division of Wolters Kluwer, is headquartered in New York. Wolters Kluwer is a market-leading global information services company focused on professionals.

Format for the Casenote® Legal Brief

Nature of Case: This section identifies the form of action (e.g., breach of contract, negligence, battery), the type of proceeding (e.g., demurrer, appeal from trial court's jury instructions), or the relief sought (e.g., damages, injunction, criminal sanctions).

Fact Summary: This is included to refresh your memory and can be used as a quick reminder of the facts.

Rule of Law: Summarizes the general principle of law that the case illustrates. It may be used for instant recall of the court's holding and for classroom discussion or home review.

Facts: This section contains all relevant facts of the case, including the contentions of the parties and the lower court holdings. It is written in a logical order to give the student a clear understanding of the case. The plaintiff and defendant are identified by their proper names throughout and are always labeled with a (P) or (D).

Palsgraf v. Long Island R.R. Co.

Injured bystander (P) v. Railroad company (D)

N.Y. Ct. App., 248 N.Y. 339, 162 N.E. 99 (1928).

Party ID: Quick identification of the relationship between the parties.

NATURE OF CASE: Appeal from judgment affirming verdict for plaintiff seeking damages for personal injury.

FACT SUMMARY: Helen Palsgraf (P) was injured on R.R.'s (D) train platform when R.R.'s (D) guard helped a passenger aboard a moving train, causing his package to fall on the tracks. The package contained fireworks which exploded, creating a shock that tipped a scale onto Palsgraf (P).

🏛 RULE OF LAW
The risk reasonably to be perceived defines the duty to be obeyed.

FACTS: Helen Palsgraf (P) purchased a ticket to Rockaway Beach from R.R. (D) and was waiting on the train platform. As she waited, two men ran to catch a train that was pulling out from the platform. The first man jumped aboard, but the second man, who appeared as if he might fall, was helped aboard by the guard on the train who had kept the door open so they could jump aboard. A guard on the platform also helped by pushing him onto the train. The man was carrying a package wrapped in newspaper. In the process, the man dropped his package, which fell on the tracks. The package contained fireworks and exploded. The shock of the explosion was apparently of great enough strength to tip over some scales at the other end of the platform, which fell on Palsgraf (P) and injured her. A jury awarded her damages, and R.R. (D) appealed.

ISSUE: Does the risk reasonably to be perceived define the duty to be obeyed?

HOLDING AND DECISION: (Cardozo, C.J.) Yes. The risk reasonably to be perceived defines the duty to be obeyed. If there is no foreseeable hazard to the injured party as the result of a seemingly innocent act, the act does not become a tort because it happened to be a wrong as to and her. If the wrong was not willful, the plaintiff must show that the act as to her had such great and apparent possibilities of danger as to entitle her to protection. Negligence in the abstract is not enough upon which to base liability. Negligence is a relative concept, evolving out of the common law doctrine of trespass on the case. To establish liability, the defendant must owe a legal duty of reasonable care to the injured party. A cause of action in tort will lie where harm,

though unintended, could have been averted or avoided by observance of such a duty. The scope of the duty is limited by the range of danger that a reasonable person could foresee. In this case, there was nothing to suggest from the appearance of the parcel or otherwise that the parcel contained fireworks. The guard could not reasonably have had any warning of a threat to Palsgraf (P), and R.R. (D) therefore cannot be held liable. Judgment is reversed in favor of R.R. (D).

DISSENT: (Andrews, J.) The concept that there is no negligence unless R.R. (D) owes a legal duty to take care as to Palsgraf (P) herself is too narrow. Everyone owes to the world at large the duty of refraining from those acts that may unreasonably threaten the safety of others. If the guard's action was negligent as to those nearby, it was also negligent as to those outside what might be termed the "danger zone." For Palsgraf (P) to recover, R.R.'s (D) negligence must have been the proximate cause of her injury, a question of fact for the jury.

▶ ANALYSIS
The majority defined the limit of the defendant's liability in terms of the danger that a reasonable person in defendant's situation would have perceived. The dissent argued that the limitation should not be placed on liability, but rather on damages. Judge Andrews suggested that only injuries that would not have happened but for R.R.'s (D) negligence should be compensable. Both the majority and dissent recognized the policy-driven need to limit liability for negligent acts, seeking, in the words of Judge Andrews, to define a framework "that will be practical and in keeping with the general understanding of mankind." The Restatement (Second) of Torts has accepted Judge Cardozo's view.

Quicknotes

FORESEEABILITY A reasonable expectation that change is the probable result of certain acts or omissions.

NEGLIGENCE Conduct falling below the standard of care that a reasonable person would demonstrate under similar conditions.

PROXIMATE CAUSE The natural sequence of events without which an injury would not have been sustained.

Concurrence/Dissent: All concurrences and dissents are briefed whenever they are included by the casebook editor.

Analysis: This last paragraph gives you a broad understanding of where the case "fits in" with other cases in the section of the book and with the entire course. It is a hornbook-style discussion indicating whether the case is a majority or minority opinion and comparing the principal case with other cases in the casebook. It may also provide analysis from restatements, uniform codes, and law review articles. The analysis will prove to be invaluable to classroom discussion.

Issue: The issue is a concise question that brings out the essence of the opinion as it relates to the section of the casebook in which the case appears. Both substantive and procedural issues are included if relevant to the decision.

Holding and Decision: This section offers a clear and in-depth discussion of the rule of the case and the court's rationale. It is written in easy-to-understand language and answers the issue presented by applying the law to the facts of the case. When relevant, it includes a thorough discussion of the exceptions to the case as listed by the court, any major cites to the other cases on point, and the names of the judges who wrote the decisions.

Quicknotes: Conveniently defines legal terms found in the case and summarizes the nature of any statutes, codes, or rules referred to in the text.

Wolters Kluwer Law & Business is proud to offer *Casenote*® *Legal Briefs*—continuing thirty years of publishing America's best-selling legal briefs.

Casenote® *Legal Briefs* are designed to help you save time when briefing assigned cases. Organized under convenient headings, they show you how to abstract the basic facts and holdings from the text of the actual opinions handed down by the courts. Used as part of a rigorous study regimen, they can help you spend more time analyzing and critiquing points of law than on copying bits and pieces of judicial opinions into your notebook or outline.

Casenote® *Legal Briefs* should never be used as a substitute for assigned casebook readings. They work best when read as a follow-up to reviewing the underlying opinions themselves. Students who try to avoid reading and digesting the judicial opinions in their casebooks or online sources will end up shortchanging themselves in the long run. The ability to absorb, critique, and restate the dynamic and complex elements of case law decisions is crucial to your success in law school and beyond. It cannot be developed vicariously.

Casenote® *Legal Briefs* represents but one of the many offerings in Legal Education's Study Aid Timeline, which includes:

- *Casenote*® *Legal Briefs*
- *Emanuel*® *Law Outlines*
- Emanuel® *Law in a Flash* Flash Cards
- Emanuel® *CrunchTime*® Series
- *Siegel's Essay and Multiple-Choice Questions and Answers Series*

Each of these series is designed to provide you with easy-to-understand explanations of complex points of law. Each volume offers guidance on the principles of legal analysis and, consulted regularly, will hone your ability to spot relevant issues. We have titles that will help you prepare for class, prepare for your exams, and enhance your general comprehension of the law along the way.

To find out more about Wolters Kluwer Law & Business' study aid publications, visit us online at *www.wolterskluwerlb.com* or email us at *legaledu@wolterskluwer.com*. We'll be happy to assist you.

A. Decide on a Format and Stick to It

Structure is essential to a good brief. It enables you to arrange systematically the related parts that are scattered throughout most cases, thus making manageable and understandable what might otherwise seem to be an endless and unfathomable sea of information. There are, of course, an unlimited number of formats that can be utilized. However, it is best to find one that suits your needs and stick to it. Consistency breeds both efficiency and the security that when called upon you will know where to look in your brief for the information you are asked to give.

Any format, as long as it presents the essential elements of a case in an organized fashion, can be used. Experience, however, has led *Casenote® Legal Briefs* to develop and utilize the following format because of its logical flow and universal applicability.

NATURE OF CASE: This is a brief statement of the legal character and procedural status of the case (e.g., "Appeal of a burglary conviction").

There are many different alternatives open to a litigant dissatisfied with a court ruling. The key to determining which one has been used is to discover *who is asking this court for what.*

This first entry in the brief should be kept as *short as possible.* Use the court's terminology if you understand it. But since jurisdictions vary as to the titles of pleadings, the best entry is the one that addresses who wants what in this proceeding, not the one that sounds most like the court's language.

RULE OF LAW: A statement of the general principle of law that the case illustrates (e.g., "An acceptance that varies any term of the offer is considered a rejection and counteroffer").

Determining the rule of law of a case is a procedure similar to determining the issue of the case. Avoid being fooled by red herrings; there may be a few rules of law mentioned in the case excerpt, but usually only one is *the* rule with which the casebook editor is concerned. The techniques used to locate the issue, described below, may also be utilized to find the rule of law. Generally, your best guide is simply the chapter heading. It is a clue to the point the casebook editor seeks to make and should be kept in mind when reading every case in the respective section.

FACTS: A synopsis of only the essential facts of the case, i.e., those bearing upon or leading up to the issue.

The facts entry should be a short statement of the events and transactions that led one party to initiate legal proceedings against another in the first place. While some cases conveniently state the salient facts at the beginning of the decision, in other instances they will have to be culled from hiding places throughout the text, even from concurring and dissenting opinions. Some of the "facts" will often be in dispute and should be so noted. Conflicting evidence may be briefly pointed up. "Hard" facts must be included. Both must be *relevant* in order to be listed in the facts entry. It is impossible to tell what is relevant until the entire case is read, as the ultimate determination of the rights and liabilities of the parties may turn on something buried deep in the opinion.

Generally, the facts entry should not be longer than three to five *short* sentences.

It is often helpful to identify the role played by a party in a given context. For example, in a construction contract case the identification of a party as the "contractor" or "builder" alleviates the need to tell that that party was the one who was supposed to have built the house.

It is always helpful, and a good general practice, to identify the "plaintiff" and the "defendant." This may seem elementary and uncomplicated, but, especially in view of the creative editing practiced by some casebook editors, it is sometimes a difficult or even impossible task. Bear in mind that the *party presently* seeking something from this court may not be the plaintiff, and that sometimes only the cross-claim of a defendant is treated in the excerpt. Confusing or misaligning the parties can ruin your analysis and understanding of the case.

ISSUE: A statement of the general legal question answered by or illustrated in the case. For clarity, the issue is best put in the form of a question capable of a "yes" or "no" answer. In reality, the issue is simply the Rule of Law put in the form of a question (e.g., "May an offer be accepted by performance?").

The major problem presented in discerning what is *the* issue in the case is that an opinion usually purports to raise and answer several questions. However, except for rare cases, only one such question is really the issue in the case. Collateral issues not necessary to the resolution of the matter in controversy are handled by the court by language known as *"obiter dictum"* or merely *"dictum."* While dicta may be included later in the brief, they have no place under the issue heading.

To find the issue, ask *who wants what* and then go on to ask *why did that party succeed or fail in getting it.* Once this is determined, the "why" should be turned into a question.

The complexity of the issues in the cases will vary, but in all cases a single-sentence question should sum up the issue. *In a few cases,* there will be two, or even more rarely, three issues of equal importance to the resolution of the case. Each should be expressed in a single-sentence question.

Since many issues are resolved by a court in coming to a final disposition of a case, the casebook editor will reproduce the portion of the opinion containing the issue or issues most relevant to the area of law under scrutiny. A noted law professor gave this advice: "Close the book; look at the title on the cover." Chances are, if it is Property, you need not concern yourself with whether, for example, the federal government's treatment of the plaintiff's land really raises a federal question sufficient to support jurisdiction on this ground in federal court.

The same rule applies to chapter headings designating sub-areas within the subjects. They tip you off as to what the text is designed to teach. The cases are arranged in a casebook to show a progression or development of the law, so that the preceding cases may also help.

It is also most important to remember to *read the notes and questions* at the end of a case to determine what the editors wanted you to have gleaned from it.

HOLDING AND DECISION: This section should succinctly explain the rationale of the court in arriving at its decision. In capsulizing the "reasoning" of the court, it should always include an application of the general rule or rules of law to the specific facts of the case. Hidden justifications come to light in this entry: the reasons for the state of the law, the public policies, the biases and prejudices, those considerations that influence the justices' thinking and, ultimately, the outcome of the case. At the end, there should be a short indication of the disposition or procedural resolution of the case (e.g., "Decision of the trial court for Mr. Smith (P) reversed").

The foregoing format is designed to help you "digest" the reams of case material with which you will be faced in your law school career. Once mastered by practice, it will place at your fingertips the information the authors of your casebooks have sought to impart to you in case-by-case illustration and analysis.

B. Be as Economical as Possible in Briefing Cases

Once armed with a format that encourages succinctness, it is as important to be economical with regard to the time spent on the actual reading of the case as it is to be economical in the writing of the brief itself. This does not mean "skimming" a case. Rather, it means reading the case with an "eye" trained to recognize into which "section" of your brief a particular passage or line fits and having a system for quickly and precisely marking the case so that the passages fitting any one particular part of

the brief can be easily identified and brought together in a concise and accurate manner when the brief is actually written.

It is of no use to simply repeat everything in the opinion of the court; record only enough information to trigger your recollection of what the court said. Nevertheless, an accurate statement of the "law of the case," i.e., the legal principle applied to the facts, is absolutely essential to class preparation and to learning the law under the case method.

To that end, it is important to develop a "shorthand" that you can use to make marginal notations. These notations will tell you at a glance in which section of the brief you will be placing that particular passage or portion of the opinion.

Some students prefer to underline all the salient portions of the opinion (with a pencil or colored underliner marker), making marginal notations as they go along. Others prefer the color-coded method of underlining, utilizing different colors of markers to underline the salient portions of the case, each separate color being used to represent a different section of the brief. For example, blue underlining could be used for passages relating to the rule of law, yellow for those relating to the issue, and green for those relating to the holding and decision, etc. While it has its advocates, the color-coded method can be confusing and time-consuming (all that time spent on changing colored markers). Furthermore, it can interfere with the continuity and concentration many students deem essential to the reading of a case for maximum comprehension. In the end, however, it is a matter of personal preference and style. Just remember, whatever method you use, underlining must be used sparingly or its value is lost.

If you take the marginal notation route, an efficient and easy method is to go along underlining the key portions of the case and placing in the margin alongside them the following "markers" to indicate where a particular passage or line "belongs" in the brief you will write:

N   (NATURE OF CASE)
RL   (RULE OF LAW)
I   (ISSUE)
HL   (HOLDING AND DECISION, relates to
           the RULE OF LAW behind the decision)
HR   (HOLDING AND DECISION, gives the
           RATIONALE or reasoning behind the
           decision)
HA   (HOLDING AND DECISION, applies the
           general principle(s) of law to the facts of
           the case to arrive at the decision)

Remember that a particular passage may well contain information necessary to more than one part of your brief, in which case you simply note that in the margin. If you are using the color-coded underlining method instead of marginal notation, simply make asterisks or checks in the margin next to the passage in question in the colors that indicate the additional sections of the brief where it might be utilized.

The economy of utilizing "shorthand" in marking cases for briefing can be maintained in the actual brief writing process itself by utilizing "law student shorthand" within the brief. There are many commonly used words and phrases for which abbreviations can be substituted in your briefs (and in your class notes also). You can develop abbreviations that are personal to you and which will save you a lot of time. A reference list of briefing abbreviations can be found on page x of this book.

C. Use Both the Briefing Process and the Brief as a Learning Tool

Now that you have a format and the tools for briefing cases efficiently, the most important thing is to make the time spent in briefing profitable to you and to make the most advantageous use of the briefs you create. Of course, the briefs are invaluable for classroom reference when you are called upon to explain or analyze a particular case. However, they are also useful in reviewing for exams. A quick glance at the fact summary should bring the case to mind, and a rereading of the rule of law should enable you to go over the underlying legal concept in your mind, how it was applied in that particular case, and how it might apply in other factual settings.

As to the value to be derived from engaging in the briefing process itself, there is an immediate benefit that arises from being forced to sift through the essential facts and reasoning from the court's opinion and to succinctly express them in your own words in your brief. The process ensures that you understand the case and the point that it illustrates, and that means you will be ready to absorb further analysis and information brought forth in class. It also ensures you will have something to say when called upon in class. The briefing process helps develop a mental agility for getting to the *gist* of a case and for identifying, expounding on, and applying the legal concepts and issues found there. The briefing process is the mental process on which you must rely in taking law school examinations; it is also the mental process upon which a lawyer relies in serving his clients and in making his living.

Abbreviations for Briefs

acceptance	acp	offer	O
affirmed	aff	offeree	OE
answer	ans	offeror	OR
assumption of risk	a/r	ordinance	ord
attorney	atty	pain and suffering	p/s
beyond a reasonable doubt	b/r/d	parol evidence	p/e
bona fide purchaser	BFP	plaintiff	P
breach of contract	br/k	prima facie	p/f
cause of action	c/a	probable cause	p/c
common law	c/l	proximate cause	px/c
Constitution	Con	real property	r/p
constitutional	con	reasonable doubt	r/d
contract	K	reasonable man	r/m
contributory negligence	c/n	rebuttable presumption	rb/p
cross	x	remanded	rem
cross-complaint	x/c	res ipsa loquitur	RIL
cross-examination	x/ex	respondeat superior	r/s
cruel and unusual punishment	c/u/p	Restatement	RS
defendant	D	reversed	rev
dismissed	dis	Rule Against Perpetuities	RAP
double jeopardy	d/j	search and seizure	s/s
due process	d/p	search warrant	s/w
equal protection	e/p	self-defense	s/d
equity	eq	specific performance	s/p
evidence	ev	statute	S
exclude	exc	statute of frauds	S/F
exclusionary rule	exc/r	statute of limitations	S/L
felony	f/n	summary judgment	s/j
freedom of speech	f/s	tenancy at will	t/w
good faith	g/f	tenancy in common	t/c
habeas corpus	h/c	tenant	t
hearsay	hr	third party	TP
husband	H	third party beneficiary	TPB
injunction	inj	transferred intent	TI
in loco parentis	ILP	unconscionable	uncon
inter vivos	I/v	unconstitutional	unconst
joint tenancy	j/t	undue influence	u/e
judgment	judgt	Uniform Commercial Code	UCC
jurisdiction	jur	unilateral	uni
last clear chance	LCC	vendee	VE
long-arm statute	LAS	vendor	VR
majority view	maj	versus	v
meeting of minds	MOM	void for vagueness	VFV
minority view	min	weight of authority	w/a
Miranda rule	Mir/r	weight of the evidence	w/e
Miranda warnings	Mir/w	wife	W
negligence	neg	with	w/
notice	ntc	within	w/i
nuisance	nus	without	w/o
obligation	ob	without prejudice	w/o/p
obscene	obs	wrongful death	wr/d

Table of Cases

CHAPTER 1

Introduction: Freedom of Disposition

Quick Reference Rules of Law

Shapira v. Union National Bank

Beneficiary (P) v. Bank (D)

Ohio Com. Pl. Ct., 39 Ohio Misc. 28, 315 N.E.2d 825 (1974).

NATURE OF CASE: Declaratory judgment action.

FACT SUMMARY: Daniel's (P) interest under his father's will was conditioned on the requirement that he marry a Jew whose parents were both Jewish within seven years of his father's death.

🏛 RULE OF LAW
A testator may validly impose a restraint on the religion of the spouse of a beneficiary as a condition precedent to inheriting under the will.

FACTS: Under Shapira's will, his son Daniel (P) could inherit only if, at the time of Shapira's death or within seven years thereafter, he was married to a Jewish woman whose parents were both Jewish. Daniel (P) sought a declaration that the will was unconstitutional since it restricted his right to marry or that such a clause violated public policy.

ISSUE: May a testator attempt to restrict the right of a beneficiary to marry within a certain religion?

HOLDING AND DECISION: (Henderson, J.) Yes. The right to receive property by will is a matter of statutory law. A testator may either disinherit his children or condition their taking in any manner without offending the Constitution. While the right to marry is a constitutionally protected right, there is no state action present herein which would trigger the Due Process or Equal Protection Clause. The courts are not being asked to enforce covenants. The only official action involves the probate of the will, and this is, in itself, insufficient to be deemed state action. Therefore, a testator may restrict a beneficiary's right to marriage without offending the Constitution. Public policy does not prohibit a limited restriction on the right to marriage restricted to members of one religion. A partial restraint of marriage which imposes only reasonable restrictions is not void as violative of public policy. Gifts conditioned on marrying within a certain religious grouping are deemed reasonable restrictions in a majority of jurisdictions. We find that it is not violative of public policy to condition a bequest on the marriage to one of a particular religion. The clause is valid, and Daniel (P) is bound by its terms.

▶ ANALYSIS

A condition requiring the beneficiary not to marry a member of a specific religion is also deemed valid. *In re Clayton's Estate*, 13 Pa. D. & C. 413 (Pa. Orphan's Ct. 1930). Where the restriction based on religion unreasonably limits the beneficiary's right to marriage, it will be deemed void, e.g., *Maddox v. Maddox*, 52 Va. (11 Grattan's) 804 (1854), where there were only four or five unmarried members of the particular sect.

■■■■

Quicknotes

BENEFICIARY A third party who is the recipient of the benefit of a transaction undertaken by another.

DUE PROCESS The constitutional mandate requiring the courts to protect and enforce individuals' rights and liberties, consistent with prevailing principals of fairness and justice and prohibiting the federal and state governments from such activities that deprive its citizens of a life, liberty, or property interest.

EQUAL PROTECTION A constitutional guarantee that no person shall be denied the same protection of the laws enjoyed by other persons in life circumstances.

TESTATOR One who executes a will.

■■■■

Hodel v. Irving

Secretary of the Interior (D) v. Sioux Indian (P)

481 U.S. 704 (1987).

NATURE OF CASE: Appeal from judgment finding a statute unconstitutional as a taking without just compensation.

FACT SUMMARY: Congress enacted the Indian Land Consolidation Act, which contained a provision that certain fractional interests owned by tribe members would escheat to the tribe.

🏛 RULE OF LAW
The complete abolition of the rights of an owner to dispose of property rights is a taking without just compensation, violating the owner's rights guaranteed under the Fifth Amendment.

FACTS: The Indian Land Acts enacted at the end of the nineteenth century provided that each Sioux Indian was allotted reservation land which was held in trust by the United States. Eventually the lands were splintered into multiple undivided interests, with some parcels having hundreds of fractional owners. In 1983, Congress passed the Indian Land Consolidation Act. Section 207 of the Act provided that certain fractional interests could not be transferred by intestacy or devise but would escheat to the tribe. No provision was made for the payment of compensation to the owners of the escheated fractional interests. Irving (P), a member of the Sioux tribe and a prospective recipient of one of the fractional interests affected by the statute, filed suit, claiming that § 207 was a taking without just compensation in violation of the Fifth Amendment. The district court found that the statute was constitutional. The court of appeals reversed and declared the statute unconstitutional. Hodel (D), the Secretary of the Interior, appealed.

ISSUE: Is the complete abolition of the rights of an owner to dispose of property rights a taking without just compensation, violating rights guaranteed under the Fifth Amendment?

HOLDING AND DECISION: (O'Connor, J.) Yes. Section 207 amounts to a virtual abrogation of the right to pass a certain type of property—the small undivided interest—to one's heirs. A right to pass property to one's family has been part of the Anglo-Saxon legal system since feudal times. The escheatable interests are not necessarily de minimis. Even though the fractional owners have the right to make inter vivos transfers of the interests, such a retained right does not obviate the total abrogation of the owner's rights to devise the property. Affirmed.

▶ ANALYSIS

In an analogous case, the Supreme Court upheld the constitutionality of a provision of the Bald Eagle Protection Act, which prohibits the right to sell or trade artifacts made from eagle feathers and eagle parts. *Andrus v. Allard*, 444 U.S. 31 (1979). The Court held that "where an owner possesses a full 'bundle' of property rights, the destruction of one 'strand' of the bundle is not a taking, because the aggregate must be viewed in its entirety." The Court pointed out that the artifact owners could still donate or devise the artifacts.

Quicknotes

INTER VIVOS TRANSFER A transfer of property that is effectuated between living persons.

JUST COMPENSATION The right guaranteed by the Fifth Amendment to the United States Constitution of a person, when his property is taken for public use by the state, to receive adequate compensation in order to restore him to the position he enjoyed prior to the appropriation.

TAKING A governmental action that substantially deprives an owner of the use and enjoyment of his or her property, requiring compensation.

Shaw Family Archives Ltd. v. CMG Worldwide, Inc.

Intellectual property owner (D) v. Decedent's successor-in-interest (P)

486 F. Supp. 2d 309 (S.D.N.Y. 2007).

NATURE OF THE CASE: Cross-motions for summary judgment in suit alleging violation of right of publicity.

FACT SUMMARY: Shaw Family Archives, LLC (SFA) (D), a limited liability company that owned photographs taken by professional photographer Sam Shaw, sold T-Shirts bearing Marilyn Monroe's image and also allowed customers to purchase licenses for the use of pictures and images of Monroe that Shaw created. CMG Worldwide, Inc. (CMG) (P), one of the successor-in-interests to Monroe's estate, filed suit against SFA (D), alleging that SFA's (D) use of Monroe's likeness violated Indiana's Right of Publicity Act.

RULE OF LAW
A postmortem right of publicity does not pass through the residuary clause in a decedent's will when the decedent did not have a statutory right of publicity at the time of her death.

FACTS: Marilyn Monroe died in 1962, leaving the remainder of her estate to Lee Strasberg and naming her attorney Frosch as her executor. Strasberg died in 1982 and left his estate to his wife, Anna. When Frosch died in 1989, Anna was appointed Administratrix of the Monroe Estate, which remained open until 2001. When the estate was closed, the residuary assets were transferred to Marilyn Monroe, LLC (MMLLC) (P). In 2006, MMLLC (P) and CMG (P) discovered that SFA (D), the company that owned the photographs taken by the famous photographer Sam Shaw, was selling T-Shirts bearing Monroe's likeness, and was also issuing licenses for others to reproduce Monroe's image from photographs that Shaw had taken. MMLLC (P) sued SFA (D) under Indiana's Right of Publicity Act, alleging that, as the successor-in-interest to Monroe's estate, it could prevent SFA (D) from selling Monroe's image because Monroe's right of publicity passed to MMLLC (P) through the residuary clause of Monroe's will. Both parties filed motions for summary judgment.

ISSUE: Does a postmortem right of publicity pass through the residuary clause in a decedent's will when the decedent did not have a statutory right of publicity at the time of her death?

HOLDING AND DECISION: (McMahon, J.) No. A postmortem right of publicity does not pass through the residuary clause in a decedent's will when the decedent did not have a statutory right of publicity at the time of her death. Here, regardless of any rights purportedly conferred after her death, Monroe could not devise by will a property right she did not own at the time of her death in 1962. Descendible postmortem publicity rights were not recognized in New York, California (the two states of which she could have been a domiciliary), or Indiana at the time of Monroe's death in 1962. As a result, any publicity rights she enjoyed during her lifetime were extinguished at her death by operation of law. MMLLC (P) makes much of Ms. Monroe's purported intent to include in her residuary estate all property "to which [she] shall be in any way entitled." In the absence of any other evidence concerning her intent, this boiler-plate language is much too slender a reed on which to hang a devise of postmortem publicity rights that did not come into being until 22 years after her death. Summary judgment granted to SFA (D) and denied to CMG (P).

ANALYSIS

In 2007, in a direct refutation of *Shaw Family Archives*, California amended its right of publicity statute to create generally devisable publicity rights, even for wills created before the enactment of the statute. The amendment was of no use to MMLLC (P) in this case because two separate courts determined that Monroe was a New York domiciliary and therefore not subject to California law.

■■■

Quicknotes

RESIDUARY ESTATE That portion of the estate that remains after all the estate has been distributed through the satisfaction of all claims.

RIGHT OF PUBLICITY The right of a person to control the commercial exploitation of his name or likeness.

■■■

Simpson v. Calivas

Beneficiary (P) v. Attorney (D)

N.H. Sup. Ct., 139 N.H. 1, 650 A.2d 318 (1994).

NATURE OF CASE: Appeal from summary judgment and dismissal of negligence and breach of contract actions.

FACT SUMMARY: Calivas (D) drafted a will for Robert Simpson Sr. that was intended to leave property to his son, but was ambiguous, causing Robert Jr. (P) to bring suit.

🏛 RULE OF LAW
Attorneys drafting wills owe a duty of reasonable care to the intended beneficiaries.

FACTS: In March 1984, Robert Simpson Sr. executed a will that had been drafted by Calivas (D). The will was ambiguously written, causing the probate court to award a life estate in Simpson's property to Robert Simpson Jr.'s (P) stepmother, although notes from meetings with Calivas (D) showed that the intent was for Simpson Jr. (P) to receive most of the property outright. Since Simpson Jr. (P) had to pay his stepmother $400,000 for the life estate, he sued Calivas (D) for malpractice in improperly drafting his father's will. The trial court dismissed the action and Simpson Jr. (P) appealed.

ISSUE: Do attorneys drafting wills owe a duty of reasonable care to the intended beneficiaries?

HOLDING AND DECISION: (Horton, J.) Yes. Attorneys drafting wills owe a duty of reasonable care to the intended beneficiaries. In order to recover for negligence a plaintiff must show that the defendant owed a duty of care. Generally, duty arises out of relation between the parties and the scope of such a duty is limited to those in privity of contract. However, there are exceptions to this privity rule. One such exception has been accepted by the overwhelming majority of jurisdictions: attorneys owe a duty to the intended beneficiary of a will. This exception to privity is accepted because of the obvious forseeability of injury upon malpractice. Accordingly, in the present case, the trial court should not have dismissed Simpson Jr.'s (P) negligence action. Reversed and remanded.

▶ ANALYSIS

The court also rejected Calivas's (D) argument that collateral estoppel barred the suit. The court found that the probate court had not expressly ruled on the question of Simpson Sr.'s (P) actual intent. Another situation in which privity is not required is where investigators for insurance companies look into claims of the insureds.

Quicknotes

COLLATERAL ESTOPPEL A doctrine whereby issues litigated and determined in a prior proceeding are binding upon all subsequent litigation between the parties regarding that issue.

DUTY OF REASONABLE CARE Duty to exercise the degree of care as would a reasonably prudent person under like circumstances.

A. v. B.

[Parties not identified.]

N.J. Sup. Ct., 158 N.J. 51, 726 A.2d 924 (1999).

NATURE OF CASE: Paternity action.

FACT SUMMARY: Father sought to restrain his former law firm from revealing to his present wife the existence of his illegitimate child.

🏛 RULE OF LAW

Rule of Professional Conduct (RPC) 1.6(c) permits a lawyer to disclose a confidential communication to the extent the lawyer believes necessary "to rectify the consequences of the client's criminal, illegal or fraudulent act in furtherance of which the lawyer's services had been used."

FACTS: In this paternity action, the mother's former law firm, which simultaneously represented the father and his wife in planning their estates, sought to disclose to the wife the existence of the father's illegitimate child. The devises in the father and wife's wills created the possibility that the other spouse's issue, whether legitimate or illegitimate, ultimately would acquire the decedent's property. Because of a clerical error, the firm's computer check did not reveal the conflict of interest in its representation of the mother and the husband. On learning of the conflict, the firm withdrew from representation of the mother in the paternity action. The husband represented by new counsel, requested restraints against the firm from disclosing to his wife the existence of the child. The restraints were denied and the appellate division reversed and remanded.

ISSUE: Does RPC 1.6(c) permit a lawyer to disclose a confidential communication to the extent the lawyer believes necessary "to rectify the consequences of the client's criminal, illegal or fraudulent act in furtherance of which the lawyer's services had been used?"

HOLDING AND DECISION: (Pollock, J.) Yes. RPC 1.6(c) permits a lawyer to disclose a confidential communication to the extent the lawyer believes necessary "to rectify the consequences of the client's criminal, illegal or fraudulent act in furtherance of which the lawyer's services had been used." This appeal involves the conflict between two fundamental obligations of lawyers: the duty of confidentiality and the duty to inform clients as to material facts. The conflict arises from the representation of two clients whose interests were, but are no longer, compatible. RPC 1.6(a) imposes a duty on the lawyer not to reveal confidential information learned in the course of representation unless the client consents after consultation. A lawyer's obligation to communicate to one client all information needed to make an informed decision qualifies the firm's duty to maintain the confidentiality of a co-client's information. The firm argues that RPC 1.6 mandates, or at least permits, the firm to disclose the existence of the husband's illegitimate child. RPC 1.6(b) requires that a lawyer disclose information relating to a client to the proper authorities if the lawyer reasonably believes that such disclosure is necessary to prevent a client from committing an unlawful act likely to result in death or substantial bodily harm or substantial injury to the financial interest or property of another. Despite the firm's argument that this section applies here, the facts of this case do not justify mandatory disclosure. The possible inheritance of the wife's estate by the husband's illegitimate child is too remote to constitute such substantial injury within the meaning of RPC 1.6(b). However, in limited circumstances RPC 1.6(c) permits a lawyer to disclose a confidential communication to the extent the lawyer believes necessary "to rectify the consequences of the client's criminal, illegal or fraudulent act in furtherance of which the lawyer's services had been used." In construing the "crime or fraud" exception to the attorney-client privilege the term fraud has been given an expansive meaning. So construed, the husband's deliberate omission of the existence of his illegitimate child constitutes a fraud on the wife. In executing reciprocal wills, the husband and wife could reasonably expect that each would disclose information material to the distribution of their estates, including the existence of children who are contingent residuary beneficiaries. The husband breached that duty. The existence of the illegitimate child could affect the distribution of the wife's estate if she predeceased him or deplete that part of his estate that would otherwise pass to the wife. The firm may inform the wife of the existence of the illegitimate child. Reversed and remanded.

▶ ANALYSIS

The court states that an attorney who is jointly representing co-clients, should first expressly agree with the clients on the sharing of confidential information. That prior agreement would clarify the expectations of the parties and preclude the need for future litigation.

━■

Quicknotes

CONFIDENTIAL COMMUNICATIONS A communication made between specified classes of persons which is privileged.

DEVISE The conferring of a gift of real or personal property by means of a testamentary instrument.

RECIPROCAL WILLS Testamentary instruments pursuant to which two or more individuals make reciprocal provisions in favor of the other.

━■

Intestacy: An Estate Plan by Default

Quick Reference Rules of Law

Janus v. Tarasewicz

Contingent beneficiary (P) v. Primary beneficiary (D)

Ill. App. Ct., 1st Dist., 135 Ill. App. 3d 936, 482 N.E.2d 418 (1985).

NATURE OF CASE: Appeal from declaratory judgment.

FACT SUMMARY: Stanley and Theresa Janus died after ingesting cyanide-laced Tylenol capsules.

🏛 RULE OF LAW
The determination of legal death must be made in accordance with the usual and customary standards of medical practice.

FACTS: Stanley and Theresa Janus, a married couple, unknowingly took Tylenol capsules laced with cyanide. Soon afterward, Stanley collapsed. Within minutes, Theresa started experiencing seizures. They were both taken to the hospital. Stanley had no blood pressure, pulse, or signs of respiration. Therefore, the medical director at the hospital pronounced him dead on September 29, 1982. Like Stanley, Theresa at first exhibited no visible vital signs when she was admitted to the hospital. However, hospital personnel were able to get her heart beating independently again and could detect a measurable, though unsatisfactory, blood pressure. Theresa was judged to be in a deep coma with very unstable vital signs and placed in the intensive care ward. One entry in her records indicated that a nurse detected a minimal reaction to light in Theresa's right pupil. On September 30, 1982, various tests were conducted to determine her brain function. As a result of these tests, Theresa was diagnosed as having sustained total brain death and was pronounced dead on October 1, 1982. The proceeds of a life insurance policy on Stanley's life were paid to the administrator of Theresa's estate, Jan Tarasewicz (D). Alojza Janus (P), Stanley's mother and the contingent beneficiary on Stanley's life insurance policy, sued Tarasewicz (D) for the proceeds. The court concluded from the evidence that Theresa survived Stanley. Janus (P) appealed, contending that there was not sufficient evidence to prove that both victims did not suffer brain death prior to their arrival to the hospital.

ISSUE: Must the determination of legal death be made in accordance with the usual and customary standards of medical practice?

HOLDING AND DECISION: (O'Connor, J.) Yes. The determination of legal death must be made in accordance with the usual and customary standards of medical practice. Both victims arrived at the hospital with artificial respirators and no obvious vital signs. There is no dispute that Stanley Janus died in both a cardiopulmonary sense and a brain death sense when his vital signs disappeared on route to the hospital and were never reestablished. In contrast, hospital personnel were able to reestablish a spontaneous blood pressure and pulse in Theresa. Efforts to preserve Theresa's life continued after more intensive efforts on Stanley's behalf had failed. In the medical director's opinion, Theresa's condition did not warrant a diagnosis of brain death, and she did not suffer irreversible brain death until much later. The record clearly establishes that the treating physician's diagnoses of death with respect to Stanley and Theresa Janus were made within the usual and customary standards of medical practice. Affirmed.

▶ ANALYSIS

The Uniform Probate Code provides that an heir or devisee who fails to survive by 120 hours is deemed to have predeceased the decedent. Attorneys provide for the "no sufficient evidence" problem by providing in a will the following language: "if any person dies with me in a common disaster, any property given to such person by this will shall pass as if such person predeceased me."

■—■

Quicknotes

CONTINGENT BENEFICIARY A third party who is the recipient of the benefit of a transaction undertaken by another, the receipt of which is based on the uncertain happening of another event.

PRIMARY BENEFICIARY The individual specified in a life insurance policy to receive the proceeds upon the insured's death.

SURVIVORSHIP Between two or more persons, such as in a joint tenancy relationship, the right to the property of a deceased passes to the survivor.

■—■

Hall v. Vallandingham

[Parties not identified.]

Md. Ct. Spec. App., 75 Md. App. 187, 540 A.2d 1162 (1988).

NATURE OF CASE: Appeal from judgment disinheriting relatives.

FACT SUMMARY: After Earl Vallandingham died, his children were adopted by Killgore, his wife's new husband.

 RULE OF LAW
An adopted child is no longer considered a child of either natural parent and loses on adoption all rights of inheritance from his natural parents.

FACTS: Earl Vallandingham died, survived by his wife Elizabeth and their four children. Elizabeth then married Jim Killgore. Killgore adopted Vallandingham's children. Earl's brother William died childless, unmarried, and intestate. His sole heirs were his surviving brothers and the children of brothers (like Earl) and sisters who predeceased him. Earl's children alleged that they were entitled to their distributive share. The court held that they were not entitled to inherit from William because they had been adopted by Killgore. They appealed.

ISSUE: Is an adopted child no longer considered a child of either natural parent, and does he lose on adoption all rights of inheritance from his natural parents?

HOLDING AND DECISION: (Gilbert, C.J.) Yes. An adopted child is no longer considered a child of either natural parent and loses on adoption all rights of inheritance from his natural parents. The Maryland Estates and Trust Code provide that on adoption, "a child no longer shall be considered a child of either natural parent." To construe this statute so as to allow dual inheritance would bestow upon an adopted child a superior status. Because an adopted child has no right to inherit from the estate of a natural parent who dies intestate, it follows that the same child may not inherit through the natural parent by way of representation. Affirmed.

▶ **ANALYSIS**

The states disagree whether or not a child continues to have inheritance rights from both natural parents when the child is adopted by a step-parent. Only a few states draw a distinction between adoption of a minor and adoption of an adult. Adult adoption has been used more frequently to prevent will contests.

■▬■

Quicknotes

MARYLAND ESTATES AND TRUSTS CODE ANN. § 1-207(a) An adopted child shall be treated as a natural child of his adopted parent or parents. On adoption, a child no longer shall be considered a child of either natural parent, except that upon adoption by the spouse of a natural parent. The child shall be considered the child of that natural parent.

■▬■

Minary v. Citizens Fidelity Bank & Trust Co.

Daughter-in-law of deceased (P) v. Trustee (D)

Ky. Ct. App., 419 S.W.2d 340 (1967).

NATURE OF CASE: Action seeking to have a will provision construed.

FACT SUMMARY: Amelia Minary placed property in trust for eventual distribution "to [her] then-surviving heirs." One of Amelia's sons adopted his own wife (P), but the Bank (D) refused to distribute the trust property to the wife (P) as Amelia's heir.

RULE OF LAW
One who adopts a spouse or other adult cannot thereby make the adoptee an heir to an estate created by an existing testamentary instrument executed by an ancestor of the adopter.

FACTS: Amelia Minary's will created a trust, the income of which was to be paid to her husband and her three sons. Upon the death of the last surviving beneficiary, the property which Amelia had placed in the trust was to be distributed "to [her] then-surviving heirs, according to the laws of descent and distribution then in force in Kentucky, and, if no such heirs, then to the First Christian Church, Louisville, Kentucky." Amelia died in 1932. Her husband passed away three years later. Two of her three sons had predeceased their father and had left no issue. Amelia's husband was survived by the couple's daughter and by Alfred, the last of the three sons who had been named beneficiaries of Amelia's trust. In 1934, Alfred married and, prior to his death, he adopted his wife (P). When Alfred died in 1959, Myra (P), the wife, demanded that the Citizens Fidelity Bank & Trust Co. (D), the trustee, distribute the corpus of Amelia's trust to her. A suit was eventually filed in which Myra (P) claimed to be, by virtue of having been adopted as Alfred's child, an heir of Amelia Minary. The trial court ruled that Myra (P) was an heir of Amelia, but the trustee (D) appealed.

ISSUE: May a party, by adopting his spouse, make his spouse an heir of one of his ancestors?

HOLDING AND DECISION: (Osborne, J.) No. One who adopts a spouse or other adult cannot thereby make the adoptee an heir to an estate created by an existing testamentary instrument executed by an ancestor of the adopter. It is clear that any adopted person, including an adult adoptee, may inherit from his adoptive parent. Moreover, the adoptee may ordinarily inherit, through an adoptive parent, the estate of an adoptive ancestor. In this case, it is probable that Amelia Minary intended her heirs to include any adopted children of her sons. Nonetheless, despite precedent to the contrary, a descendant should not be able to frustrate the declared intentions of an ancestor by adopting an adult for the sole purpose of making them an heir of the ancestor. Such a tactic, although permitted by the adoption laws, would thwart the ancestor's testamentary scheme. Therefore, the finding that Myra (P) is an heir of Amelia Minary must be reversed.

ANALYSIS

Adoption is entirely a creature of statute and was not recognized in earliest common law times. Traditionally, an adopted child was entitled to inherit from, but not through, its adoptive parents. The modern statutory trend, however, is to permit the adoptee to inherit from the ancestors of his or her adoptive parents. Of course, once a legal adoption has been consummated, the adopted child loses all right to inherit from or through his or her natural parents.

Quicknotes

RESIDUARY ESTATE The portion of the estate remaining following distribution of the assets and the payment of costs.

O'Neal v. Wilkes

Virtual adoptee (P) v. Estate executor (D)

Ga. Sup. Ct., 263 Ga. 850, 439 S.E.2d 490 (1994).

NATURE OF CASE: Appeal from judgment n.o.v. denying equitable adoption claim.

FACT SUMMARY: O'Neal (P), who had been raised by testator but never formally adopted, petitioned the court for a declaration of virtual (equitable) adoption.

🏛 RULE OF LAW
A contract to adopt may not be specifically enforced unless the contract was entered into by a person with the legal authority to consent to the adoption.

FACTS: Hattie O'Neal's (P) mother died in 1957, when O'Neal (P) was eight years old. O'Neal's (P) father never recognized her as his daughter. After O'Neal (P) had lived with a maternal aunt for four years, she was taken to live with her paternal aunt, Page. Page ultimately sent O'Neal (P) to live with the testator. She lived with the testator for more than ten years, until she was married. The testator referred to O'Neal (P) as his daughter and her children as his grandchildren. After he died intestate, O'Neal (P) claimed she was entitled to inherit, under the theory of equitable adoption, the property she would have been entitled to had she been the testator's statutorily adopted daughter. Wilkes (D), the executor of the estate, contested O'Neal's (P) claim. The court granted a judgment n.o.v. in favor of Wilkes (D) on the grounds that Page, the paternal aunt who sent O'Neal (D) to live with the testator, had no legal authority to enter into an adoption contract with the testator. O'Neal (P) appealed.

ISSUE: May a contract to adopt be specifically enforced if it is entered into by a person without authority to consent to the adoption?

HOLDING AND DECISION: (Fletcher, J) No. A contract to adopt cannot be specifically enforced if it is entered into by a person without authority to consent to the adoption. Consent to an adoption may only be given by a child's parent or legal guardian. O'Neal's (P) Aunt Page was not O'Neal's (P) legal guardian; she was merely taking over a familial obligation in caring for the child. Because Page had no legal relationship with O'Neal (P), she could not consent to her adoption by the testator. The adoption contract was, therefore, invalid, and thus, O'Neal's (P) claim for an equitable adoption is defeated. Affirmed.

DISSENT: (Sears, J.) Equity treats as done that which ought to be done. By insisting that a person be appointed as a legal guardian before agreeing to a contract to adopt, the majority is harming the very person the requirement is designed to protect—the child.

▶ ANALYSIS

The majority does not grant the adoption in this case because the aunt was not the proper party to consent. The opinion, however, recognizes that O'Neal's (P) biological father also had no right to consent since he had abandoned her. The question the court fails to address is whether the child should be punished when there is no proper party to consent through no fault of her own. The result is anything but equitable toward the child.

Quicknotes

EQUITABLE ADOPTION An oral contract to adopt a child not executed in accordance with statutory requirements, giving rise to rights of inheritance in the child, upon the death of the promisor.

INTESTATE To die without leaving a valid testamentary instrument.

LEGAL CUSTODIAN Person having responsibility for a person or his property pursuant to law.

Woodward v. Commissioner of Social Security

Applicant for survivor benefits (P) v. Federal agency (D)

Mass. Sup. Jud. Ct., 435 Mass. 536, 760 N.E.2d 257 (2002).

NATURE OF CASE: Certified question regarding the inheritance rights of a child created through posthumous reproduction in an action for survivor benefits.

FACT SUMMARY: Woodward (P) sought survivor benefits for herself and her children, who were conceived using her deceased husband's previously preserved semen.

🏛 RULE OF LAW
A child resulting from posthumous reproduction may enjoy the inheritance rights of "issue" under the intestacy statute where there is a genetic relationship between the child and the decedent and the decedent consented to posthumous conception and to the support of any resulting child.

FACTS: Three years after the Woodward's wedding, the husband was diagnosed with leukemia. The Woodwards subsequently arranged for a quantity of the husband's semen to be medically withdrawn and preserved in case he was left sterile after treatment. Shortly thereafter the husband died. Two years later, the wife (P) gave birth to twin girls conceived through artificial insemination using the husband's preserved semen. The Social Security Administration (SSA) (D) rejected the wife's (P) application for mother and child survivor benefits on the ground that she had not established that the twins were the husband's children within the meaning of the applicable law. While a series of appeals of the SSA (D) decision were pending, the Probate and Family Court entered a judgment of paternity and an order to amend both birth certificates declaring the deceased husband to be the children's father. A United States administrative law judge concluded that the children did not qualify for benefits because they were not entitled to inherit from the husband under the Massachusetts intestacy and paternity laws. The appeals counsel of the SSA (D) affirmed. The wife (P) appealed to the United States District Court for the District of Massachusetts seeking a declaratory judgment to reverse the commissioner's ruling and the United States District Court judge certified the question to this court.

ISSUE: If a married man and woman arrange for sperm to be withdrawn from the husband for the purpose of artificially impregnating his wife and she is impregnated with that sperm after the man is deceased, will children resulting from such pregnancy enjoy the inheritance rights of natural children under the law of intestate succession?

HOLDING AND DECISION: (Marshall, C.J.) Yes. A child resulting from posthumous reproduction may enjoy the inheritance rights of "issue" under the intestacy statute where there is a genetic relationship between the child and the decedent and the decedent consented to posthumous conception and to the support of any resulting child. Although the intestacy statute does not limit the class of posthumous children to those in utero at the time of the decedent's death, posthumous reproduction may at times conflict with the purpose of the intestacy law and implicate other interests. This holding reconciles that conflict. The term "issue" means all genetic descendants and both marital and nonmarital descendants. Provisions of the intestacy statute regarding nonmarital children and posthumous children of an intestate are an expression of the legislature's intent to ensure that wealth passes from and to the actual family. The former requires that such a child must obtain a judicial determination that he is the father's child. Under our intestacy law, there is no reason that children conceived after the decedent's death, who are the decedent's direct genetic descendants, may not enjoy the same succession rights as children conceived before the decedent's death who are the decedent's direct genetic descendants. Massachusetts's interests in the best interests of the children, the orderly administration of estates and the reproductive rights of the genetic parents are balanced and harmonized by this holding to effect the legislature's over-all purposes. It can be assumed based on precedent and public policy, the legislature intended that posthumously conceived children be entitled to the same rights and protections of law, such as financial support from their parents, as children conceived before death. The protection of minor children has been a forefront issue in legislative action and jurisprudence. Despite the long existence of assistive reproductive technologies, the legislature has not acted to narrow the broad statutory class of posthumous children to restrict posthumously conceived children from taking in intestacy. According succession rights under our intestacy laws to posthumously conceived children will also not deteriorate the legislative purpose of providing certainty to heirs and creditors. The orderly, prompt, and accurate administration of intestate estates will not be affected. Since death ends a marriage, a posthumously conceived child is a nonmarital child. As such, our intestacy law mandates that a nonmarital child must obtain a judicial determination of paternity as a prerequisite to succeeding to a portion of the father's intestate estate. Posthumous maternity is, uncertain until judicially established as is posthumous paternity, and neither more nor less difficult to prove. The final State interest

Continued on next page.

implicated by this certified question is the reproductive rights of the genetic parent. Individuals have a protected right to control the use of their gametes. A decedent's silence, or his equivocal indications of a desire to parent posthumously, ought not to be construed as consent, but rather the prospective donor parent must clearly and un-equivocally consent not only to posthumous reproduction but also to the support of any resulting child. That a man has medically preserved his gametes for use by his spouse may indicate only that he wished to reproduce after some contingency while he was alive, and not that he consented to the different circumstances of creating a child after his death. A rule that just required a genetic tie or the election to preserve gametes would thus be insufficient. In the present case, it is up to the wife (P) to prove that her husband consented to posthumously conceived children and that he consented to support such children.

▶ ANALYSIS

This case demonstrates what effect modern technology is having on the definition of the family in the context of intestate succession. New Jersey has come out similarly to Massachusetts on this issue, whereas Virginia and North Dakota have enacted the Uniform Status of Children of Assisted Conception Act (1988), which provides that a donor of an egg or sperm is not the parent of a child conceived through assisted conception. This case also brings up the yet-to-be-determined issue of the conflict between the State's interest in the orderly administration of estates effectuated by establishing a limitations period for the commencement of paternity claims against the intes-tate estate and the burdens such limitations period imposes on the surviving parent and child.

■=■

Quicknotes

DECENT A person who is deceased.

INTESTATE To die without leaving a valid testamentary instrument.

INTESTATE SUCCESSION The scheme pursuant to which property is distributed in the absence of a valid will or of a disposition of particular property.

■=■

In re Martin B.

[Parties not identified.]

N.Y. Surrog. Ct., 841 N.Y.S.2d 207 (2008).

NATURE OF CASE: Application for advice and direction regarding trusts.

FACT SUMMARY: Martin B. created seven trust agreements in 1969, naming himself as the life income beneficiary of all of the trusts. Martin B. had a wife and two sons, Lindsay and James. James died childless shortly before Martin B. After Martin B. died, James' wife conceived two children using sperm James had frozen prior to his death. The trustees of Martin B.'s trust petitioned the court to determine if these two children should be considered "issue" or "descendants" who were eligible for distributions from the trust.

RULE OF LAW
When a governing instrument is silent, post-conceived children should be accorded the same rights as children who are conceived prior to their father's death.

FACTS: Martin B. created seven trust agreements in 1969, naming himself as the life income beneficiary of all of the trusts. The trusts provided that upon Martin B.'s death, the trustees had the discretion to distribute portions of the trusts to Martin B.'s "issue" or "descendants" until Martin B.'s wife, Abigail, died, at which point Martin B.'s issue were to be entitled to the remainder of the trusts not appointed by Abigail in her will. Martin B.'s son James, who was married but childless, died seven months before his father passed away. Three years after Martin B. and James' deaths, James' wife underwent successful in vitro fertilization using James' frozen sperm, and she gave birth to a son, James Mitchell. She had a second son, Warren, using the same technique two years later. There was no dispute that the children were biological descendants of both James and Martin B. The trustees of Martin B.'s trusts commenced an action in the Surrogate's Court to determine whether James' two biological children met the definition of "issue" or "descendants", which would allow them to receive distributions from the trusts.

ISSUE: When a governing instrument is silent, should post-conceived children be accorded the same rights as children who are conceived prior to their father's death?

HOLDING AND DECISION: (Roth, S.) Yes. When a governing instrument is silent, post-conceived children should be accorded the same rights as children who are conceived prior to their father's death. The legislatures and the courts have tried to balance competing interests. On the one hand, certainty and finality are critical to the public interests in the orderly administration of estates. On the other hand, the human desire to have children, albeit by biotechnology, deserves respect, as do the rights of the children born as a result of such scientific advances. Although it cannot be said that in 1969 Martin B. contemplated that his "issue" or "descendants" would include children who were conceived after his son's death, the absence of specific intent should not necessarily preclude a determination that such children are members of the class of issue. Although James probably assumed that any children born as a result of the use of his preserved semen would share in his family's trusts, his intention is not controlling here. For purposes of determining the beneficiaries of these trusts, the controlling factor is the Grantor's intent as gleaned from a reading of the trust agreements. Such instruments provide that, upon the death of the Grantor's wife, the trust fund would benefit his sons and their families equally. In view of such an overall dispositive scheme, a sympathetic reading of these instruments warrants the conclusion that the Martin B. intended all members of his bloodline to receive their share. Based on all of the foregoing, it is concluded that James Mitchell and Warren are "issue" and "descendants" for all purposes of these trusts.

► ANALYSIS

Some states, including California, Florida and Louisiana, have already created laws dealing with the inheritance rights of post-conceived children. The 2008 amendments to the Uniform Probate Code (UPC) also include provisions for post-conceived children of intestate parents. The UPC allows inheritance if the deceased parent consented to the posthumous conception and the child is either, living in utero within 36 months, or born within 45 months after the distribution date. In the case of trusts, this means that a child can be posthumously conceived years after the father's death, so long as they are living or born shortly after the distribution of their share of the trust.

■■■

Quicknotes

BENEFICIARY A third party who is the recipient of the benefit of a transaction undertaken by another.

TRUST The holding of property by one party for the benefit of another.

■■■

In re Estate of Mahoney

Widow (P) v. Decedent's parents (D)

Vt. Sup. Ct., 126 Vt. 31, 220 A.2d 475 (1966).

NATURE OF CASE: Appeal from an estate distribution order.

FACT SUMMARY: Mrs. Mahoney (P) was convicted of manslaughter for killing her husband.

🏛 RULE OF LAW
A conviction of voluntary manslaughter disables the party from taking under the decedent's will or through intestate succession.

FACTS: Mrs. Mahoney (P) was convicted of voluntary manslaughter for shooting her husband. Mr. Mahoney died intestate. His estate was ordered distributed to his mother (D) and father (D) since the probate court found that a conviction of voluntary manslaughter disabled Mrs. Mahoney (P) from taking any part of her husband's estate.

ISSUE: May a party convicted of the intentional killing of another, inherit property from the decedent?

HOLDING AND DECISION: (Smith, J.) No. Conviction of murder or voluntary manslaughter disables the party convicted from inheriting any property from the decedent. Any inheritance in his favor is held as a constructive trust in favor of the other heirs or next of kin. While decisions in other jurisdictions vary with respect to voluntary manslaughter, the rule imposing a constructive trust appears to be the best solution. Although in this case there was no special finding concerning the voluntariness of Mrs. Mahoney's (P) actions, the court obviously concluded that she had been convicted of the felonious killing of her husband. While a constructive trust could be imposed on the bequest, the probate court could only apply the laws of distribution and descent and incorrectly awarded the property directly to Mr. Mahoney's parents (D). We must reverse and remand for a constructive trust action to be brought in a proper court of chancery.

▌ANALYSIS

In a majority of states, a killer is barred by statute from inheriting any interest in the estate of his victim. In jurisdictions where no such statute has been enacted, courts have shown a reluctance to impose any restraints on the killer's right to inherit. Sometimes, however, a court of equity will adopt the constructive trust approach favored by the Mahoney court, although the trust device seems to unduly complicate the nature of the relief granted. Note that at earliest common law, the commission of any felony, not only murder, deprived the wrongdoer of his right to inherit property.

Quicknotes

CONSTRUCTIVE TRUST A trust that arises by operation of law whereby the court imposes a trust upon property lawfully held by one party for the benefit of another, as a result of some wrongdoing by the party in possession so as to avoid unjust enrichment.

RESIDUE That property which remains following the distribution of the assets of the testator's estate.

Wills: Formalities and Forms

Quick Reference Rules of Law

Stevens v. Casdorph

Decedent's niece (P) v. Beneficiary (D)

W. Va. Sup. Ct. App., 508 S.E.2d 610 (1998).

NATURE OF CASE: Appeal from grant of summary judgment denying action to set aside will.

FACT SUMMARY: The testator was not in the presence of the witnesses when he signed his will and the witnesses were not in the presence of each other when they signed as subscribing witnesses to his will. The Stevenses (P) sought to have the will set aside, claiming it had not been properly executed.

🏛 RULE OF LAW
To be valid, a will must have been signed by the testator in the presence of two competent witnesses, who then must sign the will in the presence of the testator and each other.

FACTS: Miller, the testator, was brought to a bank by the Casdorphs (D) to execute his will. Miller was elderly and confined to a wheelchair. After Miller had signed his will, Pauley, a bank employee and a notary, brought it to two other bank employees, who each signed the will as witnesses. Neither of the bank employees witnessed Miller signing the will. Miller did not see either bank employee sign the will, and neither bank employee saw the other sign the will, although all were in the lobby of the bank. Miller did not acknowledge his signature on the will to either of the bank employees who had signed his will, and neither employee acknowledged her signature on the will to Miller or to each other. When Miller died, he left most of his estate to the Casdorphs (D). The Stevenses (P), nieces of Miller, filed suit to have the will set aside, asserting that it was invalid because it had been improperly executed. Both parties moved for summary judgment. The Stevenses' (P) motion for summary judgment was denied by the circuit court, but the Casdorphs' (D) motion for summary judgment was granted. The Stevenses (P) appealed.

ISSUE: Must a will be signed by the testator in the presence of two witnesses and then signed by each witness in the testator's presence and in the presence of each in order to be validly executed?

HOLDING AND DECISION: (Per curiam) Yes. A will is not validly executed unless the testator has signed it in the presence of two competent witnesses who then must sign the will in the presence of the testator and each other. Under a narrow exception in West Virginia, a will is still valid if a witness acknowledges her signature on the will in the physical presence of both the testator and the other subscribing witness. The facts in this case do not fit into this narrow exception. The testator did not sign in the presence of either witness. Neither witness signed in the

presence of the testator or in the presence of each other. Neither witness acknowledged her signature on the will in the testator's presence or the other subscribing witness. Hence the will was not properly executed. Since the will was not properly executed, it is invalid. Reversed.

DISSENT: (Workman, J.) Inflexible, technical applications of statutory requirements that a testator must be "in the presence" of the subscribing witnesses when he signs his will and that they in turn must sign in the presence of the testator and each other lead to inequitable results. The intention of the statute is to prevent fraud. Where there is no claim of fraud, incapacity, or undue influence, a will is valid if there has been substantial compliance with the statute.

▶ ANALYSIS

Not all courts interpret "in the presence of" requirement as stringently as this court did. Many jurisdictions employ the "line-of-vision" test. To meet this test, the testator must have been able to see the witness signing without adjusting his position. He need not have actually seen the witness sign the will. Other jurisdictions use the "conscious presence" test. Under this test, the testator need only sense the presence of the witnesses as they sign. The Restatement Third of Property Section 3.1, comment p, also takes the "conscious presence" approach. The current Uniform Probate Code does not have a "presence" requirement except for when a testator asks another person to sign for him. The person signing for the testator must sign "in the testator's conscious presence."

■■■

Quicknotes

TESTATOR One who executes a will.

■■■

Estate of Morea

[Parties not identified.]

N.Y. Surrog. Ct., 645 N.Y.S.2d 1022 (1996).

NATURE OF CASE: Uncontested proceeding to probate will.

FACT SUMMARY: Morea's will had three witnesses, one who was not named as a beneficiary in the will, a son who was left less than his intestate share under the will, and a friend, Buonaroba, who was also a beneficiary under the will. The court questioned whether the bequest to Buonaroba was invalid due to a lack of disinterested witnesses.

🏛 RULE OF LAW
A party who is adversely affected by the terms of a will can serve as a witness thereof because he will receive no beneficial disposition thereunder.

FACTS: Morea executed a will in 1991 in front of three witnesses. The first witness was not a beneficiary under the will. The second witness, Morea's son, Kevin, was named as a beneficiary, but his share of Morea's estate was smaller than the share that he would have received under the intestacy statute. The third witness, George Buonaroba, received a one-eighth share of Morea's tangible personal property. Under New York law, a distribution to an attesting witness is void in respect to that witness unless there are at least two other attesting witnesses who receive no beneficial disposition or appointment under the will. When Morea's will was submitted for probate, Buonaroba argued that he should receive his bequest because the will had two other witnesses that received no beneficial disposition through the will. As the basis for his argument, Buonaroba claimed that Kevin Morea, the second witness, did not receive a beneficial disposition under the will when he was given less than his intestate share of his father's estate.

ISSUE: May a party who is adversely affected by the terms of a will serve as a witness thereof because he will receive no beneficial disposition thereunder?

HOLDING AND DECISION: (Holzman, S.) Yes. A party who is adversely affected by the terms of a will can serve as a witness thereof because he will receive no beneficial disposition thereunder. The purpose of the statute requiring two disinterested witnesses in cases where a witness is also a beneficiary is to preserve the will maker's testamentary scheme to at least some extent by making all attesting witnesses competent while preserving the integrity of the process of will executions by removing the possibility that attesting witnesses who receive a disposition under the will might give false testimony in support of the will to protect their legacies. Here Kevin Morea does not forfeit his legacy as a result of being both an attesting witness and

a beneficiary because the law permits him to receive the lesser of his intestate share or his legacy under the will. The objective of the law that there be at least two attesting witnesses who have nothing to gain by the admission of the will to probate is fulfilled in this matter by the one witness who receives no disposition and by Kevin, who, although he received a bequest under the will, is actually adversely affected by the admission of the will to probate. Considering that the first definition of the word "beneficial" in Webster's Dictionary is "advantageous", it is concluded that, although Kevin received a disposition under the will, it was not beneficial to him to the extent that he would have received a larger inheritance if he testified against the validity of the will and the instrument were denied probate. Consequently, the distribution to George Buonaroba is not void.

▶ ANALYSIS

Most states that have so-called "purging statutes" deny an interested witness the benefit that he would receive under a will. Like Kevin Morea in this case, these statutes frequently allow the interested witness to receive his intestate share of the estate instead. Some states follow a harsher formula and do not allow interested witnesses to receive any bequests at all.

■▬■

Quicknotes

INTESTATE To die without leaving a valid testamentary instrument.

LEGACY A disposition of real or personal property in the form of a gift, as stipulated in a donor's will.

■▬■

In re Pavlinko's Estate

Residuary (P) v. Register of wills (D)

Pa. Sup. Ct., 394 Pa. 564, 148 A.2d 528 (1959).

NATURE OF CASE: Action to have a will admitted to probate.

FACT SUMMARY: Vasil and Hellen Pavlinko inadvertently signed one another's wills. On Vasil's death, Martin (P), a legatee under Hellen's will, sought to have that will probated as Vasil's.

🏛 RULE OF LAW
A court may not rewrite a clear and unambiguous will even for the purpose of implementing the obvious intentions of the testator.

FACTS: Vasil and Hellen Pavlinko, neither of whom spoke much English, had wills prepared for them. Both left their property to the other, and both designated Elias Martin (P), Hellen's brother, as residuary. Through inadvertence, Hellen Pavlinko signed the will that had been prepared for her husband, and he signed the will that had been prepared for her. Several years later, Hellen Pavlinko died. Some time afterward, her husband also passed away. Upon Vasil's death, Martin (P) filed Hellen's will, the only one that Vasil had signed, and asked that it be admitted to probate as Vasil's will. The will was denied probate, and the court affirmed. Martin (P) appealed.

ISSUE: If a party mistakenly signs another will instead of his own, may the will he signed be modified at his death to include the provisions of the instrument which he had intended to sign?

HOLDING AND DECISION: (Bell, J.) No. A court may not rewrite a clear and unambiguous will even for the purpose of implementing the obvious intentions of the testator. The will that Vasil Pavlinko signed leaves the entire estate to him. In order to award the property to Martin (P) as residuary legatee, it would be necessary to rewrite virtually the entire instrument, and such a procedure cannot be countenanced in the case of a will so totally lacking in ambiguity as this one. Thus, the will that Vasil signed cannot be admitted to probate as his will. The will that was prepared for him cannot, of course, be probated, because he never signed it. Therefore the regrettable result, which is supported by the holding of a case that presented a fact situation substantially the same as this, is that Martin (P), is entitled to no relief. Affirmed.

DISSENT: (Musmanno, J.) The will signed by Vasil Pavlinko should be admitted to probate. Even if it is not possible to give effect to every provision of that will, there is no reason why the court cannot enforce the residuary clause, which designates Martin (P) as beneficiary.

▶ *ANALYSIS*

This case illustrates the reluctance of courts to compromise the prophylactic objects of statutes relating to the formal execution of wills. The court declined to "bend the rules" and, thus, permitted the statute to operate as an intent-defeating device. At least one court, albeit a distant one, granted relief in a case similar to *In re Pavlinko's Estate*. In *Guardian Trust & Executors Co. of New Zealand Ltd. v. Inwood*, N.Z.L.R. 614 (1946), wills were prepared for two sisters, each of whom left their estates to the other. Jane then signed Maude's will, but a New Zealand court enforced that will after striking the word "Jane" from the body of the will.

◼▬◼

Quicknotes

PROBATE The administration of a decedent's estate.

RESIDUARY LEGATEE The recipient of the residuary estate of a testator.

◼▬◼

In re Snide

[Parties not identified.]

N.Y. Ct. App., 418 N.E.2d 656 (1981).

NATURE OF CASE: Appeal from reversal of decree admitting will to probate.

FACT SUMMARY: Snide, decedent, and his wife, Rose, intending to execute mutual wills at a common execution ceremony, each executed by mistake the will intended for the other. Rose argued that the will signed by Snide was admissible if it was reformed to substitute Snide's name (Harvey) for Rose's and vice versa.

🏛 RULE OF LAW
Where a husband and wife execute identical wills at the same time, but by mistake they each sign the other's will, upon death of one of the spouses, the will that the decedent spouse actually signed is admissible to probate provided the significance of the only variance between the two instruments is fully explained, the will is genuine, and the will was executed in accordance with law.

FACTS: Harvey Snide, decedent, and his wife Rose, intending to execute mutual wills at a common execution ceremony, each executed by mistake the will intended for the other. All the required formalities of execution were followed, and there was no question of the decedent's testamentary capacity or intention and of his belief that he was signing his last will and testament. Except for obvious differences in the names of the donors and beneficiaries on the wills, they were in all respects identical. Rose offered the instrument that her husband actually signed for probate. The guardian ad litem representing Snide's infant child objected, because denial of probate was the only way in which the minor child would receive a present share of the estate. The guardian ad litem argued that the will was inadmissible because Snide lacked the requisite testamentary intent. The surrogate court decreed that it could be admitted, and further, that it could be reformed to substitute the name "Harvey" wherever the name "Rose" appeared and the name "Rose" wherever the name "Harvey" appeared. The appellate court reversed, on the law, holding that such an instrument may not be admitted to probate, and the state's highest court granted review.

ISSUE: Where a husband and wife execute identical wills at the same time, but by mistake they each sign the other's will, upon death of one of the spouses, is the will that the decedent spouse actually signed admissible to probate provided the significance of the only variance between the two instruments is fully explained, the will is genuine, and the will was executed in accordance with law?

HOLDING AND DECISION: (Wachtler, J.) Yes. Where a husband and wife execute identical wills at the same time, but by mistake they each sign the other's will, upon death of one of the spouses, the will that the decedent spouse actually signed is admissible to probate provided the significance of the only variance between the two instruments is fully explained, the will is genuine, and the will was executed in accordance with law. The gist of the guardian ad litem's argument is that Snide lacked the required testamentary intent because he never intended to execute the document he actually signed. However, a formalistic approach, holding that this intent attaches irrevocably to the document prepared, rather than the testamentary scheme it reflects, is rejected. Here, although Snide mistakenly signed the will prepared for his wife, it is significant that the dispositive provisions in both wills, except for the names, were identical. Moreover, the significance of the only variance between the two instruments is fully explained by consideration of the documents together, as well as in the undisputed surrounding circumstances. Under such facts it would indeed be ironic—if not perverse—to state that because what has occurred is so obvious, and what was intended so clear, we must act to nullify rather than sustain this testamentary scheme. The instrument in question was undoubtedly genuine, and it was executed in the manner required by the statute. Under these unique circumstances, it was properly admitted to probate. Reversed and remitted.

DISSENT: (Jones, J.) Various jurisdictions have split on whether to admit a will under circumstances identical to the ones presented in this case. Some, while expressing regret at having to do so, have applied the traditional doctrines. Others, as the majority, have been moved by the transparency of the obvious error and the egregious frustration of undisputed intention that would ensue from failure to correct that error. In this case, precedent should be adhered to.

▶ ANALYSIS

Under the Uniform Probate Code, this case could be treated as one of harmless error. Section 2-503 of the Code provides that although a document or writing has not been executed in accordance with the Code, the document or writing is treated as if it had been executed properly if it is established by clear and convincing evidence that the decedent intended the document or writing to constitute the decedent's will or other testamentary document.

■■■■

Continued on next page.

Quicknotes

DECEDENT A person who is deceased.

HARMLESS ERROR An error, taking place during trial, that does not require the reviewing court to overturn or modify the trial court's judgment in that it did not affect the appellant's substantial rights or the disposition of the action.

■═■

In re Estate of Hall

[Parties not identified.]

Mont. Sup. Ct., 310 Mont. 486, 51 P.3d 1134 (2002).

NATURE OF CASE: Appeal from admittance of joint will to probate.

FACT SUMMARY: Hall's daughter argued that a draft of a joint will executed by Hall and his wife and notarized by their attorney in the absence of any other witnesses was invalid because it was not properly witnessed.

🏛 RULE OF LAW
It is irrelevant that a document offered for probate as a will has not been properly witnessed where clear and convincing evidence establishes the testator's intent that the document be the testator's will.

FACTS: Hall had executed a will in 1984. Then, in 1997, at the suggestion of Cannon, Hall's attorney, Hall and his wife agreed to execute a joint will. They met at Cannon's office and ironed out the will's terms. Although the document they had worked on was a draft, Hall asked Cannon if the draft could stand as a will until Cannon sent them a final version. Cannon said that it would be valid if Hall and Hall's wife executed the draft and he notarized it, and accordingly, the couple executed the draft, and Cannon notarized it with no other witnesses present. When they returned home from the meeting, Hall apparently told his wife to tear up his 1984 will, which his wife did. After Hall's death, his wife applied to informally probate the joint will. Hall's daughter objected, arguing that the draft had been improperly witnessed (the state's law requires at least two witnesses). The lower court ordered the joint will admitted to probate, and the daughter appealed. The state's highest court granted review.

ISSUE: Is it irrelevant that a document offered for probate as a will has not been properly witnessed where clear and convincing evidence establishes the testator's intent that the document be the testator's will?

HOLDING AND DECISION: (Reginier, J.) Yes. It is irrelevant that a document offered for probate as a will has not been properly witnessed where clear and convincing evidence establishes the testator's intent that the document be the testator's will. Typically, the probate statute requires that for a will to be valid, two people must witness the testator signing the will and then sign the will themselves. However, the statute also provides that if two individuals do not properly witness the document, it may still be treated as if it had been executed under certain circumstances. One such circumstance is if the proponent of the document establishes by clear and convincing evi-

dence that the decedent intended the document to be the decedent's will. Thus, here the issue is whether the lower court erred in concluding that Hall intended the joint will to be his will. The evidence indicates that the lower court did not err. First, the joint will specifically revoked all previous wills and codicils made by either Hall or his wife. Second, Hall directed that his prior will be destroyed. The evidence demonstrated that Hall and his wife believed that the joint will would stand as a will until Cannon provided one in cleaner, more final form. Affirmed.

▶ ANALYSIS

The doctrine under which a court may probate a document that was not properly executed if the court is satisfied that there can be no reasonable doubt that the deceased intended the document to constitute his will is known as the dispensing power doctrine. The dispensing power doctrine, applied in this case, is found at Uniform Probate Code § 2-503.

■=■

Quicknotes

PROBATE The administration of a decedent's estate.

TESTATOR One who executes a will.

■=■

In re Probate of Will and Codicil of Macool

Niece of decedent (P) v. Decedent's step-children (D)

N.J. App. Div., 3 A.3d 1258 (2010).

NATURE OF CASE: Plaintiff's appeal from lower court decision finding that the decedent's will was not valid because she did not review or sign it prior to her death.

FACT SUMMARY: Louise Macool sought to amend her existing will and codicil after her husband passed away. She gave her attorney a handwritten note that allegedly added her niece to her will. Her attorney then created a rough draft of her will, but Macool passed away before reviewing or signing the new will.

RULE OF LAW
For a writing to be admitted into probate as a will, the proponent of the document must prove by clear and convincing evidence that the decedent actually reviewed the document and gave his or her assent to it.

FACTS: Louise and Elmer Macool were married for forty years. Both were previously married. Louise was the step-mother to Elmer's seven children, including Muriel Macool (D) and Michael Macool (D), and raised them as her own. Louise was also very close to her niece, Mary Rescigno (P). Louise created her own will in 1995 and added a codicil in 2007 that named Elmer as her sole beneficiary. After Elmer died, Louise sought to amend her will. She provided her attorney with a handwritten note that, among other things, stated Mary Rescigno (P) should be included as a beneficiary. After Louise met and discussed the new changes to the will with her attorney, her attorney's office then created a draft will that had the word "rough" handwritten at the top of it. Louise passed away an hour after her meeting with the attorney. The trial court found that Louise never reviewed the draft will or assented to it. Accordingly, the trial court rejected Mary Resigno's (P) argument that the draft will constituted a valid will under state law. Resigno (P) appealed.

ISSUE: For a writing to be admitted into probate as a will, must the proponent of the document prove by clear and convincing evidence that the decedent actually reviewed the document and gave his or her assent to it?

HOLDING AND DECISION: (Fuentes, J.) Yes. For a writing to be admitted into probate as a will, the proponent of the document must prove by clear and convincing evidence that the decedent actually reviewed the document and gave his or her assent to it. The trial court properly distinguished between evidence that Louise desired to amend her will, which was undisputed, and evidence that she reviewed and assented to the draft will created by her attorney. Louise's death prevented her from ever reading or reviewing the document. The rough draft was clearly a work in progress that was not meant to be a final draft. Because Louise never read the document or approved it, it cannot constitute a valid will. The court also finds that a testamentary or traditional will, created by a third party for the decedent's benefit, need not actually be signed by the decedent. It is enough that the decedent reviews and assents to it, with both of those elements proved by clear and convincing evidence. Conversely, holographic wills are handwritten documents created by a decedent. These types of wills must be executed by the decedent to be valid. Affirmed.

ANALYSIS

This decision codifies the "harmless error doctrine." The doctrine is a relaxation of the formal requirement that a will must be signed for it to be valid. It allows a will to be probated where there is clear and convincing evidence that the decedent reviewed the will and assented to it. For example, in another recent state case, a decedent's actions of reviewing a will, failing to sign it but then sending it to his executor to review and sign was enough evidence to hold that the will was final and valid.

━━■

Quicknotes

CLEAR AND CONVINCING EVIDENCE An evidentiary standard requiring a demonstration that the fact sought to be proven is reasonably certain.

━━■

In re Kimmel's Estate

[Parties not identified.]

Pa. Sup. Ct., 278 Pa. 435, 123 A. 405 (1924).

NATURE OF CASE: Appeal from entry of a letter into probate.

FACT SUMMARY: Kimmel, the decedent, wrote a letter to his sons mentioning, among other things, what was to happen to his possessions if anything were to happen to him. His sons attempted to probate the letter.

🏛 RULE OF LAW
An informal document evidencing intent of a conditional gift and an intent to execute may serve as a testamentary document.

FACTS: Kimmel wrote a letter to his sons, which was mailed by him on the day of his death. The letter was very poorly written but contained a discussion of the weather, butchering, and a possible trip to town. It also stated, "if enny thing hapens all the scock money in the 3 Bank liberty lones Post office stamps and my home on Horner St goes to George Darl and Irvin Kepp [my two sons] this letter lock it up it may help you out." The letter was dated and signed "Father." The heirs at law protested the entry of the letter into probate.

ISSUE: Can an informal document evidencing intent of a conditional gift and an intent to execute serve as a testamentary document?

HOLDING AND DECISION: (Simpson, J.) Yes. An informal document evidencing intent of a conditional gift and an intent to execute can serve as a testamentary document. In this case, Kimmel's language, however poor, telling his sons what should happen if he were not to survive clearly shows a gift that is conditional upon the occurrence of something, namely Kimmel's death. Most holographic wills are informal in character, and the fact that the weather is discussed in the document does not change its testamentary effect. Also, the fact that Kimmel signed all his letters "Father" shows that he considered this letter a final and executed document. The intent to execute is more important than Kimmel's knowledge of the formal requirements for execution. Affirmed.

▍ *ANALYSIS*

Most courts interpret conditional wills as stating the testator's inducement to execute the will rather than an actual condition that must be fulfilled before the will can be probated. For example, in *Eaton v. Brown*, 193 U.S. 411 (1904), the testator's holographic will stated, "I am going on a journey and may not return. If I do not, I leave everything to my adopted son." The testator did in fact return, only to die several months later. The court held the will entitled to probate on the grounds that her statement about not returning was merely an expression of her thoughts at the time she wrote the will, not an event that must occur in order to make the will effective.

■■■

Quicknotes

HOLOGRAPHIC WILL A will that is handwritten by the testator or testatrix.

TESTAMENTARY INTENT A determination that the document was intended to be a will and, as such, reflects the writer's true wishes.

■■■

In re Estate of Gonzalez

[Parties not identified.]

Maine Sup. Jud. Ct., 855 A.2d 1146 (2004).

NATURE OF CASE: Appeal from decree allowing holographic will for probate.

FACT SUMMARY: Gonzalez filled out a preprinted will naming three of his five children as beneficiaries, but he did not have the will properly witnessed. The three named beneficiaries submitted the will for probate as a holographic will and the two omitted children objected.

 RULE OF LAW
Printed portions of a will form can be incorporated into a holographic will where the trial court finds a testamentary intent, considering all of the evidence in the case.

FACTS: Before going on a trip to Florida, Fermin Gonzalez filled in a preprinted will leaving his estate in equal shares to three of his five children. Gonzalez showed his brother Joseph, and his brother's wife Elizabeth, the completed form, and Elizabeth saw Gonzalez sign it. However, no one signed the form as a witness. Gonzalez told Joseph and Elizabeth that he was going to copy the document onto a new form so that it would be more legible, and Joseph, Elizabeth, and Gonzalez's mother all signed the blank form as witnesses. However, Gonzalez died before he filled out the second form. Because the first form was not properly witnessed, it did not qualify as a will under Maine law. Therefore, Gonzalez's three children named in the form petitioned the court to admit the form for probate as a holographic will, which is admissible as a testamentary instrument when "the signature and the material provisions are in the handwriting of the testator." Gonzalez's other two children, who were omitted on the form, objected, claiming that the material provisions of the will were preprinted and not in Gonzalez's handwriting. The Probate Court found that the form was a valid holographic will, and the omitted children appealed.

ISSUE: Can printed portions of a will form be incorporated into a holographic will where the trial court finds a testamentary intent, considering all of the evidence in the case?

HOLDING AND DECISION: (Alexander, J.) Yes. Printed portions of a will form can be incorporated into a holographic will where the trial court finds a testamentary intent, considering all of the evidence in the case. Most jurisdictions have dealt with this issue in one of two ways. Some courts have looked to the preprinted language in order to determine the context of the handwritten notes. Other courts have ignored all of the preprinted words, and determined whether the handwritten words, taken alone, fulfill the requirements of a holographic will. We agree with the first method. The Uniform Probate Code comment states that "a holograph may be valid even though immaterial parts such as date or introductory wording be printed or stamped." The preprinted words in Gonzalez's will are introductory and may be preprinted. When filled in by Gonzalez's handwriting, they become a valid statement of testamentary intent in a holographic will. Affirmed.

▶ **ANALYSIS**

Not all states have statutes permitting holographic wills, and the requirements in the states that do permit them vary widely. Some states require that the entire will is written, signed and dated in the testator's handwriting. Others, like the one at issue in this case, require that the material provisions of the document be written by hand. More modern statutes call for handwritten material portions and allow the introduction of extrinsic evidence to show testamentary intent.

■═■

Quicknotes

HOLOGRAPHIC WILL A will that is handwritten by the testator.

■═■

In re Estate of Kuralt

[Parties not identified.]

Mont. Sup. Ct., 303 Mont. 335, 15 P.3d 931 (2000).

NATURE OF CASE: Appeal from determination that a letter was a valid holographic codicil to the deceased's formal will.

FACT SUMMARY: Kuralt (famous for his "On the Road" television show) wrote a letter to his mistress, Shannon, a couple of weeks before he died, while very sick, expressing an intent that Shannon "inherit" property they had shared. Kuralt's estate argued that the letter was not a valid holographic codicil to his formal will.

> **🏛 RULE OF LAW**
> A letter written by the deceased while in extremis, expressing an intent that another "inherit" a specific bequest of the deceased's property and not the entirety of the deceased's estate, is a valid holographic codicil to the deceased's formal will.

FACTS: Charles Kuralt (Kuralt), who was a "homespun American icon" known for his television show "On the Road," had a 30-year intimate personal relationship with Shannon. Both Kuralt and Shannon desired to keep their relationship secret and were successful in doing so. In 1989, Kuralt executed a holographic will that bequeathed all of Kuralt's interest in particular real property to Shannon. Then, in 1994, Kuralt executed a formal will that did not specifically mention any of the real property owned by Kuralt. Apparently, Kuralt had intended to transfer a 90-acre parcel to Shannon in 1997, but he suddenly became very ill that year. The day he checked into a hospital, he wrote a letter to Shannon expressing his intent that she "inherit" the parcel. He sent about $17,000 with the letter. He died two weeks later, and Shannon sought to probate the letter as a valid holographic codicil to Kuralt's formal 1994 will. The estate objected, but the trial court eventually entered judgment in favor of Shannon. The state's highest court granted review.

ISSUE: Is a letter written by the deceased while in extremis, expressing intent that another "inherit" a specific bequest of deceased's property and not the entirety of the deceased's estate, a valid holographic codicil to deceased's formal will?

HOLDING AND DECISION: (Trieweiler, J.) Yes. A letter written by the deceased while in extremis, expressing an intent that another "inherit" a specific bequest of the deceased's property and not the entirety of the deceased's estate is a valid holographic codicil to deceased's formal will. The intent of the testator must be followed. Here, the record supports the lower court's decision. The relevant facts are that Kuralt and Shannon continued to have a family-like relationship until the day he died; that along with the letter at issue he sent Shannon significant sums of money; there was extrinsic evidence that he intended to convey the parcel to Shannon; he was in extremis (practically on his death bed); he used the word "inherit"; and the letter made a specific bequest, and did not purport to bequeath the entirety of the estate. For these reasons, the letter was a valid holographic codicil to Kuralt's formal 1994 will. Affirmed.

▶ ANALYSIS

The estate, and in a case that preceded this one, the dissent, argued that the letter, which said, "I'll have the lawyer visit the hospital to be sure you inherit the rest of the place . . ." was not a codicil, but was instead an expression of a future intent to make a will. That argument focused on the precatory, versus imperative, language of the letter; the majority clearly went beyond just the letter's language in rendering its decision.

Quicknotes

CODICIL A supplement to a will.

HOLOGRAPHIC WILL A will that is handwritten by the testator.

Thompson v. Royall

[Parties not identified.]

Va. Sup. Ct., 163 Va. 492, 175 S.E. 748 (1934).

NATURE OF CASE: Action to probate a will.

FACT SUMMARY: Kroll attempted to revoke her will and codicil by signing notations on the back of each that purported to render them void.

🏛 RULE OF LAW
Revocation of a will by cancellation is not accomplished unless the written words of the document are mutilated or otherwise impaired.

FACTS: Kroll executed an attested will that she gave to Brittain, her executor, for safekeeping. She then executed a codicil, which she signed in the presence of two attesting witnesses and gave to Coulling, the attorney who prepared both documents. She later instructed Coulling to destroy both documents but was persuaded by Coulling to retain the documents for her use in case she decided to execute a new will. She signed a statement written on the back of the will by Coulling, which read, "This will null and void and to be only held by H.P. Brittain instead of being destroyed as a memorandum for another will if I desire to make same." An identical statement, but substituting Coulling's name for Brittain's, was written by Coulling on the back of the codicil and was signed by Kroll. Upon her death, Kroll left an estate valued at approximately $200,000. The will and codicil were offered for probate and contested by various nieces and nephews who were not mentioned in the instruments. The jury found the documents to be the last will and testament of Kroll, and from an order sustaining that verdict and probating the will, contestants brought this writ of error.

ISSUE: May a memorandum written in another's handwriting on the reverse side of a testamentary instrument and signed by the testator, purporting to void the document, effect a revocation by cancellation of the instrument?

HOLDING AND DECISION: (Hudgins, J.) No. In order to effect revocation by cancellation, the testator must actually mutilate, erase, deface, or otherwise mark the written portions of the testamentary instrument. It is true that in *Warner v. Warner's Estate*, 37 Vt. 356 (1864), one court permitted cancellation by a writing that did not actually touch written portions of the will, but that decision has not been followed and has been justly criticized by commentators. Thus, although the testatrix obviously intended to revoke her will, she did not revoke it by cancellation. Furthermore, the contestants agree that the memorandum did not constitute a "writing indicating an intention to revoke" under the appropriate statute since it was not in testatrix's own handwriting or attested to by witnesses. Therefore, the will and codicil were not revoked, and the order admitting them to probate must be affirmed.

▶ ANALYSIS

Thompson v. Royall accords with authorities generally. If words purporting to effect the cancellation of a will are written in the margin or on the reverse side of the instrument, they are ineffective to accomplish their purpose. However, the writing of words such as "void" or "canceled" will affect a revocation of a will if written across material portions of the will. The ruling of *Warner v. Warner's Estate*, disapproved by the court, is in general disrepute.

Quicknotes

CODICIL A supplement to a will.

DEVISAVIT VEL NON A matter transferred from a court of chancery to a court of law in order to determine whether a certain document was intended to be a will.

REVOCATION The cancellation or withdrawal of some authority conferred or an instrument drafted, such as the withdrawal of a revocable contract offer prior to the offeree's acceptance.

SUBSCRIBING WITNESS A person who witnesses the execution of a document and signs his name thereto.

In re Estate of Stoker

Decedent's former girlfriend (P) v. Decedent's children (D)

Cal. Ct. App., 193 Cal. App. 4th 236, 122 Cal. Rptr. 3d 529 (2011).

NATURE OF CASE: Plaintiffs' appeal from lower court decision finding that the decedent created a will in 2005 that revoked an earlier 1997 will naming them as beneficiaries.

FACT SUMMARY: Decedent Steven Stoker created a will in 1997 that named his former girlfriend and two others as his beneficiaries. In 2005, Stoker created a handwritten document expressly revoking the 1997 will and naming his children as his sole beneficiaries. He signed the new will in the presence of one other person.

🏛 RULE OF LAW
A will shall be valid if the proponent of the will proves by clear and convincing evidence that at the time the testator executed the will, he or she intended the document to constitute his or her last will.

FACTS: Steven Stoker created a will in 1997 that named his former girlfriend, Destiny Gularte (P), and two others as beneficiaries. In 2005, Stoker drafted a handwritten will that revoked the 1997 will and named his two children, Danine Pradia (D) and Darrin Stoker (D), as sole beneficiaries. Both wills were submitted to the probate court. At trial, a witness, Anne Meier, testified that Stoker dictated the will to her in 2005 and that she wrote it down word for word. She then gave the handwritten document to Stoker who signed it. The 2005 will specifically states that Gularte (P) and the other beneficiaries in the 1997 will should receive nothing. The trial court found the 2005 will, coupled with the eyewitness testimony of the creation of the will, evidenced the intent of Stoker and that the 1997 will was validly revoked. Gularte (P) appealed.

ISSUE: Shall a will be valid if the proponent of the will proves by clear and convincing evidence that at the time the testator executed the will, he or she intended the document to constitute his or her last will?

HOLDING AND DECISION: (Gilbert, J.) Yes. A will shall be valid if the proponent of the will proves by clear and convincing evidence that at the time the testator executed the will, he or she intended the document to constitute his or her last will. Dularte's (P) argument at the trial court level and here on appeal is that Stoker's handwritten will, while executed, did not include the signature of two witnesses as required by statute. The Probate Code does allow defective written wills to be submitted to probate if the will is consistent with the decedent's intent. Dularte (P) argues the legislature did not intend this provision to apply to handwritten wills. However, there is nothing in the statute that excludes handwritten wills.

Dularte (P) also argues the 2005 will did not contain any proper testamentary language. However, no specific words are necessary as long as the language provides evidence that the document constitutes the testator's last will. Here, the 2005 will clearly states that his children will be his sole beneficiaries. The document also expressly revokes the 1997 will and states that the prior beneficiaries shall receive nothing. Meier was also present at the creation of the will. There was also separate testimony that in 2001 Stoker burned and urinated on the original 1997 will. The trial court's ruling below was correct. Affirmed.

▶ ANALYSIS

When necessary, a court will allow extrinsic or outside evidence to determine the intent of the testator as stated in the document. In this case, Meier's testimony was particularly supportive of the validity of the will. She was not only present but actually drafted the will as dictated to her by Stoker.

■■■

Quicknotes

CLEAR AND CONVINCING EVIDENCE An evidentiary standard requiring a demonstration that the fact sought to be proven is reasonably certain.

EXTRINSIC EVIDENCE Evidence that is not contained within the text of a document or contract, but which is derived from the parties' statements or the circumstances under which the agreement was made.

TESTATOR One who executes a will.

■■■

Harrison v. Bird

Beneficiary (P) v. Decedent's cousin (D)

Ala. Sup. Ct., 621 So. 2d 972 (1993).

NATURE OF CASE: Appeal from a judgment of intestacy.

FACT SUMMARY: After Speer died, Harrison (P), the sole beneficiary of Speer's will, filed for probate a document purporting to be Speer's last will and testament, despite the fact that Speer's attorney had torn Speer's will into four pieces after she informed him that she wanted to revoke her will.

> ## RULE OF LAW
> A rebuttable presumption of revocation exists where a will cannot be found among a deceased's personal effects.

FACTS: A year and a half after Speer executed a will naming Harrison (P) as the main beneficiary of her estate she advised her attorney that she wanted to revoke her will. Her attorney tore the will into four pieces, informing Speer by letter that he had "revoked" her will as instructed and was sending the pieces of the will to her. State law required that, to be lawfully revoked, a will must be destroyed in the testator's presence. When Speer died, the letter was found but not the four pieces of the will. The probate court granted letters of administration to Bird (D), Speer's cousin. Harrison (P) filed for probate a duplicate of the original will. The court ruled that, although Speer's will was not lawfully revoked, there arose a presumption that Speer had revoked the will herself since the destroyed will was not found. The court held that Harrison (P) had not rebutted the presumption of revocation and that the estate should be administered as an intestate estate and confirmed the letters of administration issued to Bird (D). Harrison (P) appealed.

ISSUE: Does a rebuttable presumption of revocation exist where a will cannot be found among a deceased's personal effects?

HOLDING AND DECISION: (Houston, J.) Yes. A rebuttable presumption of revocation exists where a will cannot be found among a deceased's personal effects. Under Alabama state law, Speer's will was not lawfully revoked because her attorney destroyed it at her direction and consent but not in her presence. However, where a testator destroys the copy of the will in her possession, a presumption arises that she has revoked her will and all duplicates, even though a duplicate exists that is not in her possession. The burden of rebutting the presumption is on the proponent of the will. Under the facts of this case, there existed a presumption that Speer destroyed her will, thus revoking it. Harrison (P) did not present sufficient evi-

dence to rebut the presumption, i.e., to convince the trier of fact that the absence of the will was not due to Speer's destroying and thus revoking the will. Affirmed.

▶ ANALYSIS

A will may be revoked either by executing a subsequent will that revokes the previous one (expressly or by inconsistency) or by physical destruction of the will, known as "performing a revocatory act on the will." Revocatory acts include tearing, burning, or obliterating the will, either completely or partially. If neither of the two steps above is taken, the will, if duly executed, will be admitted to probate.

◼️▬◼️

Quicknotes

EXECUTRIX A female person designated by a deceased individual to effectuate the disposition of his property pursuant to a testamentary instrument.

INTESTATE ESTATE The property of an individual who dies without executing a valid will.

◼️▬◼️

LaCroix v. Senecal

Deceased's niece (P) v. Deceased's friend (D)

Conn. Sup. Ct., 140 Conn. 311, 99 A.2d 115 (1953).

NATURE OF CASE: Appeal from judgment holding that a residuary devise and bequest under a codicil, which was virtually identical to a similar residuary devise and bequest in deceased's will, was void, but that there was no resulting intestacy as to that portion of the residue because it was valid under the will.

FACT SUMMARY: Dupre's niece, LaCroix (P), argued that a residuary clause in Dupre's codicil, which replaced a virtually identical clause in Dupre's will, was void because it was witnessed by the spouse of a beneficiary.

> ## RULE OF LAW
> The doctrine of dependent relative revocation sustains a gift by will when such gift has been revoked in a codicil that substantially reaffirms the gift but is void by reason of the interest of a subscribing witness.

FACTS: Dupre executed a will leaving the residue of her estate in equal shares to her nephew and her friend, Senecal (D). She then executed a codicil revoking the residuary clause of the will and replaced it with an almost identical clause. The only change was that in the will she had used her nephew's nickname and in the codicil she used both his formal name and nickname. However, Senecal's (D) husband witnessed the codicil. Under the applicable purging statute, the codicil would be valid, but the gift to Senecal (D) would be invalid. The lower court nonetheless held that the gift to Senecal (D) was valid, on the theory that the gift under the will remained valid. Dupre's niece, LaCroix (P), argued that the gift was void, and the state's supreme court granted review.

ISSUE: Does the doctrine of dependent relative revocation sustain a gift by will, when such gift has been revoked in a codicil that substantially reaffirms the gift but is void by reason of the interest of a subscribing witness?

HOLDING AND DECISION: (Brown, J.) Yes. The doctrine of dependent relative revocation sustains a gift by will when such gift has been revoked in a codicil that substantially reaffirms the gift but is void by reason of the interest of a subscribing witness. That doctrine provides that if a testator cancels or destroys a will with a present intention of making a new one immediately and as a substitute and the new will is not made or, if made, fails of effect for any reason, it will be presumed that the testator preferred the old will to intestacy, and the old one will be admitted to probate in the absence of evidence overcoming the presumption. It is a rule of presumed intention. As to the case at hand, it would be difficult to conceive of a more deserving case for the application of the doctrine of dependent relative revocation. There is no room for doubt that the sole purpose of the testatrix in executing the codicil was, by making the very minor change in referring to her nephew, to eliminate any uncertainty as to his identity. Obviously, it was furthest from her intention to make any change in the disposition of her residuary estate. When the will and codicil are considered together, as they must be, to determine the intent of the testatrix, it is clear that her intention to revoke the will was conditioned upon the execution of a codicil which would be effective to continue the same disposition of her residuary estate. Affirmed.

ANALYSIS

Most courts place limitations on the doctrine of dependent relative revocation. They require that the doctrine applies only (1) if there is an alternative plan of disposition that fails or (2) where the mistake is recited in the terms of the revoking instrument, or, is established by clear and convincing evidence.

Quicknotes

CODICIL A supplement to a will.

DEPENDENT RELATIVE REVOCATION The doctrine which states that if the same person executes a will which revokes an earlier will, the earlier will is revoked only if the latter will is effective; otherwise the earlier will remains in full effect and force.

TESTATRIX A woman who dies having drafted and executed a will or testament.

In re Estate of Alburn

[Parties not identified.]

Wis. Sup. Ct., 18 Wis. 2d 340, 118 N.W.2d 919 (1963).

NATURE OF CASE: Appeal from the admission of a will to probate.

FACT SUMMARY: Alburn revoked a will in the mistaken belief that this would reinstate an earlier revoked will.

🏛 RULE OF LAW
Where a will is mistakenly revoked in the belief that an earlier revoked will would be revived, the doctrine of dependent relative revocation may be applied to revive the mistakenly revoked will.

FACTS: Alburn, while living in Milwaukee, had a will drawn up leaving her estate to her husband's relatives. Alburn subsequently moved to Kankakee and had a new will drawn up specifically revoking the Milwaukee will. There were several changes in bequests, but the bulk of her estate was still left to the relatives of her deceased husband. Alburn then revoked the Kankakee will, in the mistaken belief that revocation of the Kankakee will would revive the Milwaukee will. Alburn subsequently died, and her heirs alleged that she died intestate. Both the Milwaukee and Kankakee wills were offered to the probate court. The court found that the Milwaukee will had been revoked and could not be admitted. The Kankakee will was deemed to be valid under the doctrine of dependent relative revocation on the grounds that Alburn had revoked it by mistake and she had not wanted to die intestate since all of her heirs at law, one a minor, had no bequests under her wills.

ISSUE: Where a will has been revoked on the mistaken belief that this would revive an earlier revoked will, may the doctrine of dependent relative revocation be applied?

HOLDING AND DECISION: (Currie, J.) Yes. The doctrine of dependent relative revocation may also be applied to situations such as the one herein where a will is revoked in the mistaken belief that it would revive any earlier revoked will. The uncontradicted evidence establishes Alburn's mistaken belief. The testamentary scheme under the Kankakee will is closer to Alburn's testamentary plan than distribution through intestate succession would be. There is no showing that Alburn wished to die intestate or that any change in circumstances had occurred. Under this type of situation, the doctrine of dependent relative revocation should be applied. Affirmed.

▶ ANALYSIS

A few jurisdictions and the English courts hold that the revocation of a subsequently executed will revives the earlier revoked will since the revocation clause in the subsequent will has, itself, been revoked. Since a will is an ambulatory document having no legal effect until the date of the testator's death, the revocation clause is ineffective if revoked before the testator's death. *Goodright v. Glazier*, 4 Burr. 2512 (1770).

Quicknotes

DEPENDENT RELATIVE REVOCATION The doctrine which states that if the same person executes a will which revokes an earlier will, the earlier will is only revoked if the latter will is effective. Otherwise the earlier will remains in full effect and force.

ESTATE ADMINISTRATOR A person designated by a court to effectuate the disposition of a decedent's estate.

EXECUTRIX A female person designated by a deceased individual to effectuate the disposition of his property pursuant to a testamentary instrument.

LEGATEE A person who is granted a legacy or bequest pursuant to a will.

RESIDUARY CLAUSE (OF WILL) A clause contained in a will disposing of the assets remaining following distribution of the estate.

In re Estate of Rigsby

Decedent's sister (P) v. Decedent's husband (D)

Okla. Ct. App., 843 P.2d 856 (1992).

NATURE OF CASE: Plaintiff's appeal from lower court decision finding that a second page of an alleged handwritten will should not be considered part of the will.

FACT SUMMARY: Decedent Jessaline Rigsby drafted a one page handwritten will with instructions to disperse various personal property and money. Found with that one page was a second handwritten page listing various personal items with names of individuals next to each item. The two pages were not connected to each other and the first page did not reference the second page.

> ### 🏛 RULE OF LAW
> In regard to handwritten or holographic wills that consist of more than one page, it must be clearly apparent that the testator intended that all pages should constitute the testator's last will and testament.

FACTS: Decedent Jessaline Rigsby drafted a one page handwritten will. The document clearly stated, "Inasmuch as I do not have a will, I would like to make the following arrangements in the event of my death." After her death, her husband, Don Rigsby (D), found the will. Next to the will, but not attached to it, was a second handwritten page. The second page included a list of personal items with names next to each item. The first page of the will made no mention of the second page. At trial, the decedent's sister, Betty Dorsey (P), argued the court should consider the second page as part of the will. The trial court found that the second page was not part of the will because the first page did not incorporate or reference the second page. There were also some inconsistencies between instructions on the first page and the second page. For example, the first page stated any money she had in the bank should go to a group that sponsored horse breeding. The second page stated the money should go to her husband. Dorsey (P) appealed.

ISSUE: In regard to handwritten or holographic wills that consist of more than one page, must it be clearly apparent that the testator intended that all pages should constitute the testator's last will and testament?

HOLDING AND DECISION: (Jones, J.) Yes. In regard to handwritten or holographic wills that consist of more than one page, it must be clearly apparent that the testator intended that all pages should constitute the testator's last will and testament. The trial court correctly concluded that it is not clearly apparent that the second page was intended to be part of the will. The decedent signed and dated the first page only. The first page did not reference or incorporate the second page at all. The second page also conflicts with various instructions clearly stated on the first page. The second page could be interpreted as a worksheet listing various items, but without clear language in the first page incorporating that list, the second page cannot be considered part of the will. Affirmed.

▶ ANALYSIS

This decision deals with the doctrine of integration. Traditional testamentary wills are usually in type-written form and stapled together. There typically is little dispute regarding the pages that constitute the will. With handwritten or holographic wills, there are often disputes over which handwritten documents constitute the testator's last will and testament. If one document clearly references another, the second document will be integrated into the will. That was not the case here.

Quicknotes

HOLOGRAPHIC WILL A will that is handwritten by the testator.

Clark v. Greenhalge

Beneficiary (P) v. Executor (D)

Mass. Sup. Jud. Ct., 411 Mass. 410, 582 N.E.2d 949 (1991).

NATURE OF CASE: Appeal from a judgment incorporating a notebook by reference into the terms of a will.

FACT SUMMARY: Although Nesmith reserved the right in her will to make a further disposition of personal property by a memorandum, Greenhalge (D), the executor, refused to comply with one of Nesmith's bequests written in a notebook.

🏛 RULE OF LAW
A properly executed will may incorporate by reference into its provisions any document or paper not so executed and witnessed if it was in existence at the time of the execution of the will and is identified by clear and satisfactory proof as the paper referred to therein.

FACTS: Nesmith executed a will, naming Greenhalge (D) as executor of her estate and also the principal beneficiary, but reserved the right to make further disposition of tangible personal property as designated by a memorandum. In addition to a memorandum list of items to be distributed, Nesmith periodically made entries into a notebook, designating bequests of personal property. One of those bequests gave Clark (P) an oil painting of a farm scene. After Nesmith's death, Greenhalge (D) complied with all her bequests, except the one for the painting. Clark (P) commenced this action to compel Greenhalge (D) to deliver the painting to her. The probate judge awarded the painting to Clark (P), and Greenhalge (D) appealed.

ISSUE: May a properly executed will incorporate by reference into its provisions any document or paper not so executed and witnessed if it was in existence at the time of the execution of the will and is identified by clear and satisfactory proof as the paper referred to therein?

HOLDING AND DECISION: (Nolan, J.) Yes. A properly executed will may incorporate by reference into its provisions any document or paper not so executed and witnessed if it was in existence at the time of the execution of the will and is identified by clear and satisfactory proof as the paper referred to therein. Here, the parties agree that the memorandum document was incorporated into the will, but Greenhalge (D) contends that the notebook was not incorporated. However, the statements in the notebook unquestionably reflect Nesmith's exercise of her right to restructure the distribution of her tangible personal property upon her death. That the notebook is not entitled "memorandum" is of no consequence. The evidence sup- ports the conclusion that Nesmith intended that the bequests in her notebook be accorded the same power and effect as those contained in the memorandum referenced in her will. Affirmed.

▶ ANALYSIS

The cardinal rule in the interpretation of wills is that the intention of the testator shall prevail, provided it is consistent with the rules of law. To narrowly construe the will to exclude the notebook contents as "a memorandum" would undermine that long-standing policy. The most recent (1991) version of the Uniform Probate Code requires that a will may refer to a separate memo or list disposing of personal property, but such a list must be signed by the testator in order to be given effect.

Quicknotes

CODICIL A supplement to a will.

SPECIFIC BEQUEST A transfer of property that is accomplished by means of a testamentary instrument.

TESTATRIX A woman who dies having drafted and executed a will or testament.

Keith v. Lulofs

Step-brother (P) v. Step-sister (D)

Va. Sup. Ct., 724 S.E.2d 695 (2012).

NATURE OF CASE: Plaintiff's appeal from lower court decision finding that the 1987 "mirror image" wills executed by his parents were revocable and not an enforceable contract.

FACT SUMMARY: Arvid Keith and Lucy Keith executed mirror image wills in 1987, leaving their entire estate to the other in the event one of them died. The couple each had a child from a prior marriage and both were named equal beneficiaries in the 1987 wills. Arvid died in 1996 and his estate passed to Lucy. Lucy then modified her will in 2006, removing her step-son Walter Keith (P) from her will and giving her entire estate to her daughter, Venocia Lulofs (D).

🏛 RULE OF LAW
When reciprocal testamentary provisions are made in mutual or reciprocal wills for the benefit of a third party, sufficient consideration is present to entitle the beneficiary to enforce the wills as a contract, provided there is clear and convincing evidence the parties intended to create a contract.

FACTS: In 1987, Arvid Keith and his wife, Lucy Keith, executed reciprocal or mirror image wills. The wills provided that if either one of them died, their estate would pass first to the surviving spouse and then equally to the couple's two children. Walter Keith (P) was Arvid's son from a prior marriage and Lulofs (D) was Lucy's daughter from a prior marriage. Arvid died in 1996 leaving his estate to Lucy. In late 1996, Lucy modified her will to exclude Walter (P) and leave her entire estate to Lulofs (D). Also, in 1994, Arvid and Lucy took out a life insurance policy naming Walter (P) and Lulofs (D) equal beneficiaries. After Arvid died, Lucy modified the policy to give Lulofs (D) 78 percent of the proceeds and Walter 22 percent. Walter (P) also testified at trial that he had several conversations with Arvid and Lucy wherein they informed him that Walter (P) and Lulofs (D) would receive equal shares of their estate and the insurance policy. At trial, Walter (P) argued that the 1987 wills were irrevocable and constituted a contract for the benefit of Walter (P) and Lulofs (D). The trial court denied his arguments and found in favor of Lulofs (D). Walter (P) appealed.

ISSUE: When reciprocal testamentary provisions are made in mutual or reciprocal wills for the benefit of a third party, is sufficient consideration present to entitle the beneficiary to enforce the wills as a contract, provided there is clear and convincing evidence the parties intended to create a contract?

HOLDING AND DECISION: (Powell, J.) Yes. When reciprocal testamentary provisions are made in mu-tual or reciprocal wills for the benefit of a third party, sufficient consideration is present to entitle the beneficiary to enforce the wills as a contract, provided there is clear and convincing evidence the parties intended to create a contract. The proof may be express language in the documents, or it can be provided by competent witnesses who can testify to admissions of the testators, or can be provided by implication based upon the relationship of the parties. Here, there is no evidence the parties intended their mutual wills to constitute a contract and be irrevocable. The wills do not contain such language themselves. Agreeing with Walter's argument would mean that any surviving spouse who had executed a reciprocal will could not modify it to provide for a future spouse. That position is untenable. Also, the attorney who assisted Arvid and Lucy to draft the wills could not recall whether or not the parties intended the wills to constitute a binding contract between them. Lastly, Walter (P) cannot provide as evidence his recollection of statements made to him by Arvid and Lucy, as they have both passed away. In these circumstances, Walter (P) is required to provide independent evidence to corroborate his testimony regarding Arvid's and Lucy's statements relating to the contractual nature of the wills. The existence of the insurance policy does not assist his argument as it was created seven years after the wills were created. Accordingly, Walter (P) has not proven by clear and convincing evidence the 1987 wills constituted an enforceable, irrevocable contract. Affirmed.

▶ ANALYSIS
In regard to joint or reciprocal wills, courts will be hesitant to find that a contract exists to benefit a third party unless the documents include express language to that effect. Also, Walter's (P) inability to testify as to his parents' statements was in accordance with the Dead Man's statute. Most states have such statutes that prevent a beneficiary from testifying as to the testator's statements unless those statements can be corroborated by independent evidence.

■=■

Quicknotes

JOINT WILLS A jointly signed single instrument that is made the will or two or more persons.

RECIPROCAL WILL Testamentary instruments pursuant to which two or more individuals make reciprocal provisions in favor of the other.

■=■

CHAPTER 4

Wills: Capacity and Contests

Quick Reference Rules of Law

In re Wright's Estate

Decedent's daughter (P) v. Executrix (D)

Cal. Sup. Ct., 60 P.2d 434 (1936).

NATURE OF CASE: Executrix's appeal from lower court decision finding that the decedent lacked the required testamentary capacity at the time he created his will.

FACT SUMMARY: Lorenzo Wright created a will with the assistance of a notary public. Two other persons signed Wright's will as witnesses. After Wright's death, the notary public and the witnesses claimed Wright was of unsound mind at the time he created his will.

🏛 RULE OF LAW
Testamentary capacity to create a will cannot be destroyed by testimony regarding a testator's few isolated acts, idiosyncrasies or mental irregularities unless they bear directly upon the testamentary act of creating the will itself.

FACTS: Decedent Lorenzo Wright drafted a list of his beneficiaries and then met with Grace Thomas, a notary public, to prepare his will. She prepared his will accordingly. The will bequeathed one house to his daughter, Maud Wright Angell (P), and another house to a friend. He instructed that various personal items be given to relatives. He also instructed that his nephew and some friends should receive one dollar each. James Thomas and G.W. Madden signed the will as witnesses. After Wright's death, Angell (P) contested the will. The notary public, the two witnesses and several other persons testified at trial as to Wright's alleged lack of mental capacity. The notary public testified she thought Wright was of unsound mind because his will was the "funniest" will she had ever seen. James Thomas testified that he believed Wright was of unsound mind. G.W. Madden, the other witness, also testified that he believed Wright had been of unsound mind for some years. Other witnesses testified to Wright's odd behavior during his lifetime. One witness described how Wright presented her with a fish soaked in kerosene and how he offered to buy all of her furniture, even though it was not for sale. Others testified that Wright drank alcohol in excess and often left his house without enough clothing. Another witness testified that Wright would leave his house for days and return without any explanation for his absence. The trial court found Wright was of unsound mind at the time he created his will and denied the will admission to probate. The executrix of the will appealed.

ISSUE: Can testamentary capacity to create a will be destroyed by testimony regarding a testator's few isolated acts, idiosyncrasies or mental irregularities unless they bear directly upon the testamentary act of creating the will itself?

HOLDING AND DECISION: (Seawell, J.) No. Testamentary capacity to create a will cannot be destroyed by testimony regarding a testator's few isolated acts, idiosyncrasies or mental irregularities unless they bear directly upon the testamentary act of creating the will itself. The legal presumption is that a testator was sane at the time he created his will. At trial, the contestant, Angell (P), did not present any medical testimony relating to any injury or medical condition that would affect Wright's mental capacity to create a will. No evidence was submitted that Wright could not transact business for himself or take care of himself personally. Wright drafted his own list of beneficiaries and then went to meet with the notary public to create a formal will. There is no evidence he was not mindful of the property he owned. He specifically bequeathed one house to his daughter and another to a friend. All of the testimony given at trial was trivial in nature and did not establish that Wright lacked the appropriate mental capacity to enter into the will. In addition, it is the duty of the subscribing witnesses to ensure that the testator was of sound mind at the time he created the will. Any adverse testimony from witnesses to a will who failed to object to the testator's mental capacity at the time will be subject to heightened judicial scrutiny. Because they did not object at the time, their credibility as witnesses that the testator lacked capacity is severely weakened. Accordingly, the trial court improperly found that Wright lacked the capacity to create his will. Reversed.

▶ ANALYSIS

At the time the will is created, a testator must understand the nature and extent of his estate, the recipients of his property and the effects of his disposition of his estate. When challenging the mental capacity of a decedent, a contestant must show the testator lacked the capacity at the precise time the testator created the will. Anecdotal evidence in the form of a past history of mental irregularities is not sufficient. The contestant needs to admit medical records or testimony relating to a medical condition or injury that affected the testator's capacity around the time the testator created the will.

━━━

Quicknotes

TESTAMENTARY CAPACITY The requisite level of mental capacity required by law at the time a testator executes a testamentary instrument in order for the document to

Continued on next page.

be valid; this generally requires a finding that the testator understood the nature and extent of his estate, the natural recipients of his property and the effects of his disposition of his estate.

TESTAMENTARY INCAPACITY Absence of the requisite level of mental capacity required by law at the time a testator executes a testamentary instrument in order for the document to be valid.

Wilson v. Lane

Caveator (P) v. Executrix (D)

Ga. Sup. Ct., 279 Ga. 492, 614 S.E.2d 88 (2005).

NATURE OF CASE: Appeal from judgment notwithstanding the verdict in action challenging testators' testamentary capacity.

FACT SUMMARY: Wilson (P) challenged Greer's testamentary capacity on the grounds that she was elderly, eccentric, and feeble.

🏛 RULE OF LAW
Evidence that a testator was eccentric, elderly, and feeble at the time she signed her will by itself is not indicative of a lack of testamentary capacity.

FACTS: Lane (D), the executrix for Greer's will, offered the will for probate. Wilson (P) filed a caveat, challenging Greer's testamentary capacity. Wilson (P) presented evidence that Greer had been eccentric, elderly, and feeble at the time she made her will; and that she had difficulty engaging in daily activities without help: and that she had some irrational fears. Wilson (P) also presented evidence of a guardianship petition filed for Greer a few months after the will was executed, the testimony of an expert witness, and a letter written by Greer's physician. The expert, however, had never examined Greer, and his testimony was based solely on a cursory review of some of her medical files. He also was equivocal in his testimony that Greer was in some form of the early to middle stages of a dementia like Alzheimer's. Similarly, Greer's physician testified that Greer suffered from senile dementia, but that he was not sure whether she in fact had senile dementia at the time. The evidence also showed that Lane (D) had filed a guardianship petition after the will was executed, but that this was done solely to satisfy the Department of Family and Children Services' concerns regarding Greer's ability to continue living on her own, and thus to allow Greer to remain in her home. On the other hand, Lane (D) and the drafting attorney, as well as numerous other friends and acquaintances, testified that Greer was mentally competent at the time she selected her beneficiaries and had a clear mind at the time she signed the will. A jury held for Wilson (P), but the court granted Lane's (D) motion for judgment notwithstanding the verdict. The state's highest court granted review.

ISSUE: Is evidence that a testator was eccentric, elderly, and feeble at the time she signed her will by itself indicative of a lack of testamentary capacity?

HOLDING AND DECISION: (Fletcher, C.J.) No. Evidence that a testator was eccentric, elderly, and feeble at the time she signed her will by itself is not indicative of a lack of testamentary capacity. Here, the evidence presented by Lane (D) established a presumption that Greer possessed testamentary capacity. Despite Wilson's (P) evidence, the law does not withhold from the aged, the feeble, the weak-minded, the capricious, or the notionate, the right to make a will, provided such person has a decided and rational desire as to the disposition of his or her property. Eccentric habits and absurd beliefs by themselves do not establish testamentary incapacity. All that is required to sustain the will is proof that Greer was capable of forming a certain rational desire with respect to the disposition of her assets. The evidence offered by Wilson's (P) expert and by Greer's physician was insufficient to deprive Greer of her right to make a valid will, as none of it showed that she was incapable of forming a rational desire as to the disposition of her property. Regardless of the stigma associated with the term "Alzheimer's," the expert's testimony did not show how Greer would have been unable to form a rational desire regarding the disposition of her assets, and the expert did not explain how having Alzheimer's would affect her testamentary capacity. Similarly, the physician's vague reference to senile dementia cannot eliminate such capacity. Finally, even though Greer was unable to live alone, that fact would have no bearing on her ability to form a rational desire regarding the disposition of her property. Because no evidence was offered to show that at the time the will was executed Greer suffered from a form of dementia sufficient in form or extent to render her unable to form a decided and rational desire regarding the disposition of her assets, the trial court did not err in finding that the evidence demanded a verdict upholding the validity of the will and in reversing the jury's verdict. Affirmed.

DISSENT: (Carley, J.) The jury found that Greer lacked testamentary capacity and the court must decide if the evidence supports the jury's finding. When the totality of the evidence as to Greer's condition during the time period, is considered, a jury certainly would be authorized to find that she suffered from serious dementia. Since the evidence supports such a finding, the trial court erred in granting Lane's (D) motion for judgment notwithstanding the verdict.

▶ ANALYSIS

In general, the standard for testamentary capacity—which is a legal standard, not a medical standard—is relatively low. Accordingly, courts have found testamentary capacity even where the testator was suffering from Alzheimer's

Continued on next page.

disease or senile dementia, and even after a guardian or conservator was appointed to manage the testator's affairs.

■═■

Quicknotes

CAVEAT A formal warning provided to the court by an interested party urging the court to refrain from certain action.

CONSERVATOR A court-appointed custodian of property belonging to a person found to be unable to manage his property.

EXECUTRIX A female person designated by an individual to effectuate the disposition of the individual's property pursuant to a testamentary instrument after the individual's death.

GUARDIANSHIP A legal relationship whereby one party is responsible for the care and control over another and his property due to some legal incapacity on the part of the ward.

JUDGMENT NOTWITHSTANDING THE VERDICT A judgment entered by the trial judge reversing a jury verdict if the jury's determination has no basis in law or fact.

PROBATE The administration of a decedent's estate.

TESTAMENTARY CAPACITY The requisite level of mental capacity required by law at the time a testator executes a testamentary instrument in order for the document to be valid; this generally requires a finding that the testator understood the nature and extent of his estate, the natural recipients of his property, and the effects of his disposition of his estate.

TESTATOR One who executes a will.

■═■

In re Strittmater's Estate

Cousins of decedent (P) v. Court (D)

N.J. Ct. Err. & App., 140 N.J. Eq. 94, 53 A.2d 205 (1947).

NATURE OF CASE: Appeal from decree admitting will to probate.

FACT SUMMARY: Strittmater left her estate to the National Women's Party out of an extreme hatred for men.

🏛 RULE OF LAW
If a will is a product of an insane delusion, it will not be probated.

FACTS: Strittmater, upon her death, bequeathed her estate to the National Women's Party rather than to her cousins with whom she had very little to do. The cousins (P) contested the will. Strittmater's personal physician testified that she felt Strittmater had suffered from schizophrenia all her adult life. Strittmater's mental illness was manifested by her angry comments about her deceased parents; her vocal, intense hatred of men; and her fervent support of the women's movement. However, her relationships with her bankers and lawyer were entirely normal. The orphan's court admitted the will to probate, the cousins (P) appealed and the probate was set aside.

ISSUE: Will a will that is the product of an insane delusion be probated?

HOLDING AND DECISION: (Per curiam) No. A will that is the product of an insane delusion will not be probated. The testator must have been sane at the time of the will's execution to enforce the will. Strittmater's extreme hatred of men and "feminism to a neurotic extreme" demonstrated her obvious mental illness. This is true even though she had the capacity to transact ordinary business. While Strittmater gave her money to this organization, to which she belonged for eleven years, she did not involve herself enough in the party to justify her bequest. Strittmater's will was the result of mental illness and, thus, will not be entered into probate. Affirmed.

▌ *ANALYSIS*

There are three historical rationales for the sanity requirement. First of all, wills should carry out a person's intent; if the will is a product of insanity, it cannot represent his wishes. Secondly, an insane person is not a "person" as a recognized legal entity and therefore cannot be allowed to bequeath possessions. Thirdly, mental capacity is required in order to protect the family, which relies on the decedent for economic support.

Quicknotes

PROBATE The administration of a decedent's estate.

TESTATRIX A woman who dies having drafted and executed a will or testament.

Breeden v. Stone

Heirs at law (D) v. Executor (P)

Colo. Sup. Ct., 992 P.2d 1167 (2000).

NATURE OF CASE: Appeal from admittance of will to probate.

FACT SUMMARY: Spicer Breeden executed a holographic will shortly before committing suicide. When the will was admitted to probate, Breeden's relatives (D) challenged Breeden's testamentary capacity due to his excessive drug and alcohol use.

RULE OF LAW
An objector to a will may challenge a testator's capacity based on both or either of the *Cunningham* and insane delusion tests.

FACTS: Spicer Breeden and his friend Peter Schmitz struck and killed another motorist while they were driving drunk and high on cocaine. For two days following the accident, Breeden continued to consume copious amounts of cocaine and alcohol. When the police finally arrived at Breeden's house, he barricaded the door and wrote out a handwritten will leaving his entire estate to a friend named Sydney Stone (P). Breeden then shot his dog and killed himself. When Stone (P) submitted the will to probate, Breeden's relatives (D) objected, claiming that Breeden lacked testamentary capacity because his excessive drug use made him insane. The trial court applied two tests of testamentary capacity, the *Cunningham* test and the insane delusion test. The *Cunningham* test [*Cunningham v. Stender*, 255 P.2d 977, 981-82 (Colo. 1953)], is usually used when objectors claim that there are numerous reasons for testamentary incapacity, such as mental illness and dementia. It asks whether (1) the testator understands the nature of his act; (2) knows the extent of his property; (3) understands the proposed disposition; (4) knows the natural objects of his bounty; and (5) executed a will that represents his wishes. The insane delusion test is used when the testator is generally sane but suffering from a temporary delusion or break with reality when he executes his will. The probate court applied both tests and determined that Breeden had testamentary capacity. Breeden's relatives (D) appealed, claiming that the trial court should not have applied both tests and that the trial court improperly merged the two tests.

ISSUE: Can an objector to a will challenge a testator's capacity based on both or either of the *Cunningham* and insane delusion tests?

HOLDING AND DECISION: (Rice, J.) Yes. An objector to a will may challenge a testator's capacity based on both or either of the *Cunningham* and insane delusion tests. The trial court correctly applied these two exclusive tests to find that Breeden was of sound mind at the time that he executed his holographic will. Despite evidence showing Breeden's severe drug and alcohol abuse, the court applied the *Cunningham* test and found that the decedent: (1) could index the major categories of the property comprising his estate; (2) knew his home and rental address; and (3) identified the devisee by name and provided her current address. In addition, testimony of handwriting experts indicated that Breeden was in command of his motor skills and his handwriting was unremarkable when compared to other samples. Therefore, the trial court found that Breeden met the *Cunningham* test for sound mind. The court then applied the insane delusion test and found that although Breeden was suffering from insane delusions at the time he executed the will, the delusions did not affect or influence the disposition of his property. The court considered testimony which indicated that he was not close to his family, and also noted that Breeden did not make provisions for his father or sister in his previous will. In sum, the probate court correctly applied the two exclusive tests for testamentary capacity, and the probate court order reflects that the court thoroughly considered all of the evidence presented by the parties and concluded that (1) the testator met the *Cunningham* test for sound mind and (2) the insane delusions from which Breeden was suffering did not materially affect or influence his testamentary disposition. Affirmed.

ANALYSIS

The Court applied the majority view of the insane delusion test when it found that Breeden had testamentary capacity because his insane delusions did not "materially affect or influence" the will. The minority view asks whether the insane delusion "might have caused or affected" the testamentary disposition.

Quicknotes

CAPACITY The legal or physical ability to act or to understand the consequences of one's actions.

HOLOGRAPHIC WILL A will that is handwritten by the testator.

TESTATOR One who executes a will.

Estate of Lakatosh

Guardian of estate (P) v. Primary beneficiary (D)

Pa. Super. Ct., 656 A.2d 1378 (1995).

NATURE OF CASE: Defendant's appeal from lower court decision finding that decedent's will should not be probated because of his undue influence exerted upon the decedent prior to her death.

FACT SUMMARY: Rose Lakatosh was an elderly woman who lived alone with little contact with her family or the outside world. After first gaining her trust doing odd jobs, Roger Jacobs (D) had her execute a power of attorney making him her attorney in fact. Lakatosh then created a will leaving almost all of her $268,000 estate to Roger (D).

🏛 RULE OF LAW
If the contestant to a will proves by clear and convincing evidence that there was a confidential relationship between the testator and a beneficiary, that the person enjoying the relationship received the bulk of the estate, and that the testator's intellect was weakened, the burden of proof shifts to the beneficiary to disprove that he exerted undue influence upon the testator.

FACTS: Rose Lakatosh was an elderly woman who lived alone and had little contact with her family or the outside world. Roger Jacobs (D) began doing odd jobs for her around the house. Eventually he began visiting Rose several times a day. At Roger's (D) suggestion, Rose executed a power of attorney making Roger (D) her attorney in fact. Separately Rose was sued by a nephew for slander. Roger had his second cousin, Attorney Richard Jacobs, defend Rose in that suit. Attorney Jacobs drafted the power of attorney and a will for Rose. In the will, Rose left her entire estate to Roger (D) with the exception of $1,000 left to her church. Three days after drafting the will for Rose, Attorney Jacobs filed a petition in the slander action to have Rose evaluated to determine if she was mentally competent to assist her counsel in defense of that claim. While the power of attorney was in place, Roger (D) converted $128,000 of Rose's estate for his benefit or others while she was still alive. Also, Rose was living in squalor and filth in the years before she died. In 1990, she revoked the power of attorney but not the will. Rose died in 1993. The guardian of her estate, Donald Spry (P), contested her will on the grounds Roger (D) exerted undue influence over Rose. He petitioned the court to revoke the will. The trial court agreed and revoked the will. Roger (D) appealed.

ISSUE: If the contestant to a will proves by clear and convincing evidence that there was a confidential relationship between the testator and a beneficiary, that the person enjoying the relationship received the bulk of the estate,

and that the testator's intellect was weakened, does the burden of proof shift to the beneficiary to disprove that he exerted undue influence upon the testator?

HOLDING AND DECISION: (Cirillo, J.) Yes. If the contestant to a will proves by clear and convincing evidence that there was a confidential relationship between the testator and a beneficiary, that the person enjoying the relationship received the bulk of the estate, and that the testator's intellect was weakened, the burden of proof shifts to the beneficiary to disprove that he exerted undue influence upon the testator. The trial court properly concluded there was a confidential relationship between Rose and Roger (D). Because she had little contact with others, she depended on Roger and granted him power of attorney over her finances. There is also no dispute that Roger was to receive the bulk of her estate at her death. Lastly, Rose suffered from weakened intellect at the time she created her will. Evidence revealed Rose had trouble understanding the nature of her assets. Also, it is significant that three days after drafting Rose's will, Attorney Jacobs filed a petition in the slander suit to evaluate Rose's mental capacity. Lastly, an audiotape recording created when Rose executed her will revealed Rose could not remain focused on what she was doing. She referred to Roger as an "angel of mercy," a comment putting her out of touch with reality. She was also living in squalor, despite having several hundred thousand dollars in the bank. The combined evidence supports that Rose suffered from a weakened intellect at the time she created her will. The trial court properly revoked the will because Roger failed to carry his burden that he did not exert undue influence upon Rose when she created her will. Affirmed.

▶ ANALYSIS

There is some overlap between the concepts of undue influence and mental incapacity. Undue influence contains one element related to mental incapacity, but the testator need not be of unsound mind for the doctrine of undue influence to apply. The testator needs only a weakened intellect. Undue influence focuses more on the conduct of the outside party, while the mental incapacity doctrine focuses on the testator.

■═■

Quicknotes

UNDUE INFLUENCE Improper persuasion that deprives an individual of freedom of choice.

■═■

In re Estate of Reid

Heir of decedent (P) v. Decedent's adopted son (D)

Miss. Sup. Ct., 825 So. 2d 1 (2002).

NATURE OF CASE: Defendant's appeal from lower court decision finding that decedent's will, property deed and adoption of defendant should be set aside due to defendant's undue influence exerted upon the decedent prior to her death.

FACT SUMMARY: Decedent Mary Reid, a seventy-eight-year-old woman, developed a close relationship with twenty-four-year-old Michael Cupit (D). Over several years, Reid conveyed her 205-acre property to Cupit (D), named him as her only beneficiary, and adopted him as her son. Cupit (D) initiated these transactions by bringing Reid to a law firm and often meeting with Reid's various attorneys himself.

🏛 RULE OF LAW

If the contestant to a will proves by clear and convincing evidence that there was a confidential relationship between the testator and a beneficiary, the beneficiary can overcome the presumption of undue influence by showing: (a) good faith on the part of the beneficiary; (b) the grantor's full knowledge and deliberation; and (c) the grantor's independent consent.

FACTS: In 1979, twenty-four-year-old Michael Cupit (D) appeared uninvited at the door of Mary Reid, a seventy-eight-year-old woman. Over several years, the two developed a close relationship that some say was intimate. Cupit (D) was a law student at the time. In 1982, Cupit (D) took Reid to the law firm of Allen, Allen and Boutwell. Cupit (D) met with Boutwell to discuss the possibility of Reid adopting Cupit (D). Cupit (D) also had Boutwell draft a deed conveying Reid's property to Cupit (D), leaving Reid with a life estate. The deed was filed the next day. A year later, Cupit (D) helped Reid draft a handwritten or holographic will devising her entire estate to him. Reid then went to the same law firm and was represented by Emmett Allen, one of the other partners in the firm. Allen created a will for Reid that was a duplicate of the holographic will. In 1986, Reid adopted Cupit (D) as her son. Reid passed away in 1997 and a possible heir to her estate, Thomas Pluskat (P), contested the deed, the will and Reid's adoption of Cupit (D). A lower court found that a confidential relationship existed between Cupit (D) and Reid. Accordingly, a presumption arose that Cupit (D) exerted undue influence upon Reid relating to both the property deed and the will. The lower court found Cupit (D) did not present evidence to overcome the presumption. The court then invalidated the deed and the will. The lower court also

invalidated Reid's adoption of Cupit (D). Cupit (D) appealed.

ISSUE: If the contestant to a will proves by clear and convincing evidence that there was a confidential relationship between the testator and a beneficiary, can the beneficiary overcome the presumption of undue influence by showing: (a) good faith on the part of the beneficiary; (b) the grantor's full knowledge and deliberation; and (c) the grantor's independent consent?

HOLDING AND DECISION: (Diaz, J.) Yes. If the contestant to a will proves by clear and convincing evidence that there was a confidential relationship between the testator and a beneficiary, the beneficiary can overcome the presumption of undue influence by showing: (a) good faith on the part of the beneficiary; (b) the grantor's full knowledge and deliberation; and (c) the grantor's independent consent. First, the court properly determined that a confidential relationship existed between Reid and Cupit (D). Factors in that analysis include the close relationship between the testator and beneficiary, whether one person maintains the finances of the other, whether a power of attorney exists, and whether the testator is physically or mentally weak. The lower court concluded a confidential relationship existed that gave rise to the presumption of undue influence. Cupit (D) was in a position of dominance over Reid, Reid was elderly and Cupit (D) had power of attorney over Reid. The lower court then properly concluded that Cupit (D) did not overcome the presumption of undue influence relating to the creation of the property deed and the will. When considering the issue of good faith, a court will examine which party initiated the gift, where it was executed, the existence of valid consideration for the gift, and the transparency of the gift. Cupit (D) initiated the preparations of the deed and the will and even drove Reid to an attorney's office to prepare both transactions. Cupit's (D) deliverance of ten dollars to Reid does not qualify as proper consideration for the deed. Therefore, Cupit (D) cannot show he acted in good faith. In addition, Reid did not obtain valid, independent counsel when she met with Attorney Emmett Allen. Allen was a partner in the same firm that represented Cupit (D). Moreover, the will Allen drafted was a duplicate of the holographic will Reid created with Cupit's (D) assistance. Accordingly, Cupit (D) failed to prove he did not exert undue influence over Reid in regards to the creation of the deed and the will. Separately, Cupit (D) argues on appeal that Pluskat (P), as a nonfamily member, did not have standing to

Continued on next page.

challenge Reid's adoption of Cupit (D). Only a natural parent has the right to challenge an adoption. However, other states have concluded that possible heirs of a deceased person have standing to challenge an adoption. The lower court properly concluded that the adoption was the product of a long-term scheme by Cupit (D) to defraud Reid (D). The adoption court was not aware that Cupit (D) had power of attorney over Reid or that Reid created the property deed and will, all for Cupit's (D) benefit. Affirmed.

▶ *ANALYSIS*

This decision is an example of how difficult it can be to overcome the presumption of the existence of undue influence. Once a confidential relationship has been established, the beneficiary faces a heavy burden to establish good faith on his or her part. Here, Cupit's (D) initiation of the relevant transactions coupled with the lack of independent counsel for Reid supported the court's conclusion that the presumption was not overcome.

■══■

Quicknotes

UNDUE INFLUENCE Improper persuasion that deprives an individual of freedom of choice.

■══■

Lipper v. Weslow

Son of decedent (D) v. Disinherited grandchildren of decedent (P)

Tex. Ct. Civ. App., 369 S.W.2d 698 (1963).

NATURE OF CASE: Appeal from refusal to admit will to probate.

FACT SUMMARY: The will of a testatrix was refused probate on the basis that it had been procured by undue influence of her son (D), who was also the lawyer who had prepared the document. The challenge was brought by three grandchildren (P) of the testatrix who had been specifically disinherited by the terms of the will.

🏛 RULE OF LAW
Undue influence is shown when such control was exercised over the mind of the testator so as to overcome his free agency and free will and to substitute the will of another so as to cause the testator to do what he would not otherwise have done but for such control.

FACTS: Shortly before her death, Mrs. Block executed a will that in large measure left her estate to her two surviving children. The will specifically disinherited three of her grandchildren (P) who were descendants of a son who had died some years before. The will contained a lengthy explanation of her reasons for excluding the grandchildren (P). The basic theme of this portion of the will was that the grandchildren's mother had been unfriendly toward the testatrix and that the grandchildren (P) themselves had shown no interest in the testatrix and had refrained from any contact with her. The will had been prepared by the testatrix's son (D), who was also a lawyer and had maintained close ties with his mother. The disinheritance of the grandchildren (P) had the effect of increasing his share of the estate by redistributing that portion that would otherwise have gone to the grandchildren (P). The grandchildren [the Weslows (P)] challenged the admission of the will to probate, contending that it had been procured through the undue influence of Lipper (D), the lawyer-son. The Weslows (P) contended the disinheritance clause had been inserted because Lipper (D) disliked his deceased brother. Further, the Weslows (P) disputed the factual assertions in the will that they had neglected their grandmother and contended that their attempts at contact with her had somehow been thwarted by Lipper (D). A jury returned a verdict that the will had been procured by undue influence, and the will was refused probate. Lipper (D) then brought this appeal, contending the verdict did not have a factual basis.

ISSUE: Is undue influence shown when such control was exercised over the mind of the testator as to overcome his free agency and free will and to substitute the will of another so as to cause the testator to do what he would otherwise have done but for such control?

HOLDING AND DECISION: (McDonald, C.J.) Yes. The evidence produced at trial showed that although the testatrix was 81 years old at the time this will was executed, she was sound both physically and mentally. The Weslows (P) were able to show opportunity and motive for Lipper (D) to exercise influence over the testatrix in the preparation of her will. There was a factual dispute over whether the recitation of neglect by the Weslows (P) was a true picture of what actually occurred. However, a showing of undue influence requires more than circumstantial evidence of opportunity and motive. There must be a positive showing that such control was exercised over the mind of the testator as to overcome his free will and free agency and to substitute the will of another so as to cause the testator to do what he would not otherwise have done but for such control, the groundwork for such confidential relationship and motive in the form of an unilateral disposition of the testator's estate. But thereafter, the party contending that undue influence existed must bear the burden of proof that the will of the testator was replaced by that of another. The Weslows (P) laid the groundwork but failed to carry the burden of proof thereafter required. The absence of the required proof of actual influence is sufficient to warrant a reversal of the judgment below.

▶ ANALYSIS

A principle ignored by the appellate court was that any bequest to the attorney preparing the will is presumed to have resulted from undue influence. The ABA Model Rules of Professional Conduct strongly recommend that where a client wishes to name his attorney as a beneficiary, the attorney should refer the client to another disinterested attorney for preparation of the will. The clause in the will outlining the reasons for the exclusion of the grandchildren would seem to be entitled to little weight in determining the issue of undue influence. If the will was induced by such influence, then this clause would have been no more valid than any other portion and would become merely a self-serving attempt by the influencer to cover his acts.

■=■

Quicknotes

PROBATE The administration of a decedent's estate.

Continued on next page.

TESTATRIX A woman who dies having drafted and exe-cuted a will or testament.

UNDUE INFLUENCE Improper influence that deprives the individual freedom of choice or substitutes another's choice for the person's own choice.

■=■

Latham v. Father Divine

Cousins of decedent (P) v. Beneficiary (D)

N.Y. Ct. App., 85 N.E.2d 168 (1949).

NATURE OF CASE: Suit in equity to impose constructive trust on proceeds from a will.

FACT SUMMARY: The natural heirs of a testatrix sought to gain control of a will distribution made to a religious leader who had been named sole beneficiary. The heirs claimed that the testatrix had been prevented from executing a new will in their favor by the fraud and undue influence of the religious leader.

RULE OF LAW
Where a testator is prevented from executing a new will in favor of an intended beneficiary by the fraud, duress, or undue influence of a present beneficiary or heir, the property intended to go to the new beneficiary will pass to the present beneficiary subject to a constructive trust in favor of the intended beneficiary.

FACTS: Mary Lyon died, leaving a will which devised her entire estate to Father Divine (D), the leader of a religious cult, and to two corporations controlled by him. The will was accepted for probate after a contest filed by two first cousins (P) of the testatrix. Thereafter, the cousins (Latham [P]), who were the testatrix's only close relatives, instituted this suit, claiming that the testatrix had expressed an intention to alter her will so as to bequeath to them property in the amount of $350,000. Latham (P) further alleged that the testatrix had been prevented from doing so by the false representations, undue influence, and physical force of Father Divine (D). Latham (P) requested that a constructive trust in the cousins' favor be imposed on the proceeds of the will to the extent of the property that would otherwise have gone to them if the testatrix had not been prevented from executing the new will. The suit was dismissed for failure to state a cause of action, and Latham (P) appealed that dismissal.

ISSUE: Where a testator is prevented from executing a new will in favor of an intended beneficiary by the fraud, duress, or undue influence of a present beneficiary or heir, will the property intended to go to the new beneficiary pass to the present beneficiary subject to a constructive trust in favor of the intended beneficiary?

HOLDING AND DECISION: (Desmond, J.) Yes. In reviewing an appeal of a dismissal of a complaint for insufficiency, the allegations of that complaint must be taken as true. If, on that basis, the complaint fails to state a cause of action, then the dismissal must be affirmed. Therefore, we must assume that the allegations of fraud, undue influence, and physical coercion actually occurred. Father Divine (D) states that a showing of the alleged acts cannot empower a court to write a new will for the testatrix. In this contention he is correct. But, where a testator is prevented from executing a new will by the wrongful acts of a present beneficiary or heir to the detriment of an intended beneficiary, and the existing will is otherwise valid, then the existing beneficiary takes his bequest subject to a constructive trust as to that portion that would have gone to the intended beneficiary but for the wrongful acts. A court of equity, attempts to the extent possible, to render complete justice. By imposing a constructive trust to avoid the result of the wrongful prevention of the execution of a new will, the court does not violate the Statute of Frauds or ignore the requirements for a valid will. The will itself is not affected; it is only the property passed under that will. If Latham (P) is able to show that the testatrix intended a different testamentary disposition than is reflected in the probated will, then Father Divine (D) cannot profit by his misconduct. The dismissal is reversed.

ANALYSIS

The constructive trust remedy has also been applied where an impatient beneficiary has killed the testator in order to advance the date of the inheritance. In one instance, a number of beneficiaries were named in a will. The testatrix expressed a desire to change her will, substantially cutting out the presently named beneficiaries. Some of the present beneficiaries succeeded in physically preventing the testatrix from executing the newly drawn will. The result was a trust imposed on the entire proceeds of the will, even though this disinherited some beneficiaries who did not participate in the wrongful acts. The court reasoned that had the testatrix's intent not been thwarted, even the innocent beneficiaries would have lost their bequests. They should not be allowed to profit unjustly by the wrongful acts of the others.

■■■

Quicknotes

CONSTRUCTIVE TRUST A trust that arises by operation of law whereby the court imposes a trust upon property lawfully held by one party for the benefit of another, as a result of some wrongdoing by the party in possession so as to avoid unjust enrichment.

DURESS Unlawful threats or other coercive behavior by one person that causes another to commit acts he would not otherwise do.

Continued on next page.

FRAUD A false representation of facts with the intent that another will rely on the misrepresentation to his detriment.

LEGATEE A person who is granted a legacy or bequest pursuant to a will.

UNJUST ENRICHMENT The unlawful acquisition of money or property of another for which both law and equity require restitution is made.

■=■

Schilling v. Herrera

Disinherited brother of decedent (P) v. Decedent's caretaker (D)

Fla. Dist. Ct. App., 952 So. 2d 1231 (2007).

NATURE OF CASE: Appeal from dismissal of claim for intentional interference with an expectancy of inheritance.

FACT SUMMARY: Schilling (P) claimed that Herrera (D), who was his sister's caretaker, intentionally interfered with his expectancy of inheritance after Herrera (D) helped Ms. Schilling execute a new will naming Herrera (D) as her sole beneficiary and then fraudulently failed to inform Schilling (P) of Ms. Schilling's death until after probate was discharged.

🏛 RULE OF LAW
A party who would have contested a will but was prevented from doing so by another person's fraudulent conduct may bring a claim for intentional interference with an expectancy of inheritance.

FACTS: In 1996, Mignonne Helen Schilling (Ms. Schilling) executed a will, naming her brother, Edward Schilling (Schilling) (P), as her personal representative and sole beneficiary. Over the following years, Ms. Schilling's health declined, and Schilling (P), who lived in New Jersey, traveled to Florida on several occasions to assist his sister. In 2001, Ms. Schilling met Maria Herrera (D), who became Ms. Schilling's caretaker. After several years, Ms. Schilling moved into Herrera's (D) renovated garage, where she paid Herrera (D) rent and fees for her services. Ms. Schilling became entirely dependent on Herrera (D), and in September 2003, Herrara (D) had Ms. Schilling prepare a new will, naming Herrera (D) as her personal representative and sole beneficiary. Ms. Schilling died in August 2004, and Herrera (D) filed a petition for administration with the probate court. Despite numerous phone calls from Schilling (P) in the months following Ms. Schilling's death, Herrara (D) never informed Schilling (P) that his sister had died. Schilling (P) did not find out that his sister was dead until December 6, 2004, and shortly thereafter, the probate court entered a final order of discharge closing Ms. Schilling's estate. Schilling (P) filed suit against Herrera (D) for intentional interference with an expectancy of inheritance, but the trial court dismissed his suit, finding that Herrera (D) had no duty to inform Schilling (P) of his sister's death and that Schilling (P) had not exhausted all of his remedies in the probate court. Schilling (P) appealed.

ISSUE: May a party who would have contested a will but was prevented from doing so by another person's fraudulent conduct bring a claim for intentional interference with an expectancy of inheritance?

HOLDING AND DECISION: (Rothenberg, J.) Yes. A party who would have contested a will but was prevented from doing so by another person's fraudulent conduct may bring a claim for intentional interference with an expectancy of inheritance. To state a cause of action for intentional interference with expectancy of inheritance, the complaint must allege the following elements: (1) the existence of an expectancy; (2) intentional interference with the expectancy through tortuous conduct; (3) causation; and (4) damages. In the instant case, the trial court's ruling was based on the fact that Schilling's (P) complaint failed to allege that Herrera (D) breached a legal duty owed to Schilling (P). However, breach of a duty is not one of the elements of the cause of action. We therefore review Schilling's (P) complaint to determine if it sufficiently pleads the cause of action. We conclude that Schilling's (P) complaint states a cause of action because it alleges that Schilling (P) was named as Ms. Schilling's sole beneficiary, that based on the last will and testament, Schilling (P) expected to inherit Ms. Schilling's estate, that Herrera (D) intentionally interfered with Schilling's (P) expectancy by "convincing" the decedent, while she was ill and completely dependent on Herrera (D), to execute a new will naming Herrera (D) as the sole beneficiary, and that Herrera's (D) fraudulent actions and undue influence prevented Schilling (P) from inheriting his sister's estate. A review of the amended complaint reflects that Schilling (P) has alleged two separate frauds. The first stems from Herrera's (D) undue influence in procuring the will, and the second stems from Herrera's (D) actions in preventing Schilling (P) from contesting the will in probate court. If only the first type of fraud was involved, Schilling's (P) collateral attack on the will would be barred. However, the cause of action may be permitted when "the circumstances surrounding the tortuous conduct effectively preclude adequate relief in the probate court". As the facts in the amended complaint sufficiently allege that Schilling (P) was prevented from contesting the will in the probate court due to Herrera's (D) fraudulent conduct, we find that the trial court erred in finding that Schilling's (P) claim for intentional interference with an expectancy of inheritance was barred. Reversed and remanded.

▶ ANALYSIS

As the textbook editors point out, intentional interference with an expectancy of inheritance is not a will contest. Typically, the statute of limitations for the action is the longer statute for tort actions, which does not begin to run until a plaintiff discovers or should have discovered the

Continued on next page.

fraud. However, if a plaintiff challenges the will in a pro-bate action and loses, most states bar the plaintiff from then asserting the tort claim.

■■■

Quicknotes

EXPECTANCY The expectation or contingency of obtaining possession of a right or interest in the future.

EXPECTANCY INTEREST The expectation or contingency of obtaining possession of a right or interest in the future.

■■■

Wills: Construction

Quick Reference Rules of Law

Mahoney v. Grainger

[Parties not identified.]

Mass. Sup. Jud. Ct., 283 Mass. 189, 186 N.E. 86 (1933).

NATURE OF CASE: Appeal from a decree denying a petition for distribution of a legacy under a will.

FACT SUMMARY: After a trial judge found that a testatrix's sole heir at law was her maternal aunt, ruling that statements of the testatrix were admissible only insofar as they gave evidence of the material circumstances surrounding the testatrix at the time of the execution of the will, her first cousins appealed the ruling, contending they were her heirs at law.

> **🏛 RULE OF LAW**
> A will duly executed and allowed by the court must, under the statute of wills, be accepted as the final expression of the intent of the person executing it.

FACTS: Sullivan told her attorney she wanted to make a will. She left the bulk of her estate to two first cousins and told the attorney that the rest of the estate should be shared equally by "about twenty-five first cousins." The attorney subsequently drafted the will containing a residuary clause stating in part: "all the rest and residue of my estate, both real and personal property, I give, devise and bequeath to my heirs at law living at the time of my decease." After Sullivan's death, the trial judge found that Sullivan's sole heir at law at the time of her death was her maternal aunt, Frances Greene. The first cousins argued that Sullivan's statement regarding the twenty-five first cousins should be admitted to prove her testamentary intention. However, the trial judge ruled that the statements were not admissible to prove intention and dismissed the cousins' petition. They appealed.

ISSUE: Must a will duly executed and allowed by the court, under the statute of wills, be accepted as the final expression of the intent of the person executing it?

HOLDING AND DECISION: (Rugg, C.J.) Yes. A will duly executed and allowed by the court must, under the statute of wills, be accepted as the final expression of the intent of the person executing it. It is only where testamentary language is not clear in its application to facts that evidence may be introduced in order to clarify the language. In this case, there is no doubt as to Sullivan's heirs at law. The aunt alone falls within that description. The cousins are excluded. The circumstance that the plural word "heirs" was used does not prevent one individual from taking the entire gift. Decree affirmed.

▶ **ANALYSIS**

Most courts subscribe to the rule that when an instrument has been proved and allowed as a will, oral testimony as to the meaning and purpose of a testator cannot be used to disturb the plain meaning of a will. The fact that a will does not conform to the instructions given to the draftsman who prepared it, by reason of mistake or otherwise, does not authorize a court to reform or alter the will or remold it by amendments. Where no doubt exists as to the property bequeathed or the identity of the beneficiary, there is no room for extrinsic evidence.

■■■

Quicknotes

EXTRINSIC EVIDENCE Evidence that is not contained within the text of a document or contract but which is derived from the parties' statements or the circumstances under which the agreement was made.

RESIDUARY CLAUSE (OF WILL) A clause contained in a will disposing of the assets remaining following distribution of the estate.

TESTATRIX A woman who dies having drafted and executed a will or testament.

■■■

In re Estate of Cole

Decedent's personal representative (P) v. Decedent's friend (D)

Minn. Ct. App., 621 N.W.2d 816 (2001).

NATURE OF CASE: Defendant's appeal from lower court decision finding that decedent intended to bequeath her $25,000 and not $200,000.

FACT SUMMARY: Decedent Ruth Cole's will stated that she bequeathed to the defendant Veta Vining (D) "the sum of two hundred thousand dollars ($25,000)." The trial court found that Ms. Cole intended to bequeath Vining (D) $25,000.

RULE OF LAW
A court may resort to extrinsic evidence if, after examining the circumstances surrounding the creation of a will, an ambiguity or inconsistency remains.

FACTS: Decedent Ruth Cole's will stated that she bequeathed the defendant Veta Vining (D) "the sum of two hundred thousand dollars ($25,000)." Cole's personal representative petitioned the court to interpret the gift as $25,000 while Vining (D) argued Cole's intent was to provide her with $200,000. At trial, the attorney who drafted the will testified he cut and paste another provision from the will where Cole actually did provide a gift of $200,000. For the gift to Vining (D), the attorney changed the figures to $25,000 but failed to change the wording of the gift. The trial court determined that Cole intended to give Vining (D) $25,000 and granted summary judgment to Cole's personal representative (P). Vining (D) appealed.

ISSUE: May a court resort to extrinsic evidence if, after examining the circumstances surrounding the creation of a will, an ambiguity or inconsistency remains?

HOLDING AND DECISION: (Crippen, J.) Yes. A court may resort to extrinsic evidence if, after examining the circumstances surrounding the creation of a will, an ambiguity or inconsistency remains. Historically, courts have examined inconsistencies in the will depending on whether they were latent or patent ambiguities. Extrinsic evidence can be allowed in to determine latent ambiguities. Such ambiguities are provisions that could apply to one or more persons. Patent ambiguities are inconsistencies readily apparent on the face of the document. In those situations, extrinsic evidence is not admissible and the provision will usually be found void for uncertainly. The common trend now is to do away with the distinction between latent and patent ambiguities. A reviewing court should examine the circumstances surrounding the gift in question first. If the ambiguity persists, whether latent or patent, extrinsic evidence may be allowed to assist with the determination of the testator's intent. Here, the court properly allowed the testimony of the drafting attorney which was undisputed by Vining (D). Affirmed.

ANALYSIS

The decision aptly summarizes the trend regarding the admissibility of evidence for ambiguities in certain provisions of the will. Some states still prohibit introduction of evidence for patent ambiguities. The historical rationale is that the words of the testator were paramount and courts were reluctant to rewrite any section of the will with the use of outside evidence.

Quicknotes

EXTRINSIC EVIDENCE Evidence that is not contained within the text of a document or contract, but which is derived from the parties' statements or the circumstances under which the agreement was made.

Arnheiter v. Arnheiter

[Parties not identified.]

N.J. Super. Ch. Div., 42 N.J. Super. 71, 125 A.2d 914 (1956).

NATURE OF CASE: Application to correct mistake in probated will.

FACT SUMMARY: Executrix (P) of Guterl's will applied to the court to correct an obvious mistake in the will by changing the street number of property devised to correctly identify property owned by Guterl.

🏛 RULE OF LAW
An erroneous description of a particular devise will not cause the devise to fail where less essential particulars can be eliminated leaving a resulting description that is clearly accurate.

FACTS: Upon Guterl's death, her will was duly probated. The will provided that the executrix (P) was to sell Guterl's half interest in the property known as "304" Harrison Avenue, and to use the proceeds to establish trusts for her nieces. At the time of the execution of her will and at her death, Guterl owned a half interest in "317" Harrison Avenue, not "304" Harrison Avenue. This was the only property on Harrison Avenue in which Guterl held any interest. The executrix (P) applied to the court to correct the will, changing "304" to "317."

ISSUE: Will an erroneous description of a particular devise cause a devise to fail where less essential particulars can be eliminated leaving a resulting description that is clearly accurate?

HOLDING AND DECISION: (Sullivan, J.) No. An erroneous description of a particular devise, will not cause the devise to fail, where less essential particulars can be eliminated leaving a resulting description that is clearly accurate. The court is powerless to reform the will in the manner requested by the executrix (P), because reformation is not available to change a testamentary instrument. But where there is an obvious mistake, the court may delete particulars from the description of a particular devise so long as the resulting description fits. Here, the mistake was clear, Guterl owned no interest in "304" Harrison Avenue. By disregarding the street number, the rest of the description is sufficient to identify the property described, as her interest in "317" Harrison Avenue, and the will should be so construed. Judgment entered construing decedent's will.

▶ ANALYSIS

This is the doctrine of "*Falsa Demonstratio Non Nocet,*" which allows courts to prevent devises from failing. The key in applying the doctrine is that after the "false" or less important particular is dropped from the description, whether the object or subject of the devise can be identified with sufficient certainty. If not, the devise will still fail.

■■■

Quicknotes

EXECUTRIX A female person designated by a deceased individual to effectuate the disposition of his property pursuant to a testamentary instrument.

■■■

In re Gibbs' Estate

Former employee of decedent (P) v. Named beneficiary (D)

Wis. Sup. Ct., 111 N.W.2d 413 (1961).

NATURE OF CASE: Defendant's appeal from lower court decision finding that decedents intended to bequeath one percent of their estate to a man with the same first and last name but with a different middle initial.

FACT SUMMARY: Decedents George and Lena Gibbs stated in their will that Robert J. Krause should receive one percent of their estate. Robert W. Krause, a long-time employee and family friend of the Gibbs, contested the will and argued the Gibbs intended to make the bequest to him.

🏛 RULE OF LAW
When minor details of identification in a will are at issue, including middle initials or street addresses, courts should admit extrinsic evidence and should disregard such minor details when the proof establishes that a mistake in identification was actually made.

FACTS: In wills executed in the years before their deaths, both George Gibbs and Lena Gibbs bequeathed one percent of their combined estate as follows: "To Robert J. Krause, now of 4708 North 46th Street, Milwaukee, Wisconsin." A man with that exact name lived at that address. However, when the Gibbs' wills were probated, Robert W. Krause (P) contested the provision. He argued that he was an employee of George Gibbs for thirty years at the Gibbs Steel Plant. Robert W. (P) also provided testimony that he visited the Gibbs' home often and even did work around the house. The Gibbs' housekeeper also testified that Robert W. (P) was a friend of the family by virtue of his long service at the steel plant and his many visits to the home. The will also included sequential one percent bequest to three other long-time employees of the steel mill. Robert J. Krause (D) actually lived at 4708 North 46th Street. However, his only connection to the Gibbs family was a taxi ride he allegedly gave to Mrs. Gibbs in 1955. The lower court concluded the Gibbs made a mistake of identification in the will and ordered that the one percent bequest go to Robert W. (P). Robert J. (D) appealed.

ISSUE: When minor details of identification in a will are at issue, including middle initials or street addresses, should courts admit extrinsic evidence and disregard such minor details when the proof establishes that a mistake in identification was actually made?

HOLDING AND DECISION: (Fairchild, J.) Yes. When minor details of identification in a will are at issue,

including middle initials or street addresses, courts should admit extrinsic evidence and should disregard such minor details when the proof establishes that a mistake in identification was actually made. At common law, no reformation of this will would be possible. The terms of the one percent provision, without reference to any extrinsic evidence, apply to Robert J. Krause (D) and no one else. There is no ambiguity in the language. Typically, only when there is ambiguity in the language will outside evidence be admitted to interpret a will. When there is no ambiguity, extrinsic evidence is typically barred. The rationale for the strict rule was to prohibit plausible claims of mistaken identity by disappointed heirs made after a testator is no longer present to refute such claims. However, courts have relaxed the prohibition on extrinsic evidence somewhat. Details such as middle initials and addresses should not be accorded the same level of sanctity as full names so as to frustrate the testator's intent. When circumstances tend to show a mistake was made, courts should allow contestants to admit evidence to prove that in fact the testator made a mistake in the will. Here, the evidence was clear that the Gibbs intended to give the one percent gift to their long-time friend and employee, Robert W. Krause (P). Affirmed.

▶ ANALYSIS

While the modern trend is to admit extrinsic evidence when there is an ambiguity in the contract, not all courts would have reached the same conclusion as the court did here. Here, the will was not ambiguous. Many courts would refuse to reform the will based on the long held doctrine that extrinsic evidence is only allowed if there is a latent ambiguity in the language. In addition, this decision was criticized because it did not specifically define "minor details of identification" and many commentators felt the decision provided courts with unlimited ability to reform wills as they saw fit.

■▬■

Quicknotes

EXTRINSIC EVIDENCE Evidence that is not contained within the text of a document or contract, but which is derived from the parties' statements or the circumstances under which the agreement was made.

LATENT AMBIGUITY Language capable of more than one interpretation that seems clear on its face, but the introduction of extrinsic evidence proves it to have a different meaning.

■▬■

In re Estate of Herceg

Executrix of will (P) v. Heirs of estate (D)

N.Y. Surrog. Ct., 747 N.Y.S.2d 901 (2002).

NATURE OF CASE: Probate court's consideration of decedent's will that failed to name a beneficiary of the will's residuary provision.

FACT SUMMARY: Decedent Eugenia Herceg's will failed to name a beneficiary for the residue and remainder of her property. A prior version of the will named her nephew or her nephew's wife as the beneficiary of the residuary of the estate.

RULE OF LAW
A will, even though unambiguous, may be reformed to conform the language of the text to the testator's intention if it is established by clear and convincing evidence: (1) that a mistake of law or fact affected the terms of the document; and (2) what the specific intent of the donor was.

FACTS: Decedent Eugenia Herceg's will failed to name a beneficiary for the residue and remainder of her property. Herceg's prior will had a similar provision but added that the residuary of her estate should go to her nephew or her nephew's wife if he failed to survive her. The executrix (P) of the will petitioned that the nephew should receive the residuary. Heirs of the will (D) consented to the petition. At a hearing the drafting attorney testified that when he sought to redraft the prior will, some lines from the earlier will were accidently deleted. The issue for the probate court was whether it could correct the will by supplying the name of beneficiary.

ISSUE: May a will, even though unambiguous, be reformed to conform the language of the text to the testator's intention if it is established by clear and convincing evidence: (1) that a mistake of law or fact affected the terms of the document; and (2) what the specific intent of the donor was?

HOLDING AND DECISION: (Peckham, J.) Yes. A will, even though unambiguous, may be reformed to conform the language of the text to the testator's intention if it is established by clear and convincing evidence: (1) that a mistake of law or fact affected the terms of the document; and (2) what the specific intent of the donor was. This fairly modern rule allowing for reformation of a will is a response to two long-held doctrines for the interpretation of wills. First, a court is not supposed to supply terms that a testator has failed to add. In contrast, the paramount rule of will construction is to determine the intention of the testator in order to avoid intestacy, or the invalidation of the will. It is also presumed that a testator's goal in creating a will is to avoid intestacy. When a mistake of law or fact exists, extrinsic evidence may be admitted to determine the testator's intent. The evidence must be clear and convincing, and not simply a preponderance of the evidence. Here, the evidence is clear, by virtue of the prior will, Herceg sought to give the residuary to her nephew. Because her nephew is deceased, the residuary will go to this wife.

ANALYSIS

Not all jurisdictions have adopted this rule allowing for reformation of the will when the testator failed to provide the name of the beneficiary. The modern trend is to allow extrinsic evidence to determine the intent of the testator. However, a contestant to a will must prove by clear and convincing evidence that the testator intended to name a particular person as a beneficiary. That is a higher standard than proof by a preponderance of evidence.

Quicknotes

CLEAR AND CONVINCING EVIDENCE An evidentiary standard requiring a demonstration that the fact sought to be proven is reasonably certain.

INTESTACY To die without leaving a valid testamentary instrument.

PREPONDERANCE OF THE EVIDENCE A standard of proof requiring the trier of fact to determine whether the fact sought to be established is more probable than not.

In re Estate of Russell

[Parties not identified.]

Cal. Sup. Ct., 69 Cal. 2d 200, 444 P.2d 353 (1968).

NATURE OF CASE: Appeal from a determination of heirship.

FACT SUMMARY: The testator left her $10 gold piece and diamonds to Hembree, her only heir-at-law, and the residue of her estate to Charles Quinn and Roxy Russell, the latter being her dog, who predeceased her.

🏛 RULE OF LAW
When an uncertainty arises upon the face of a will, it cannot always be determined whether the will is ambiguous or not before the circumstances surrounding the writing of the will are first considered.

FACTS: The testatrix left her $10 gold piece to her sister, Hembree, who was her only heir-at-law, and the residue of her estate to Charles Quinn and Roxy Russell. Charles was a longtime friend and confidante, while Roxy was the testatrix's dog. Roxy predeceased the testatrix but was alive at the time of execution of the will. Extrinsic evidence was introduced to establish Roxy's identity. The trial court found that it was the testatrix's intention that Charles was to receive the entire residue and that the gift to Roxy was merely precatory in nature. It further found that there was no lapse of the gift to Charles, but that the gift was to maintain Roxy. Hembree appealed, arguing that the gift of one-half of the residue to a dog was clear and unambiguous; that it was void and passed to her under the laws of intestate succession; and that the admission of extrinsic evidence did not cure the invalidity of the gift.

ISSUE: When an uncertainty arises upon the face of a will, can it always be determined whether the will is ambiguous or not before the circumstances surrounding its writing are first considered?

HOLDING AND DECISION: (Sullivan, J.) No. When an uncertainty arises upon the face of a will, it cannot always be determined whether the will is ambiguous or not before the circumstances surrounding the writing of the will are first considered. The exclusion of extrinsic evidence regarding surrounding circumstances merely because no ambiguity appears can easily lead to giving the will a meaning never intended. California probate code § 105 provides that if, after the admission of extrinsic evidence, the will is not susceptible to two or more meanings, then no ambiguity exists. The statute simply delineates the manner of ascertaining testator's intention. Here, the trial court's conclusion was unreasonable. No words gave the residuary all to Charles or appeared to be merely precatory in nature. A distribution in equal shares to two persons cannot be said to be for one to use whatever portion is necessary in behalf of the other. No extrinsic evidence should have been admitted that would lead to a meaning to which the will was not reasonably susceptible. As for the gift to Roxy, it was clearly void so it lapsed and passed to the heirs-at-law by intestacy. Hembree, as the only heir-at-law, should take the gift. Reversed.

▶ ANALYSIS

Few definite guidelines can be given as to interpretation of wills. Rules and "trends" are conflicting. The rules of the case above apply not only to wills but to contracts and deeds also. They are important in evidence cases as well. What evidence to admit is usually the tough question; the student can only consider the appropriate statutory provisions and the various theories presented in the cases and resolve the problem in his own mind.

■══■

Quicknotes

EXTRINSIC EVIDENCE Evidence that is not contained within the text of a document or contract but which is derived from the parties' statements or the circumstances under which the agreement was made.

RESIDUE That property which remains following the distribution of the assets of the testator's estate.

TESTATRIX A woman who dies having drafted and executed a will or testament.

■══■

Ruotolo v. Tietjen

[Parties not identified.]

Conn. App. Ct., 890 A.2d 166 (2006).

NATURE OF CASE: Appeal of lower court's refusal to apply antilapse statute.

FACT SUMMARY: John Swanson's will left one-half of the residue of his estate to his stepdaughter, Hazel Brennan, "if she survives me". When Brennan predeceased Swanson, her daughter attempted to take her mother's share under an antilapse statute.

🏛 RULE OF LAW
Words of survivorship alone do not constitute sufficient evidence of a contrary intent on the part of the testator so as to prevent the application of an antilapse statute.

FACTS: John Swanson executed a will in 1990, leaving one-half of the residue of his estate, to his stepdaughter, Hazel Brennan, "if she survives me." Brennan predeceased Swanson, and when the will was submitted for probate, Brennan's daughter Kathleen argued that the Connecticut Antilapse Statute allowed her to take her mother's share under the will. The antilapse statute provided that "when a devisee or legatee, being a child, stepchild, grandchild, brother or sister of the testator, dies before him, and no provision has been made in the will for such contingency, the issue of such devisee or legatee shall take the estate so devised or bequeathed." The superior court held that Swanson's use of the phrase "if she survives me" addressed the contingency that Brennan might not survive him, refused to apply the antilapse statute, and applied the rules of intestacy to Brennan's share of the estate, bypassing Kathleen who appealed the ruling.

ISSUE: Do words of survivorship alone constitute sufficient evidence of a contrary intent on the part of the testator so as to prevent the application of an antilapse statute?

HOLDING AND DECISION: (Lavery, C.J.) No. Words of survivorship alone do not constitute sufficient evidence of a contrary intent on the part of the testator so as to prevent the application of an antilapse statute. At common law, if a named beneficiary under a will predeceased the testator, the beneficiary's share did not pass to his descendants. Antilapse statutes were designed to avoid unintended disinheritances. Connecticut conditioned operation of the antilapse statute on the intent of the testator as expressed in the will. Accordingly, the critical inquiry is whether intent contrary to the statute is so manifested, and the burden is on those who seek to deny the statutory protection rather than on those who assert it. We are mindful that our statute was enacted to prevent operation of the rule of lapse. Our statute is remedial in nature and must be liberally construed. Accordingly, we resolve any doubt in favor of the operation of the statute. In 1990, a revised uniform probate code contained a substantially altered antilapse statute, which provides that "words of survivorship, such as in a devise to an individual 'if he survives me' . . . Are not, in the absence of additional evidence, a sufficient indication of an intent contrary to the application" of the antilapse statute. Our conclusion today effectuates the intent of the general assembly in enacting this remedial statute. Should a testator desire to avoid application of the antilapse statute, the testator must either unequivocally express that intent or simply provide for an alternate bequest. Because the testator in the present case did neither, the protections of the antilapse statute apply. Accordingly, the bequest to Brennan does not lapse, but rather descends to her issue. Reversed and remanded.

▶ ANALYSIS
The Connecticut Supreme Court upheld the appellate court's decision. Many, if not the majority, of the states have concluded that the survivorship clause at issue here is sufficient evidence to prevent the application of the antilapse statute. The presumption in those states is that the testator, often relying upon experienced counsel, specifically chose to include the survivorship clause, and that a clear intent to override the antilapse statute should be attributed to the testator in those cases.

━■━

Quicknotes
ANTILAPSE STATUTE State statute providing for the substitution of a recipient of a devise made pursuant to a testamentary instrument, if the beneficiary of the gift predeceases the testator and no alternative disposition is made.

TESTATOR One who executes a will.

━■━

Dawson v. Yucus

Beneficiary (P) v. Executrix (D)

Ill. App. Ct., 97 Ill. App. 2d 101, 239 N.E.2d 305 (1968).

NATURE OF CASE: Appeal from a judgment for defendants in an action to construe a will.

FACT SUMMARY: Wilson (P), the remaining beneficiary of a will, argued that the gift was made to a class, and therefore, as survivor of the class, he was entitled to the entire interest bequeathed to the class.

🏛 RULE OF LAW

Where the number of beneficiaries to a gift is certain, and the share each is to receive is also certain and in no way dependent for its amount upon the number who shall survive, it is not a gift to a class but to the individuals.

FACTS: Nelle Stewart left a duly executed will containing ten clauses. The second clause gave the one-fifth interest in farm lands that Stewart inherited from her husband to two of his nephews, Stewart Wilson and Gene Burtle. Each was to receive one-half of Stewart's one-fifth interest. After the will was admitted to probate, Wilson (P) filed suit against the executrix, Yucus (D), to construe the will, alleging that the devise was a class gift, that Burtle had died after the date of execution of the will but before the testatrix, and that Wilson (P), as the survivor of the class, was entitled to the entire one-fifth interest in the farm. Burtle's two children, Dawson (P) and Burtle (P), were subsequently substituted as plaintiffs. The trial court held that clause two did not create a class gift, and therefore the gift to Burtle lapsed and passed into the residue of the estate upon his death. Dawson (P) and Burtle (P) appealed.

ISSUE: Where the number of beneficiaries to a gift is certain, and the share each is to receive is also certain and in no way dependent for its amount upon the number who shall survive, is it a gift to a class?

HOLDING AND DECISION: (Jones, J.) No. Where the number of beneficiaries to a gift is certain, and the share each is to receive is also certain and in no way dependent for its amount upon the number who shall survive, it is not a gift to a class but to the individuals. In this case, Stewart named the individuals, giving them each a specified portion of her interest in the farm, thus making certain the number of beneficiaries and the share each was to receive. The shares in no way depend upon the number who shall survive Stewart's death. She did, however, create a survivorship gift of the residue of her estate, thus indicating she knew how to manifest such intent. Hence, the language of clause two, phrased differently, was intended to create a gift to individuals distributively. Affirmed.

▶ ANALYSIS

A testator is deemed to be "group minded," that is, intends to create a class gift, if she uses a generic class label such as "to my nephews" in devising her property. Stewart stated in her bequest in clause two that she believed the farm lands should go back to her late husband's "side of the house." Wilson (P) argued unsuccessfully that this phrase, together with the extrinsic evidence admitted by the court as to Stewart's intentions, clearly required class gift construction.

━■━

Quicknotes

CLASS GIFT A gift to a group of unspecified persons whose number, identity, and share of the gift will be determined sometime in the future.

EXTRINSIC EVIDENCE Evidence that is not contained within the text of a document or contract but which is derived from the parties' statements or the circumstances under which the agreement was made.

REMAINDER An interest in land that remains after the termination of the immediately preceding estate.

RESIDUE That property which remains following the distribution of the assets of the testator's estate.

━■━

In re Estate of Anton

Beneficiary (P) v. Executor (D)

Iowa Sup. Ct., 731 N.W.2d 19 (2007).

NATURE OF CASE: Appeal of order denying claim against an estate.

FACT SUMMARY: Hester Mary Lewis Anton (Anton) executed a will leaving one-half of her interest in a piece of property to her stepdaughter Gretchen Coy (Coy) (P). Anton's daughter, acting as her mother's agent under a durable power of attorney, sold the property in 2003 to pay for Anton's nursing home care. After Anton died, Coy (P) filed a claim against the estate (D) to recover the value of her share of the property.

🏛 RULE OF LAW
The identity rule adeeming bequests not specifically found in an estate will not be applied to cases where specifically devised property is removed from the testator's estate through an act that is involuntary to the testator.

FACTS: In 1981, Anton executed a will leaving one-half of her interest in her duplex to her stepdaughter Coy (P). Anton was injured in a car accident in 1996 and spent the rest of her life living in several nursing homes, where she was also treated for Huntington's Chorea, a progressive neurological disorder. After the accident, Anton executed a valid durable power of attorney naming her daughter Nancy Ezarski (Ezarski) as her attorney-in-fact. Ezarski managed her mother's financial affairs from 1986 until Anton died in 2003, and gradually sold off Anton's assets to pay for her nursing home care. By 2003, Anton was suffering from what one social services progress report referred to as advanced dementia, and was apparently not competent to handle her financial affairs. Ezarski, having run out of assets to sell, finally sold the duplex and used approximately $29,000 out of the $133,263 net proceeds from the sale to pay for Anton's care up until Anton's death. When Anton's will was submitted for probate, Coy (P) filed a claim against the estate (D), claiming that she was entitled to one-half of the net proceeds from the sale of the duplex. The estate (D) claimed that Coy (P) was not entitled to any of the funds because the identity theory of ademption extinguished any specific bequests not in Anton's estate. The trial court denied the claim and the court of appeals upheld the denial. Coy (P) appealed to the Iowa Supreme Court.

ISSUE: Will the identity rule adeeming bequests not specifically found in an estate be applied to cases where specifically devised property is removed from the testator's estate through an act that is involuntary to the testator?

HOLDING AND DECISION: (Appel, J.) No. The identity rule adeeming bequests not specifically found in an estate will not be applied to cases where specifically devised property is removed from the testator's estate through an act that is involuntary to the testator. Our cases hold that the identity rule will not be rigidly applied in all cases. This includes cases where the property is sold by a guardian, or conservator, or is destroyed contemporaneously with the death of the testator. The rationale of our cases is that ademption occurs where a testator had knowledge of a transaction involving a specific devise, realizes the effect of the transaction on his or her estate plan, and has an opportunity to revise the will. Where these elements are not present, no ademption occurs. The focus of the analysis is on the testator and whether the testator has made a deliberate decision not to revise the will, and not on the nature of the agency causing the involuntary act. If Anton was aware of the transaction, was aware of the impact the transaction had on her estate plan, and did not change her will, ademption would, of course, occur. Here, however, Anton only had a general knowledge that assets would need to be sold for her support at some time in the future. Therefore, ademption does not apply. Reversed and remanded.

▶ ANALYSIS

The Iowa Supreme Court refused to award Coy (P) one-half of the net proceeds from the sale, but instead ordered the trial court to award Coy (P) one-half of the proceeds remaining from the sale after Anton's cost of care was deducted. This is in keeping with most modern statutes; however, some states still award the full value of the property regardless of what happened to the funds between the time of the sale and the testator's death.

Quicknotes

ADEMPTION Revocation of a specific devise or bequest made pursuant to a testamentary instrument if the particular property is not part of the decedent's estate at the time of death.

BEQUEST A transfer of property that is accomplished by means of a testamentary instrument.

DEVISE The conferring of a gift of real or personal property by means of a testamentary instrument.

DURABLE POWER OF ATTORNEY A written document pursuant to which one party confers the authority to act as an agent on his behalf to another party and which is to become effective if the grantor should later become incapacitated.

Trusts: Characteristics and Creation

Quick Reference Rules of Law

Jimenez v. Lee

Trustee's daughter (P) v. Trustee (D)

Or. Sup. Ct., 274 Or. 457, 547 P.2d 126 (1976).

NATURE OF CASE: Action for an accounting.

FACT SUMMARY: Jimenez (P) sought an accounting from her father, Lee (D), for his use of trust funds to satisfy his legal support obligations to her.

RULE OF LAW
Where funds are held in trust for a specific purpose, the trustee will be liable for all expenditures not related to that purpose.

FACTS: Jimenez's (P) grandmother purchased a $1,000 savings bond shortly after Jimenez's (P) birth in the joint names of Jimenez (P) and/or her father, Lee (D). The bond was for Jimenez's (P) educational needs. Another $500 bond was purchased by a third party for Jimenez's (P) education. Lee (D) subsequently cashed the bonds in and invested the proceeds in common stock, which Lee (D) held as custodian for Jimenez (P) under the Uniform Gift to Minors Act. Lee (D) had held these funds as trustee and could use them only for a proper trust purpose, Jimenez's (P) education. Jimenez (P) sought an accounting. Lee (D) alleged that no trust existed and that all funds had been used for Jimenez's (P) benefit. The trial court dismissed Jimenez's (P) complaint.

ISSUE: May a trustee use trust funds for the benefit of the beneficiary but for purposes not authorized under the trust?

HOLDING AND DECISION: (O'Connell, C.J.) No. A trustee may only use trust funds in a manner authorized under the trust. He may not expand his powers to include unauthorized uses. The evidence indicates that the bonds were to be used for Jimenez's (P) education and were held in trust by Lee (D) for this purpose. The evidence clearly establishes that Lee (D) could not expand his powers by using the bonds to purchase stock, with Lee (D) acting as custodian under the Uniform Gift to Minors Act. The stock is directly traceable to the bonds, and the trust is impressed on the stock. As trustee, Lee (D) was obligated to keep exact records of all expenditures made for Jimenez's (P) education. Failure to keep accurate records can result in a surcharge to the trustee for unaccounted sums. The trustee is also liable for expenditures not related to the purpose of the trust. Reversed and remanded.

▶ ANALYSIS

Jimenez is important for a number of reasons. First, it points out the importance of keeping adequate records of expenditures. Even if the trustee has acted entirely properly, he will be liable for any unaccounted-for funds.

White v. Rankin, 46 N.Y.S. 228 (1897). Next, *Jimenez* indicates that the trustee must be able to establish that all expenditures are within the areas permitted under the trust instrument. Bogart on *Trusts and Trustees* § 972(1) (1962).

■■■

Quicknotes

TRUSTEE A person who is entrusted to keep or administer property for the benefit of another.

■■■

Hebrew University Assn. v. Nye

[Parties not identified.]

Conn. Sup. Ct., 169 A.2d 641 (1961).

NATURE OF CASE: Appeal from judgment in action over property ownership.

FACT SUMMARY: Yahuda owned an extensive library that she promised to give to a university in Jerusalem but never delivered before her death.

🏛 RULE OF LAW
An imperfect gift due to lack of delivery may not be turned into a trust without an express manifestation of intent.

FACTS: Yahuda became the owner of a collection of rare manuscripts on the death of her husband. In January 1953, Yahuda went to Israel and had discussions about the library with the university officers and announced her gift of the manuscripts to them at a luncheon. Thereafter, Yahuda told everyone that she had given the library of books to the university, and she refused offers to sell. In 1954, Yahuda began arranging and cataloguing the materials for shipment to Israel. However, before her tasks were finished and the books delivered, Yahuda died. Yahuda's will left her estate to another charitable institution. The university filed suit, claiming that it was entitled to the library because it was the rightful owner. The trial court ruled for the university on the basis that Yahuda had created a trust with regard to the library in favor of the university. The decision was appealed.

ISSUE: May an imperfect gift due to lack of delivery be turned into a trust without an express manifestation of intent?

HOLDING AND DECISION: (King, J.) No. An imperfect gift due to lack of delivery may not be turned into a trust without an express manifestation of intent. If an intended gift fails because there was not actual or constructive delivery, the intent can be carried out in equity under the fiction that the donor presumed to constitute himself as trustee to make the delivery. However, this is not true unless there is an express trust, which may be oral, created by the donor. In the present case, there are no facts suggesting that Yahuda ever intended to impose on herself the duties of a trustee with regard to the library. The only evidence is that she had a donative intent but failed to make the delivery. There simply is no evidence to support the trial court's conclusion that she established a trust in favor of the university. Reversed and remanded for a new trial so that the university can present another theory of ownership.

▶ ANALYSIS

Other jurisdictions may have reached a different conclusion on these facts. The Connecticut opinion here represents a strict and narrow view of what is required to show that a donor considers him or herself to be a trustee. While the court seemed to realize that Yahuda had clearly intended the university to receive the library, they seemed concerned that it was subverting the rules on gifts and trusts to fit it in.

Quicknotes

DONOR A person who gives real or personal property or value.

TRUSTEE A person who is entrusted to keep or administer property for the benefit of another.

Hebrew University Assn. v. Nye

[Parties not identified.]

Conn. Super. Ct., 223 A.2d 397 (1966).

NATURE OF CASE: Action to resolve ownership of decedent's property.

FACT SUMMARY: The ownership of Yahuda's rare book collection was disputed because she intended to give it as a gift but died before delivering it.

🏛 RULE OF LAW
Constructive delivery of a gift through an informal document is permitted if accompanied by acts and declarations showing an intention to complete the gift.

FACTS: Yahuda became the owner of a collection of rare manuscripts on the death of her husband. In January 1953, Yahuda went to Israel and had discussions about the library with the university officers and announced her gift of it to them at a luncheon. Thereafter, Yahuda told everyone that she had given the library of books to the university, and she refused offers to sell. In 1954, Yahuda began arranging and cataloguing the materials for shipment to Israel. However, before her tasks were finished and the books delivered, Yahuda died. Her will left her estate to another charitable institution. The university filed suit, claiming that it was entitled to the library because it was the rightful owner. The trial court ruled for the university on the basis that Yahuda had created a trust with regard to the library in favor of the university. After the Supreme Court reversed, the case was remanded so that the university could present alternative theories.

ISSUE: Is constructive delivery of a gift through an informal document permitted if accompanied by acts and declarations showing an intention to complete the gift?

HOLDING AND DECISION: (Parskey, J.) Yes. Constructive delivery of a gift through an informal document is permitted if accompanied by acts and declarations showing an intention to complete the gift. Constructive delivery must be the reasonable equivalent of actual delivery depending on the nature of the property and the circumstances. In the present case, Yahuda clearly indicated her intent to give the library of rare books to the university. She was preparing it for actual delivery when she died, and she had already given the university a memorandum containing a list of the contents of the library. If this memorandum was a formal document the gift would have been unquestionably valid. But the lack of formalism is not fatal here, especially given the other facts that show a clear intention to provide the gift to the university. While the court realizes that the facts here stretch the concept of constructive delivery, courts of equity must do their best to effectuate the wishes of the decedent. Thus, the university is entitled to the possession of Yahuda's library.

▶ ANALYSIS

The result reached here seems to be the fairest one possible. However, even the court was a bit apprehensive at stretching the rules to make sure that Yahuda's intent was carried out. They acknowledged that loose rules could give rise to fraudulent claims.

◼═◼

Quicknotes

CONSTRUCTIVE DELIVERY The transfer of title or possession of property by means other than actual delivery indicative of the parties' intent to effect a transfer.

◼═◼

Unthank v. Rippstein

Promisee (P) v. Executor (D)

Tex. Sup. Ct., 386 S.W.2d 134 (1964).

NATURE OF CASE: Action to declare a trust.

FACT SUMMARY: Craft sent a letter to Rippstein (P) promising to give her $200 per month.

🏛 RULE OF LAW
A mere promise to give periodic gifts in the future will not support a finding that a trust has been established.

FACTS: Craft sent Rippstein (P) a letter a few days before his death, promising to give her $200 per month. The letter stated that Craft's estate would be liable for such payments if he died. Rippstein (P) alleged that the letter created an enforceable trust. Unthank (D), the executor of Craft's will, alleged this was an unenforceable gift or a voluntary trust that was unenforceable for lack of consideration.

ISSUE: Is a mere promise to make payments in the future enforceable as a trust?

HOLDING AND DECISION: (Steakley, J.) No. A gift or voluntary trust is merely a promise, without consideration to make payments in the future. As such, it is unenforceable under the rules governing gifts. It is not a trust since there is no res and no intention expressed to hold all of the alleged trustor's property liable for payment. Upon the death of the promisor, the promise cannot be enforced against the estate since the gift of payments after death is a will substitute lacking the requisite testamentary requirements. The gift is unenforceable. Reversed and trial court affirmed.

▶ ANALYSIS

Before a trust may be found to be enforceable, the equitable title must sufficiently rest in the beneficiary so as to allow him to maintain an action for the conversion of the trust property. *Flick v. Baldwin*, 141 Tex. 340. Where there is no specific trust res to which the trust is to attach, the beneficiary has no beneficial interest in any particular property. Additionally, of course, the absence of trust res would in and of itself, cause the trust to fail in most instances.

■=■

Quicknotes

HOLOGRAPHIC CODICIL A handwritten provision added to a testamentary instrument.

RES Thing; subject matter of a dispute to establish rights therein.

TRUST The holding of property by one party for the benefit of another.

TRUST CORPUS The aggregate body of assets placed into a trust.

VOLUNTARY TRUST A trust established by a settlor voluntarily, as opposed to by operation of law, with the intent to make a gift of the trust property for the benefit of another.

■=■

Clark v. Campbell

[Parties not identified.]

N.H. Sup. Ct., 133 A. 166 (1926).

NATURE OF CASE: Will contest.

FACT SUMMARY: The trustees of the estate were directed to give decedent's personal effects to the friends they knew she wished to receive them.

🏛 RULE OF LAW
Where the beneficiaries of a noncharitable trust cannot adequately be determined, the trust fails.

FACTS: Decedent left her personal property to her trustees in trust to "make disposal by way of memento . . . to such of my friends as they, my trustees, shall select." Decedent further stated that her trustees were familiar with her friends and her wishes. Heirs alleged that the trust was void for lack of definite beneficiaries or ascertainable standards to identify them.

ISSUE: Must there be a definite beneficiary of a trust or ascertainable standards for determining the identity of beneficiaries?

HOLDING AND DECISION: (Snow, J.) Yes. To be valid, a trust must have an identifiable beneficiary, or there must be adequate standards provided under the trust instrument for their identification in the future. "Friends" is too indefinite a class of beneficiaries. Appointment of property by the trustee could not be opposed, in most cases, since the permissible class is too vague for the court to determine whether the distribution was proper. The trust therefore fails, and the trustee holds for the taker under the will. Case discharged.

▶ ANALYSIS

The Attorney General of the state administers charitable trusts and can protect against trustee abuses. Therefore, charitable trusts will not fail for lack of a definite beneficiary. *Harrington v. Pier*, 105 Wis. 485 (1900). Personal wishes conveyed to the trustee by the testator are not sufficient to render an otherwise indefinite description of beneficiaries definite. *Olliffe v. Wells*, 130 Mass. 221 (1881).

━━━

Quicknotes

CESTUI QUE TRUST Beneficiary; the party for whose benefit a trust is established.

UNJUST ENRICHMENT The unlawful acquisition of money or property of another for which both law and equity require restitution to be made.

━━━

In re Searight's Estate

Department of Taxation (P) v. Executor (D)

Ohio Ct. App., 95 N.E.2d 779 (1950).

NATURE OF CASE: Appeal from probate decision.

FACT SUMMARY: The testator, by will, left $1,000 to his executor (D) to pay another to care for his dog for the rest of the dog's life, and the probate court found it was a valid honorary trust.

RULE OF LAW
An "honorary trust" is valid where it is for a legal purpose and the trustee accepts the testator's wishes, even though there is no beneficiary who can enforce the trust.

FACTS: The testator, by will, left $1,000 to his executor (D) to pay Florence Hand $0.75 per day to care for his dog for the rest of the dog's life. The probate court found that it was a valid "honorary trust."

ISSUE: Is an "honorary trust" valid where it is for a legal purpose and the trustee accepts the testator's wishes, even though there is no beneficiary who can enforce the trust?

HOLDING AND DECISION: (Hunsicker, J.) Yes. An "honorary trust" is valid where it is for a legal purpose and the trustee accepts the testator's wishes, even though there is no beneficiary who can enforce the trust. Normally, attempts to create a trust where there is no ascertainable beneficiary will fail, but an exception permits an "honorary trust" to survive. The requirements are that the trust, have some legal purpose and that the trustee accepts the wishes of the testator. Here, the testator attempted to further no illegal purpose but rather a worthy one; and Florence accepted the dog and the responsibilities of care. The transfer into trust does not violate the rule against perpetuities since there is only $1,000 plus accumulated interest involved, which, at $0.75 per day, would be exhausted within 5 years. (The R.A.P. requires the transfer to vest within a life or lives in being plus twenty-one years.) Affirmed.

ANALYSIS

Most jurisdictions do not recognize "honorary trusts." But no jurisdiction recognizes such a trust where the testator "requests" or "hopes" that the trustee will perform the stated tasks in the purported trust instrument. This would be an aleatory suggestion, which the trustee could ignore while keeping the transfer into trust for his own benefit. It would then be void due to no affirmative trust intent.

Quicknotes

CHARITABLE TRUST A trust that is established for the benefit of a class of persons or for the public in general.

RULE AGAINST PERPETUITIES The doctrine that a future interest that is incapable of vesting within twenty-one years of lives in being at the time it is created is immediately void.

In re Estate of Fournier

[Parties not identified.]

Me. Sup. Jud. Ct., 902 A.2d 852 (2006).

NATURE OF CASE: Appeal from denial of petition seeking declaratory judgment that an oral trust had been created for an individual.

FACT SUMMARY: Fournier asked a couple to hold $400,000 for him and to turn the money over to his sister, Fogarty (P), when he died since Fogarty (P) needed the money more than his other sister, Flanigan (D). Fogarty (P), the personal representative of Fournier's estate, contended that Fournier had created an oral trust with the couple and that she was the personal beneficiary of that trust.

> ## 🏛 RULE OF LAW
> An enforceable oral trust is created where clear and convincing evidence shows that the settlor intended to create it.

FACTS: Fournier asked a couple who were his trusted friends to hold $400,000 for him and to turn the money over to his sister, Fogarty (P), when he died since Fogarty (P) needed the money more than his other sister, Flanigan (D). Fournier told Flanigan (D) and her daughter about the money. He also gave Fogarty (P) $100,000 during his life. After Fournier died, Fogarty (P) became the personal representative of Fournier's estate. She met with the couple, who turned the $400,000 over to her. Fogarty (P) petitioned for a declaratory judgment to establish that during his lifetime Fournier had created an oral trust for her benefit. The probate court denied her petition because it concluded that by telling Flanigan (D) and her daughter about the money, Fournier had sought to pass the money through his estate, and that by giving Fogarty the $100,000 gift, he decreased her financial need, potentially obviating the need for a trust for her benefit. The state's highest court granted review.

ISSUE: Is an enforceable oral trust created where clear and convincing evidence shows that the settlor intended to create it?

HOLDING AND DECISION: (Dana, J.) Yes. An enforceable oral trust is created where clear and convincing evidence shows that the settlor intended to create it. The creation of an oral trust must be established by clear and convincing evidence. Here, the evidence, primarily in the form of testimony from the couple, clearly and convincingly showed that Fournier intended Fogarty (P) to get the money in her individual capacity, not as the estate's personal representative. It also showed that he did not want Flanigan (D) to get the money. Accordingly, the probate court clearly erred in determining that Fournier wanted the money to pass through his estate. Thus, Fournier created an oral trust in which the couple was to hold the money during his lifetime and turn it over to Fogarty (P) personally after his death. Vacated and remanded.

▶ ANALYSIS

Oral trusts are valid in all but a few states, and, as in this case, may be proved by oral testimony.

■■■

Quicknotes

TRUST The holding of property by one party for the benefit of another.

■■■

Olliffe v. Wells

Family of deceased (P) v. Executor (D)

Mass. Sup. Jud. Ct., 130 Mass. 221 (1881).

NATURE OF CASE: Action to have legacy of estate residue declared lapsed and to have property distributed among heirs at law and next of kin.

FACT SUMMARY: Testatrix devised residue of estate to the executor with an instruction to distribute it, according to his discretion, so as to carry out the testatrix's pre-expressed wishes.

🏛 RULE OF LAW
Where a will on its face shows that the devisee takes the legal title only and not the beneficial interest, and the trust is not sufficiently defined by the will to take effect, the equitable interest goes by way of resulting trust to the heirs or next of kin as property of the deceased not disposed of by his will.

FACTS: Testatrix left a will, and after giving various legacies, she devised to Wells (D), the named executor, the residue of the estate, which the executor (D) was empowered to distribute in such manner as in his discretion was best calculated to carry out the wishes of the testatrix as expressed to him. In an action by the heirs (P) and next of kin (P) of the testatrix to have the executor (D) distribute the residue to them, the executor (D) claimed prior to her death, the testatrix orally instructed him to give the residue to charities.

ISSUE: Where a will on its face gives legal title but not any beneficial interest to a devisee, and there is no express trust indicated, will a resulting trust arise in favor of heirs or next of kin?

HOLDING AND DECISION: (Gray, C.J.) Yes. The purported trust in favor of the charities did not appear on the face of the will; therefore, it cannot be established by extrinsic evidence. Thus, the executor (D) only has discretion in the manner of distribution; he cannot choose the beneficiaries. Since the trust cannot be carried out, the bequest falls within the residue of the estate and goes to the heirs (P) and next of kin (P). If the charities had been expressly named, they could have enforced the trust against the executor (D), who received only a legal title, and no beneficial interest, in the devise. Decision for plaintiffs.

▌ ANALYSIS

Where a testamentary trust fails for any reason, the assets that were to be a part of that trust must still be distributed. In some instances the testator's will may provide for the distribution of such assets. But if no contingent provision was prepared, the assets must pass intestate. This has resulted, in some cases, in the assets going to heirs or next of kin specifically excluded by the testator. A statement by a testator in his will that certain individuals are not to share in his estate does not constitute a testamentary scheme.

■=■

Quicknotes

DEVISEE A person upon whom a gift of real or personal property is conferred by means of a testamentary instrument.

EXTRINSIC EVIDENCE Evidence that is not contained within the text of a document or contract but which is derived from the parties' statements or the circumstances under which the agreement was made.

RESIDUARY ESTATE That portion of the estate that remains after all the estate has been distributed through the satisfaction of all claims and is conditional upon something remaining after the claims on the testator's estate are satisfied.

RESULTING TRUST An equitable trust that is established from the inferred intent of the parties to create a trust.

■=■

Nonprobate Transfers and Planning for Incapacity

Quick Reference Rules of Law

Farkas v. Williams

Estate administrators (P) v. Beneficiary (D)

Ill. Sup. Ct., 5 Ill. 2d 417, 125 N.E.2d 600 (1955).

NATURE OF CASE: Action to determine who, between the administrators of the estate and the beneficiary of the trust, had a right to four stock certificates.

FACT SUMMARY: The Administrators (P) of Farkas's estate claim the right to four stock certificates that Farkas held in trust for Williams (D).

RULE OF LAW
Even though the settlor retains the power to revoke the trust and appoints himself as trustee, if the beneficiary obtains any interest in the trust before the settlor dies, a valid inter vivos trust may have been formed.

FACTS: Albert Farkas executed a written declaration of trust for four separate stock certificates and named Williams (D) as beneficiary of all four. Farkas retained the power to revoke the trust and the power to vote, sell, redeem, exchange, or otherwise deal with the stock. He also appointed himself as trustee. If Farkas didn't revoke the trust, Williams (D) was required to be alive when Farkas died or the trust would be automatically revoked. Farkas died without having revoked the trust and the Administrators (P) of his estate brought this action to obtain a declaration of rights to the stock certificates. The Administrators (P) claimed that the trust was testamentary and not valid because Farkas had not complied with the statute of wills in making his declarations of trust. They claimed that Farkas had retained so much control over the trust that it didn't qualify as an inter vivos trust. The circuit court held that the trust was an invalid testamentary trust, and so the stock was an asset of the Farkas estate.

ISSUE: Must a beneficiary obtain some interest in the trust before the settlor dies to have a valid inter vivos trust?

HOLDING AND DECISION: (Hershey, J.) Yes. It is necessary that a beneficiary obtain some interest in the trust prior to the time the settlor dies or the trust will be considered to be a testamentary trust. This means that the settlor cannot retain absolute control over the trust res in making an inter vivos trust. It is true that Farkas retained a great deal of control over the trust res, but Williams (D) did have an interest in the trust before Farkas died. Farkas had to administer the trust in accordance with the declaration of trust, which limited his control over the stock. Even though Williams (D) was required to be living when Farkas died in order to have any right to the stock, which meant that he did not have an interest that he could bequeath to anyone, he still had a small right to the stock in that, if the trust were not revoked and Farkas, as trustee, committed a breach of trust, Williams (D) could hold the estate liable. A valid inter vivos trust was established in Williams's (D) favor. Reversed and remanded with instructions.

ANALYSIS

There is a split of opinion among the different jurisdictions as to the amount of power and control the settlor can retain and still have a valid inter vivos trust. The more recent cases seem to hold as the court in this case did. They allow the settlor to retain a great deal of control over the trust.

Quicknotes

INTER VIVOS TRUST Property that is held by one person for the benefit of another and which is created by an instrument that takes effect during the life of the grantor.

REVOCABLE TRUST The holding of property by one party for the benefit of another pursuant to an instrument in which the creator reserves the right to revoke the trust.

TESTAMENTARY DISPOSITION A disposition of property that is effective upon the death of the grantor.

Moon v. Lesikar

Sister (P) v. Brother (D)

Tex. Ct. App., 230 S.W.3d 800 (2007).

NATURE OF CASE: Appeal from lower court decision finding that a contingent beneficiary did not have standing to challenge a transaction completed by the settlor of a revocable trust.

FACT SUMMARY: Woodrow Lesikar created an Amended Family Trust in 1997 providing that all net income from the trust go to him during his lifetime. The document stated that special trusts would be set up for his son, Woody Lesikar (D) and daughter, Carolyn Lesikar Moon (P), upon his death. Prior to his death, Mr. Lesikar sold 10,000 shares of stock in an airport to Woody (D) directly for a small dollar amount. Carolyn (P) challenged the sale as a breach of a fiduciary duty.

> 🏛 **RULE OF LAW**
> A contingent beneficiary of a revocable trust has no legally enforceable interest while the settlor of the trust is alive and the trust remains revocable.

FACTS: Woodrow Lesikar, the owner of the West Houston Airport, created an Amended Family Trust in 1997. A prior version of the family trust stated that 10,000 shares of the West Airport Corporation would go to a trust established for the benefit of the children of his son, Woody Lesikar (D). The 1997 trust set up special trusts for Woody (D) and for Lasikar's daughter, Carolyn Lesikar Moon (P). However, the 1997 trust removed the provision giving 10,000 shares to Woody's (D) children. Instead, in 1998, Lesikar sold the 10,000 shares of Airport Stock to Woody (D) directly for the low price of $2,000. The sale included an assignment of the stock to a trust that would be set up for Woody's (D) two children. After Lesikar died in 2001, Carolyn (P) filed a petition for construction of the trust, claiming Lesikar breached a fiduciary duty to her as a contingent beneficiary by selling the Airport Stock to Woody (D) at an artificially low price. The lower court granted summary judgment to Woody (D) on the grounds a contingent beneficiary did not have standing to challenge a transaction completed by the settlor of a revocable trust. The 1997 trust was revocable with Lesikar acting as both the settlor and trustee of the trust. Carolyn (P) appealed.

ISSUE: Does a contingent beneficiary of a revocable trust have a legally enforceable interest while the settlor of the trust is alive and the trust remains revocable?

HOLDING AND DECISION: (Hudson, J.) Yes. A contingent beneficiary of a revocable trust has no legally enforceable interest while the settlor of the trust is alive and the trust remains revocable. Carolyn (P) argues that any interested person in the trust may bring an action relating to the fiduciary duties of the trustee. An interested person is defined as a trustee, beneficiary, or any other person who has an interest or claim in the trust. An interest includes both vested and contingent interests. Carolyn (P) clearly has a contingent interest in the trust. However, Lesikar has the power to revoke or amend the trust until his death. Moreover, he was the sole beneficiary of the trust during his lifetime. Courts in other jurisdictions have concluded that where a settlor of a trust has the power to revoke during his lifetime, a contingent beneficiary does not have standing to sue the trust or the settlor based on any dispositions of the trust assets completed by the settlor while he was alive. Accordingly, the lower court properly granted summary judgment to Woody (D). Affirmed.

▶ ANALYSIS

While the settlor of a revocable trust is still alive, only the settlor may file a complaint with the trustee regarding a breach of the trustee's duties. Here, Lesikar was the settlor and the trustee. In addition, Carolyn (P) claimed that Lesikar failed to notify the trustee of the sale of the Airport stock. Consistent with other jurisdictions, the court found that Lesikar did not have a duty to notify himself of the sale.

■=■

Quicknotes

REVOCABLE TRUST A trust where trustor reserves the right to revoke the trust.

SETTLOR The grantor or donor of property that is to be held in trust for the benefit of another.

■=■

Patterson v. Patterson

Brother (P) v. Brother (D)

Utah Sup. Ct., 266 P.3d 828 (2011).

NATURE OF CASE: Appeal from lower court decision invalidating amendment to trust that removed one of the settlor's sons as a beneficiary.

FACT SUMMARY: Darlene Patterson executed an amendment to the Patterson Family Protection Trust that removed one of her sons, Ronald Patterson (P), as a beneficiary. The original trust document did not include a specific provision providing the manner in which an amendment could be completed.

▥ RULE OF LAW

If the terms of a revocable trust do not provide a method for amendments or revocation, the settlor of the trust may amend or revoke the trust document by any method that manifests clear and convincing evidence of the settlor's intent.

FACTS: Darlene Patterson executed an amendment to the Patterson Family Protection Trust that sought to remove one of her sons, Ronald Patterson (P), as a beneficiary. Randy Patterson (D), another son, acted as the trustee of the trust. The original trust document did not include a provision that provided the method for any amendments or revocation of the trust. After Darlene's death, Ronald (P) petitioned the court to invalidate the amendment, on the grounds that Darlene improperly sought to divest Ronald (P) of his interest without revoking the entire trust first. The lower court agreed and granted Ronald (P) partial summary judgment. Randy (D) appealed.

ISSUE: If the terms of a revocable trust do not provide a method for amendments or revocation, may the settlor of the trust amend or revoke the trust document by any method that manifests clear and convincing evidence of the settlor's intent?

HOLDING AND DECISION: (Parrish, J.) Yes. If the terms of a revocable trust do not provide a method for amendments or revocation, the settlor of the trust may amend or revoke the trust document by any method that manifests clear and convincing evidence of the settlor's intent. Under prior case law, where a trust states that beneficiaries' vested interest remains valid until the trust is revoked or terminated, only a complete revocation of the trust document could divest a beneficiary's interest. Any piecemeal attempt to amend a trust was invalidated. In 2004, Utah joined other states in adopting the Uniform Trust Code which acknowledges the increased use of living and revocable trusts in place of wills. The Code treats a living trust essentially as a will and grants similar rights to amend living trusts just as a testator has to amend his or her will. Moreover, while the settlor of the living trust is alive, all of the rights of the beneficiaries are controlled by the settlor. Specifically, the new Code allows a living trust to be amended by any later trust amendment or codicil even if the trust document does not provide for such amendments. Here, Darlene's trust did not provide a method for amendments. Her properly executed amendment to her trust removing Ronald (P) as a beneficiary manifested clear and convincing evidence of her intent to amend the trust. Accordingly, the amendment is valid and the lower court should not have granted summary judgment to Ronald (P). Reversed.

▶ ANALYSIS

The decision notes the significant rise in the use of living trusts in place of wills. During a testator's lifetime, the testator has the ability to amend the will via the use of other documents. The prior rule for revocable trusts was that unless the trust specifically laid out a procedure for amendments, a trust could not be amended to remove a specific provision. The entire document needed to be revoked. The Uniform Trust Code's 2004 amendments sought to allow modifications to revocable trusts similar to the ability to amend wills.

Quicknotes

REVOCABLE TRUST A trust where trustor reserves the right to revoke the trust.

SETTLOR The grantor or donor of property that is to be held in trust for the benefit of another.

State Street Bank & Trust Co. v. Reiser

Lending bank (P) v. Estate of decedent (D)

Mass. App. Ct., 389 N.E.2d 768 (1979).

NATURE OF CASE: Appeal from order upholding an inter vivos trust.

FACT SUMMARY: After Dunnebier created an inter vivos trust funded with the capital stock of five closely held corporations that owned certain real estate regarded by State Street Bank (P) as evidence of Dunnebier's solvency, the Bank (P) made an unsecured loan to him without knowledge of the trust and sought to recover assets of the trust after Dunnebier's death for repayment.

🏛 **RULE OF LAW**
Where a person places property in trust and reserves the right to amend and revoke and direct disposition of principal and income, the settlor's creditors, after his death, may reach all assets of the trust subjected to those powers.

FACTS: Dunnebier held the majority of the capital stock of five closely held corporations that in turn owned real estate development projects and interests. Dunnebier approached Bank (P) for a loan of $75,000 and showed its officer certain of the projects under construction. Regarding these projects as evidence of Dunnebier's solvency, an unsecured loan was approved for that amount, though Bank (P) was unaware of the fact that Dunnebier had placed his stock in an inter vivos trust. The trust provided that Dunnebier was to have the right to amend or revoke the trust and to direct the disposition of all principal and income during his life. The trial court upheld the trust, insulating the assets from Bank's (P) claim for the unpaid portion of the debt remaining after Dunnebier's death. Bank (P) appealed.

ISSUE: Where a person places property in trust and reserves the right to amend and revoke and direct disposition of principal and income, may the settlor's creditors, after his death, reach all assets of the trust subjected to those powers?

HOLDING AND DECISION: (Kass, J.) Yes. When a person creates a discretionary trust, such as one where virtually all powers to administer the property remain in the settlor, his creditors can reach the assets under the settlor's power during the settlor's lifetime. After death, all power goes either to beneficiaries or to the trustee. However, since the right to use principal and income rested in the settlor, he could have used it to pay debts and may have been forced to do so. The internal revenue code provides that where substantial control resides in the settlor of an inter vivos trust, ownership for tax purposes resides in him after death. By analogy, creditors may reach the assets of a trust subject to a settlor's rights to amend and revoke and direct disposition and death of the settlor does not terminate this right. Reversed.

▶ **ANALYSIS**

The loan here was unsecured. Bank (P) held no interest in the real estate shown to it by Dunnebier, however, it relied upon the existence of these assets for future collection purposes. Dunnebier's death was unexpected, and it was not unreasonable in fact to speculate that he would have used his power to invade the corpus or to apply interest in such a way as to pay bank (P). Where a settlor retains so much control as to make a trust "discretionary," however, these points need not even be considered. The settlor has not given up control enough to insulate the assets from his creditors.

▬▬▮

Quicknotes

CLOSELY HELD CORPORATION A corporation whose shares (or at least voting shares) are held by a closely knit group of shareholders or a single person.

CORPUS The principal property comprising a trust, not including interest or income.

DISCRETIONARY TRUST A trust pursuant to which the trustee is authorized to make decisions regarding the investment of the trust funds and the distribution of such funds to beneficiaries.

INTER VIVOS TRUST Property that is held by one person for the benefit of another and which is created by an instrument that takes effect during the life of the grantor.

▬▬▮

Clymer v. Mayo

Administrator of estate (P) v. Decedent's husband (D)

Mass. Sup. Jud. Ct., 473 N.E.2d 1084 (1985).

NATURE OF CASE: Appeal from lower court decision finding that a couple's divorce revoked a husband's interest in his former wife's will but not his interest in her revocable trust.

FACT SUMMARY: Decedent Clara Mayo created a will and a revocable trust that was to be funded from the residuary of her will upon her death. Her husband, James Mayo (D), was the primary beneficiary of the will and the trust. The couple divorced in 1978 and Clara Mayo passed away in 1981.

🏛 RULE OF LAW
A state statute that terminates a spouse's interest in the other spouse's will when the couple divorces also applies to a revocable pour-over trust that is funded entirely by the will of the deceased spouse.

FACTS: Decedent Clara Mayo created a will and revocable trust in 1973. Her husband, James Mayo (D), was the primary beneficiary of the will and her trust. The revocable trust was unfunded and would only be funded upon Clara's death. The will provided that upon her death, the residuary of the estate would pour over into the trust for James Mayo's (D) benefit. The couple divorced in 1978. Clara died in 1981. Litigation ensued among the administrator of the estate, Clymer (P), and Mayo (D), as well as other beneficiaries in the will. The issue at trial was whether the state statute that revoked James Mayo's (D) interest in Clara's will when the couple divorced also applied to the revocable trust. The lower court found that it did not. Clymer (P) appealed.

ISSUE: Does a state statute that terminates a spouse's interest in the other spouse's will when the couple divorces apply to a revocable pour-over trust that is funded entirely by the will of the deceased spouse?

HOLDING AND DECISION: (Hennessey, C.J.) Yes. A state statute that terminates a spouse's interest in the other spouse's will when the couple divorces also applies to a revocable pour-over trust that is funded entirely by the will of the deceased spouse. Like many other states, Massachusetts has a statute that terminates a spouse's interest in the other spouse's will upon divorce. Here, Clara's trust was unfunded during her lifetime and it would only be funded from the residuary of her will at the time of her death. Accordingly, it was clear that the will and the trust were part of a single testamentary scheme. It would be incongruous to revoke Mayo's (D) interest in the will but not the revocable trust that was only funded via the will's residuary provision. Accordingly, the statute terminating the interest in the will also terminates the spouse's interest in the revocable trust that is entirely funded through the will at the testator's death. Reversed.

▶ ANALYSIS

The court noted that its holding was confined only to those revocable trusts that received their funding entirely from the will at the time of the testator's death. The court found that this holding was consistent with the legislative purposes behind enactment of the state statute terminating one spouse's interest in the other spouse's will upon divorce. The statute was enacted to conform the law to the expectations of people that upon divorce, the couple's financial interests will be completely separated.

Quicknotes

POUR-OVER PROVISION A provision pursuant to a testamentary instrument, providing that the residuary estate be distributed to a different testamentary instrument; i.e., will to trust or trust to will.

REVOCABLE TRUST A trust where trustor reserves the right to revoke the trust.

Cook v. Equitable Life Assurance Society

Administrator of estate (D) v. Decedent's life insurance company (P)

Ind. Ct. App., 428 N.E.2d 110 (1981).

NATURE OF CASE: Appeal from lower court decision finding that decedent's use of a will to modify the beneficiary of his life insurance policy was ineffective.

FACT SUMMARY: Decedent Douglas Cook's life insurance policy named his first wife as beneficiary. After his divorce and remarriage, Cook drafted a holographic will that attempted to change the beneficiary of the insurance policy to his new wife and child.

RULE OF LAW

Any attempt to change the beneficiary of a life insurance policy by will or other testamentary instrument will be ineffectual because that type of modification fails to follow the prescribed method as stated in the insurance policy.

FACTS: Douglas Cook's life insurance policy named his former wife Doris as beneficiary. After Douglas and Doris divorced, Douglas married Margaret Cook (D). The two of them had a son, Daniel (D). After his remarriage, Douglas created a handwritten will that attempted to change the beneficiary of his life insurance policy to Margaret (D) and Daniel (D). After his death, the life insurance company, Equitable Life Assurance Society (P), brought this interpleader action alleging that Douglas's attempt to change his life insurance policy via a will was ineffectual. The trial court agreed and granted summary judgment to Equitable Life (P). Margaret (D) and Daniel (D) appealed.

ISSUE: Is an attempt to change the beneficiary of a life insurance policy by will or other testamentary instrument ineffectual because that type of modification fails to follow the prescribed method as stated in the insurance policy?

HOLDING AND DECISION: (Ratliff, J.) Yes. Any attempt to change the beneficiary of a life insurance policy by will or other testamentary instrument will be ineffectual because that type of modification fails to follow the prescribed method as stated in the insurance policy. There are some exceptions to the strict rule requiring compliance with the policy's provisions for beneficiary changes. The insurance company may waive compliance. The insured may be unable to comply with the policy requirement due to infirmity or disability. Lastly, compliance may be excused if the deceased took the necessary steps to change the beneficiary but passed away before the change went into effect. Here, none of those exceptions apply. Douglas was not prevented in any way from modifying the beneficiary in accordance with the requirements of the policy. He also did not take any steps at all to attempt to comply with the policy. Insurance companies have a substantial interest in requiring their insureds to comply with specified procedures regarding the change of beneficiaries. This will prevent insurance companies from being subjected to claims of others of whom the insurance company has no notice or knowledge. It is also in the interest of the beneficiaries of policies to be entitled to prompt payment without the insurance company having to investigate competing claims from others. Here, Douglas's attempted modification to change his beneficiary did not include some type of notice to Equitable Life (P). While Douglas may have intended that the insurance proceeds of $3,154.00 dollars go to his new wife, the valid interests of insurance companies and the judiciary in support of settled expectations is primary and trumps his stated intentions. Affirmed.

▌ ANALYSIS

This decision summarizes the prevailing view regarding modification of life insurance beneficiaries via a will. The concept of settled expectations for insurance companies and named beneficiaries is paramount. Any opposite decision would allow hosts of competing claims based upon alleged testamentary documents created by the testator. The law of contracts is present here as well. A life insurance policy is a contract and it can only be modified in accordance with the terms of the contract.

■=■

Quicknotes

TESTAMENTARY INSTRUMENT An instrument that takes effect upon the death of the maker.

■=■

Nunnenman v. Estate of Grubbs

Named beneficiary of IRA (P) v. Decedent's mother (D)

Ark. Ct. App., 374 S.W.3d 75 (2010).

NATURE OF CASE: Appeal from lower court decision finding that decedent's use of a will to modify the beneficiary of his individual retirement account was effective.

FACT SUMMARY: Decedent Donald Grubbs' individual retirement account (IRA) named a friend, Jeannie Nunnenman (P), as beneficiary. Just prior to his death, Grubbs drafted a brief will with assistance of counsel that left his entire estate to his mother, Shervena Grubbs (D). While the will did not mention the IRA account, Grubbs allegedly drafted a separate handwritten note that stated his mother should be the named beneficiary of his IRA.

🏛 RULE OF LAW
A change in the beneficiary of a life insurance policy or individual retirement account may be accomplished via a will so long as the language of the will specifically identifies the insurance policy or IRA involved and evidences the testator's clear intent to change the beneficiary.

FACTS: Decedent Donald Grubbs named a friend, Jeannie Nunnenman (P), as the beneficiary of his individual retirement account (IRA). Six days prior to his death in 2009, Grubbs had an attorney draft a formal will for him. The will stated that his entire estate should go to his mother, Shervana Grubbs (D). Grubbs also allegedly drafted a separate handwritten note stating that his mother should be the beneficiary of his IRA. Allegedly, Shervana Grubbs (D) found this note in a Bible after Grubbs' death. The trial court found the note evidenced intent on Grubbs' part to change the beneficiary of his IRA to his mother. Nunnenman (P) appealed.

ISSUE: May a change in the beneficiary of a life insurance policy or individual retirement account be accomplished via a will so long as the language of the will specifically identifies the insurance policy or IRA involved and evidences the testator's clear intent to change the beneficiary?

HOLDING AND DECISION: (Pittman, J.) Yes. A change in the beneficiary of a life insurance policy or individual retirement account may be accomplished via a will so long as the language of the will specifically identifies the insurance policy or IRA involved and evidences the testator's clear intent to change the beneficiary. The significant determination is whether the testamentary instrument clearly identifies the policy or IRA to be modified. Here, Grubbs' will, drafted with assistance of counsel,

did not mention the IRA. Instead, it only stated that Grubbs' entire estate should be left to his mother. The will therefore was not effective in changing the beneficiary of the IRA. As to the handwritten note, the note is of dubious authenticity. Even if it was authentic, the existence of the formal last will and testament drafted just days before Grubbs' death revoked the holographic will. If the handwritten note is viewed simply as an attempt to modify the beneficiary of the IRA, it did not comply with the procedures as specified in the IRA. Grubbs was able to summon an attorney just days before his death to draft a will. If he wanted to modify the IRA's beneficiary, he had the opportunity to do so with the assistance of counsel. Reversed.

▶ ANALYSIS

This decision summarizes the minority view regarding modifications of life insurance or IRA beneficiaries via a will. In these jurisdictions, the will or trust document must specifically identify the policy or IRA in order for the modification to be valid. Most jurisdictions do not allow modifications of such beneficiaries via a will.

Quicknotes

HOLOGRAPHIC WILL A will that is handwritten by the testator.

TESTAMENTARY INSTRUMENT An instrument that takes effect upon the death of the maker.

Egelhoff v. Egelhoff

Decedent's child (P) v. Decedent's ex-wife (D)

532 U.S. 141 (2001).

NATURE OF CASE: Appeal from decision distributing proceeds of insurance policy and pension plan.

FACT SUMMARY: Donna Rae Egelhoff (D) received the proceeds from an insurance plan and a pension plan provided by her ex-husband's employer after he died intestate from injuries incurred in a traffic accident. The decedent had not removed her name as beneficiary. The decedent's two children from a previous marriage, David and Samantha Egelhoff (P), his statutory heirs, sued Donna Egelhoff (D) for the proceeds from the plans.

RULE OF LAW
ERISA preempts a state statute that provides for the automatic revocation of a spouse as the designated beneficiary of a nonprobate asset upon the couple's divorce.

FACTS: David A. Egelhoff had named his wife, Donna Rae Egelhoff (D), beneficiary of an insurance policy and a pension plan provided through his employer, Boeing Company. Both plans were governed by the Employee Retirement Income Security Act of 1974 (ERISA). Two months after the couple's divorce, David died intestate after a traffic accident. He had not removed Donna's (D) name as beneficiary under either plan. Donna (D) received $46,000 from the life insurance policy. David and Samantha Egelhoff (P), the decedent's children from a previous marriage and his statutory heirs, sued Donna (D) for the life insurance proceeds, relying on a Washington statute that provided that the designation of a spouse as beneficiary of a nonprobate asset would be revoked automatically upon the couple's divorce. David and Samantha (P) also filed a separate action to recover the pension plan proceeds. [The trial courts granted summary judgment for Donna (D), holding that both the insurance policy and the pension should follow ERISA's procedures. The appellate court consolidated the case and concluded that ERISA did not preempt the state statute and that David and Samantha (P) were not entitled to the proceeds. The state supreme court affirmed. The U.S. Supreme Court granted review.]

ISSUE: Does ERISA preempt a state statute that provides for the automatic revocation of a spouse as the designated beneficiary of a nonprobate asset upon the couple's divorce?

HOLDING AND DECISION: (Thomas, J.) Yes. ERISA preempts a state statute that provides for the automatic revocation of a spouse as the designated beneficiary

of a nonprobate asset upon the couple's divorce. Under ERISA's preemption section, 29 U.S.C. Section 1144(a), ERISA supersedes all state laws that relate to employee benefit plans that are covered by ERISA. The provision must be given broad effect. A state law "relates to" an ERISA plan, if there is a "connection with" the plan. Here, the Washington statute impermissibly restricts ERISA plan administrators' choice of rules in determining whom to designate as beneficiary. Hence, it has a connection with ERISA plans. Further, the statute interferes with ERISA's ability to administer a plan uniformly throughout the country. An ERISA administrator should not be burdened with the task of trying to find out if a purported beneficiary has in fact had her beneficiary's status revoked. Reversed and remanded.

DISSENT: (Breyer, J.) Merely because a state's law imposes some burden on the administration of an ERISA plan does not by itself mandate preemption. The statute at issue here is no different from many such state laws. It imposes at most an administrative burden, but in substance it promotes ERISA objectives—it transfers an employee's pension assets at death to those individuals whom the worker would likely have wanted to receive them. The assumption under the state statute here—that a divorced worker would prefer that a child rather than a divorced spouse receive those assets—is embodied in the uniform probate code and is consistent with human experience. The effect of the majority's holding that statute preempted is that the ex-wife will receive a windfall at the expense of the deceased's children. Applying the majority's rationale would also preempt other transfer statutes, such as those involving simultaneous deaths or spousal murder.

ANALYSIS

Although it is not federal common law, divorce sets aside a revocable beneficiary designation of a former spouse under both the Restatement (Third) of Property and the Uniform Probate Code.

Quicknotes

POWER OF REVOCATION The power to revoke an existing interest.

Varela v. Bernachea

Joint account holder (D) v. Joint account holder (P)

Fla. Dist. Ct. App., 917 So. 2d 295 (2005).

NATURE OF CASE: Appeal from judgment declaring a sole owner of a joint account.

FACT SUMMARY: Bernachea (P) added his girlfriend Varela (D) as a joint tenant with right of survivorship to his CMA account. When they broke up and Varela (D) subsequently withdrew $280,000 from the account, Bernachea (P) sued to settle ownership of the account.

🏛 RULE OF LAW
A gift is presumed when a joint bank account is established with the funds from one person, and the presumption can be overcome only through clear and convincing evidence to the contrary.

FACTS: Varela (D) and Bernachea (P), both Argentine citizens, began an affair in 2000. In 2001 Varela (D) moved in with Bernachea (P), and in early 2002 Bernachea (P) added Varela (D) to his Merrill Lynch CMA account as a joint tenant with a right of survivorship. Bernachea (P) never restricted access to the account, and Varela (D) could access the account with a check card or a written check. Bernachea (P) had a heart attack in late 2002, and while he was in the hospital his daughters threw Varela (D) out of Bernachea's (P) house. Varela (D) moved out, but wrote herself a check withdrawing $280,000 from the CMA account. When Bernachea (P) learned of the withdrawal, he had Merrill Lynch return the funds and he sued both Merrill Lynch and Varela (D) to settle ownership of the account. The trial court found that Bernachea (P) lacked donative intent and awarded him full ownership of the entire account. Varela (D) appealed.

ISSUE: Is a gift presumed when a joint bank account is established with the funds from one person, and can the presumption only be overcome through clear and convincing evidence to the contrary?

HOLDING AND DECISION: (Per curiam) Yes. A gift is presumed when a joint bank account is established with the funds from one person, and the presumption can be overcome only through clear and convincing evidence to the contrary. The only evidence in support of Bernachea's (P) claim that he lacked donative intent was his own dubious testimony. Bernachea's (P) account representative testified that he specifically explained the details of joint tenancy with right of survivorship in Spanish without any questions from Bernachea (P), a former attorney, and Bernachea (P) admitted that Varela (D) had the ability to make check card purchases and write checks on the CMA account. Clearly, Bernachea (P) did not rebut Varela's (D)

gift presumption when he openly admitted that he gave Varela (D) access to their joint account via check card. The record does not support the trial court's finding, as a matter of law, that Bernachea (P) demonstrated an absence of donative intent. Reversed and remanded with instructions.

▶ ANALYSIS

This case illustrates the dangers of making someone a joint tenant on an account. The Uniform Portable Code attempts to solve this problem by creating a presumption that funds in a joint account belong to the person who placed the funds into the account unless there is clear and convincing evidence to the contrary. However, some states go in the opposite direction and have a conclusive presumption that naming someone as a joint owner is a gift of the entire account.

■━■

Quicknotes

DONATIVE INTENT Donor's intent to make a gift.

JOINT BANK ACCOUNT A bank account in which two or more persons have equal interests usually with right of survivorship.

JOINT TENANCY An interest in property whereby a single interest is owned by two or more persons and created by a single instrument; joint tenants possess equal interests in the use of the entire property and the last survivor is entitled to absolute ownership.

RIGHT OF SURVIVORSHIP Between two or more persons, such as in a joint tenancy relationship, the right to the property of a deceased passes to the survivor.

■━■

In re Estate of Kurrelmeyer

[Parties not identified.]

Vt. Sup. Ct., 895 A.2d 207 (2006).

NATURE OF CASE: Appeal of grant of summary judgment setting aside a trust.

FACT SUMMARY: Kurrelmeyer's wife Martina created a trust in Kurrelmeyer's name under a durable power of attorney and transferred Kurrelmeyer's home into the trust. When Kurrelmeyer died, his son asked the court to set aside the trust.

🏛 RULE OF LAW
A durable power of attorney that authorizes the attorney-in-fact to "execute and deliver any assignments, stock powers, deeds or trust instruments" allows the attorney-in-fact to create and fund a revocable living trust, and the creation of the trust is not an invalid usurpation of the principal's will.

FACTS: Kurrelmeyer executed a durable power of attorney naming his wife Martina as his attorney-in-fact. In his durable power of attorney, Kurrelmeyer gave his attorney-in-fact the ability "to add all of my assets deemed appropriate by my said attorney to any trust of which I am the donor" and also granted the power to "execute and deliver any assignments, stock powers, deeds or trust instruments". When Kurrelmeyer became incompetent, Martina, pursuant to what she presumed to be her powers under the durable power of attorney, created a revocable living trust for Kurrelmeyer's lifetime benefit and she transferred a piece of his property into the trust. Under the terms of the trust, Martina was allowed to live on the property for the remainder of her life, the trust could pay expenses for the property's upkeep, upon Martina's request the property could be sold with the proceeds used as trust principal or to purchase a new home, and the entire trust principal was available for Martina's support at the trustee's discretion. These terms differed from Kurrelmeyer's will, which only provided Martina with a life estate in the property. Both the trust and the will distributed the remainder of Kurrelmeyer's estate to his children. When Kurrelmeyer's estate entered probate, his son objected to the exclusion of the trust's property from the inventory, and he asked the court to rescind the trust and distribute the property according to the terms of the will. The probate court rejected the request, but on appeal the superior court granted summary judgment in favor of Kurrelmeyer's children and set aside the trust. Martina appealed.

ISSUE: Does a durable power of attorney that authorizes the attorney-in-fact to "execute and deliver any assignments, stock powers, deeds, or trust instruments" allow the attorney-in-fact to create and fund a revocable living trust, and is the creation of the trust an invalid usurpation of the principal's will?

HOLDING AND DECISION: (Burgess, J.) Yes, a durable power of attorney that authorizes the attorney-in-fact to "execute and deliver any assignments, stock powers, deeds or trust instruments" allows the attorney-in-fact to create and fund a revocable living trust, and, no, the creation of the trust is not an invalid usurpation of the principal's will. As its title suggests, this power of attorney is indeed "general" and quite broad. The first subsection, empowering the attorney to add any and all assets to a trust of which he is the donor, does refer to a trust already in existence, but does not suggest a lack of authority to create a new trust when considered together with the second subsection granting the power "to execute and deliver . . . trust instruments." Furthermore, we do not agree that delegation of authority to create a trust through a durable power of attorney to serve the interests of the principal violates public policy as a matter of law, even when a trust's dispositive terms may serve a function similar to a will. When the principal expressly granted his attorney-in-fact the power to convey realty from his estate, he must have anticipated that the terms of his will might be so altered. It is not clear, then, why conveyance of the property to a trust would be a per se impermissible alteration of the will, when the power of attorney expressly authorized Martina to convey any real estate outright to others. Reversed and remanded for further proceedings to determine if Martina breached her fiduciary duty as an agent when she transferred the property into trust.

▶ ANALYSIS

The textbook editors report that on remand the trial court upheld the trust and found that Martina did not breach her fiduciary duty. That decision was also appealed.

Quicknotes

DURABLE POWER OF ATTORNEY A written document pursuant to which one party confers the authority to act as an agent on his behalf to another party and which is to become effective if the grantor should later become incapacitated.

LIFE ESTATE An interest in land measured by the life of the tenant or a third party.

REVOCABLE TRUST A trust where trustor reserves the right to revoke the trust.

TRUST The holding of property by one party for the benefit of another.

Limits on Freedom of Disposition: Protection of the Spouse and Children

Quick Reference Rules of Law

Sullivan v. Burkin

Widow (P) v. Successor trustee (D)

Mass. Sup. Jud. Ct., 390 Mass. 864, 460 N.E.2d 572 (1984).

NATURE OF CASE: Appeal from a dismissal of a complaint for determination of estate assets.

FACT SUMMARY: Sullivan (P) contended that the value of real estate placed in trust by her late husband should be considered part of his estate for purposes of providing her a portion of the estate.

RULE OF LAW
The surviving spouse has no claim against the assets of a valid inter vivos trust created by the deceased spouse even when the deceased spouse retained substantial rights and powers under the trust instrument.

FACTS: Sullivan's (P) husband, the decedent, executed during his life a deed of trust by which he transferred real estate to a trust with himself as sole trustee. The net income of the trust was payable to him during his life, and the trustee was instructed to pay to him all or such part of the principal that he might request. Upon his death, the trust indicated that the trustee was to pay the principal amount and any undistributed income to third parties. Sullivan executed a will wherein he stated that he intentionally neglected to make any provision for his wife, Sullivan (P). Following her husband's death, Sullivan (P) made a claim against the estate, contending that the property in the trust should be considered part of the estate. Burkin (D) was the successor in interest to the third parties to whom the decedent left the residue of the trust. The probate court held that a valid inter vivos trust was created and that the property of the trust was not to be considered part of the estate. Sullivan (P) appealed.

ISSUE: May a surviving spouse claim against the assets of a valid inter vivos trust created by the deceased spouse even when the deceased spouse retained substantial rights and powers under the trust instrument?

HOLDING AND DECISION: (Wilkins, J.) No. The surviving spouse may not claim against the assets of a valid inter vivos trust created by the deceased spouse even when the deceased spouse retained substantial rights and powers under the trust instrument. Merely because the inter vivos trust was testamentary does not indicate that it was invalid. Merely because the settlor retained a broad power to modify or revoke the trust, the law of the state is quite clear in upholding inter vivos trusts which become testamentary in nature. Further, Sullivan (P) has no special interest that should be recognized in breaking the trust. As a result, because this trust was created under the then-established law, the assets of the trust cannot be applied to the estate. Affirmed.

ANALYSIS

The court indicated quite clearly that although it felt obligated to apply the general rule in this case, it announced that in the future any inter vivos trust created or amended after the date of this opinion shall no longer follow the previously announced rule. In the future, if the settlor retains the same type of substantial rights the decedent did in the principal case, then the assets of the trust will be considered part of the estate for purposes of distribution to the heirs of the estate.

■=■

Quicknotes

INTER VIVOS TRUST Property that is held by one person for the benefit of another and which is created by an instrument that takes effect during the life of the grantor.

REMAINDER INTEREST An interest in land that remains after the termination of the immediately preceding estate.

SUCCESSOR TRUSTEE A trustee who succeeds a previous trustee.

■=■

In re Estate of Myers

Named beneficiaries of checking account (P) v. Decedent's husband (D)

Iowa Sup. Ct., 825 N.W.2d 1 (2012).

NATURE OF CASE: Appeal from lower court decision finding that decedent's checking account, a certificate of deposit and an annuity should be included in the elective share of the decedent's surviving spouse.

FACT SUMMARY: Decedent Karen Myer's assets included a checking account, a certificate of deposit and an annuity that all named her children as beneficiaries in case of her death. The lower court determined that those accounts should be included in Karen Myer's husband's elective share.

🏛 RULE OF LAW
Assets that are payable on death to a specific beneficiary, such as checking accounts, certificates of deposit and annuities, shall not be included in the elective share of the surviving spouse.

FACTS: Decedent Karen Myer's assets included a checking account, a certificate of deposit and an annuity that all named her children (P) as beneficiaries in case of her death. Her husband, Howard (D), became the sole of owner of their real estate because he and Karen were joint tenants with rights of survivorship. The checking account and certificate of deposit were worth $91,000 and the annuity was worth $18,000. After Karen's death, Howard (D) chose to receive his statutory elective share of Karen's estate in lieu of what he would have received via her will. The trial court found that the decedent's checking account, a certificate of deposit and an annuity should be included in the elective share of the decedent's surviving spouse. Karen's children (P) appealed.

ISSUE: Shall assets that are payable on death to a specific beneficiary, such as checking accounts, certificates of deposit and annuities, be included in the elective share of the surviving spouse?

HOLDING AND DECISION: (Waterman, J.) No. Assets that are payable on death to a specific beneficiary, such as checking accounts, certificates of deposit and annuities, shall not be included in the elective share of the surviving spouse. Prior case law held that a revocable trust with named beneficiaries other than the spouse should be included in the surviving spouse's elective share. The decedent had discretion to revoke or modify the trust during his or her lifetime and the property would properly be considered part of the decedent's estate. However, in 2009, the state legislature modified the elective share statute. The statute does not include any assets that are payable on death (POD) such as checking accounts. POD accounts are nonprobate assets. The legislative history of the 2009 amendment reveals the legislature intended to prevent POD accounts from being included in the surviving spouse's elective share. Accordingly, Karen Myer's three POD accounts will not be considered part of Howard's (D) elective share. Reversed.

▶ ANALYSIS

The purpose of elective share statutes is to prevent spouses from disinheriting their surviving spouse. The statute allows the surviving spouse to elect a one-third or one-half share of the decedent's estate in lieu of what they would receive under the will. Each state's elective share statute is different. Some states include POD accounts as part of the elective share on the grounds that excluding them would frustrate the purpose of the statute.

━━■

Quicknotes

ELECTIVE SHARE Election by the surviving spouse to take either what the deceased spouse gave under the will or a share of the deceased spouse's estate as set forth by statute.

━━■

Reece v. Elliott

Widow (P) v. Executrix (D)

Tenn. Ct. App., 208 S.W.3d 419 (2006).

NATURE OF CASE: Appeal from dismissal of declaratory judgment action to have antenuptial agreement invalidated.

FACT SUMMARY: Ms. Reece (P) claimed that the antenuptial agreement she entered with Mr. Reece, who died intestate, was invalid because the value of stock held by Mr. Reece had not been disclosed.

🏛 RULE OF LAW
The failure to disclose the value of an asset is not fatal to an antenuptial agreement where the parties thereto have entered the agreement freely, with full disclosure available, and with the assistance of separate, independent counsel.

FACTS: Mr. Reece and Ms. Reece (P) entered an antenuptial agreement. They had each previously been married, had children from their prior marriages, and had their own property. The agreement indicated that they each waived their right to the separate property of the other, and that they had each consulted with independent counsel and that a full disclosure of assets had been made. The value of some of the assets disclosed by each party was not stated, including certain stock owned by Mr. Reece. Although Ms. Reece (P) and her counsel had the opportunity to inquire about the value of this stock, Ms. Reece did not do so because she fully understood this asset would not belong to her in the event of Mr. Reece's death, and that she would have no interest in it. Mr. Reece died intestate, and Ms. Reece (P) brought a declaratory judgment action against the executrixes (D) of his estate to invalidate the antenuptial agreement on the grounds that it did not state the value of the stock, which, it turned out, was substantial. The trial court ruled that the agreement was enforceable, since it was obvious from looking at Mr. Reece's list of property that he was a wealthy man, without taking into account the value of the stock, since all assets were revealed on the list and Ms. Reece (P) could have investigated any items that she wanted to. The court reasoned that it was not important that the value of some of the assets had not been identified because they both agreed the assets would go to their respective children. The state's intermediate appellate court granted review.

ISSUE: Is the failure to disclose the value of an asset fatal to an antenuptial agreement where the parties thereto have entered the agreement freely, with full disclosure available, and with the assistance of separate, independent counsel?

HOLDING AND DECISION: (Franks, J.) No. The failure to disclose the value of an asset is not fatal to an antenuptial agreement where the parties thereto have entered the agreement freely, with full disclosure available, and with the assistance of separate, independent counsel. State law favors the enforcement of antenuptial agreements where they have been entered into "voluntarily and knowledgeably." The term "knowledgeably" means that there was full and fair disclosure of the nature, extent and value of the proponent spouse's holdings, or that such disclosure was unnecessary because the other spouse had independent knowledge of the same. Also, "full and fair" disclosure depends on the facts of each particular case. While specific appraisals are not a necessity, the spouse must have a general knowledge of the proponent spouse's overall net worth and must not have been misled when entering the agreement. Representation by independent counsel also is a strong indication that the agreement has been entered into freely and knowingly. Here, Ms. Reece (P) had full knowledge that her husband was a man of wealth, as shown by the list of assets that was provided; she consulted with independent counsel and clearly understood that the agreement meant she would have no claim to any of Mr. Reece's assets; she admitted that Mr. Reece was never dishonest with her, and was very straightforward and open with her about his financial dealings and never misled her. For these reasons, Ms. Reece (P) was not misled, and the agreement is enforceable and binding. Affirmed.

▶ ANALYSIS

A fairly straightforward and effective way of avoiding the disclosure issue presented by this case would have been for the parties to have attached a net worth schedule of assets, liabilities, and income to the agreement itself. The value of the assets, where not apparent from the face of the assets (e.g., cash), should be determined through a good-faith, independent valuation.

Quicknotes

ANTENUPTIAL AGREEMENT An agreement entered into by two individuals, in contemplation of their impending marriage, in order to determine their rights and interests in property upon dissolution or death.

Lambeff v. Farmers Co-operative Executors & Trustees Ltd.

Decedent's daughter (P) v. Estate's executors (D)

So. Australia Sup. Ct., 56 S.A.S.R. 323, 1991 WL 1121294 (1991).

NATURE OF CASE: Claim for maintenance against decedent's estate under Australia's Inheritance (Family Provision) Act.

FACT SUMMARY: Lambeff (P), decedent's daughter, who was abandoned by decedent when she was ten, claimed that she was entitled to support (provision) in the form of a legacy out of decedent's estate under Australia's Inheritance (Family Provision) Act because decedent had failed to support her "advancement in life."

> ## 🏛 RULE OF LAW
> Under Australia's Inheritance (Family Provision) Act, an independent adult child of a decedent, who was abandoned by the decedent as a child, has a claim of support (provision) against decedent's estate where the child has done nothing disentitling and would have done better with proper support for the child's proper advancement in life.

FACTS: Lambeff (P) was abandoned by decedent when she was ten. Decedent left Lambeff (P) and her mother and started another family, in which he had two sons. Lambeff (P) was not married, had a steady job, and had considerable equity in a flat. Decedent's will left his entire estate to his two sons, after payment of all debts and funeral expenses. Both sons had families to support and few assets. Lambeff (P) claimed that she was entitled to support (provision) under Australia's Inheritance (Family Provision) Act, which provides in pertinent part that a decedent's family member who is left without adequate provision for proper advancement in life may make a claim for support against the decedent's estate, which may be granted at the court's discretion.

ISSUE: Under Australia's Inheritance (Family Provision) Act, does an independent adult child of a decedent, who was abandoned by the decedent as a child, have a claim of support (provision) against decedent's estate where the child has done nothing disentitling and would have done better with proper support for the child's proper advancement in life?

HOLDING AND DECISION: (Matheson, J.) Yes. Under Australia's Inheritance (Family Provision) Act, an independent adult child of a decedent, who was abandoned by the decedent as a child, has a claim of support (provision) against decedent's estate where the child has done nothing disentitling and would have done better with proper support for the child's proper advancement in life. The statute's words "advancement in life" have a wide meaning and are not restricted to early childhood. In every case, the court must place itself in the testator's position and consider what he or she should have done as a "wise and just" testator. Here, although it is true that Lambeff (P) has done reasonably well in life without her father's support, she would have done better with proper support for her advancement in life. Given all the circumstances of the case—that she is independent and that the sons need to support families and do not have many assets—the legacy to Lambeff (P) should be modest. It is ordered that she be paid a legacy of $20,000 out of the estate.

▶ ANALYSIS

The model under which this case was decided is known as the Family Maintenance Model, which gives courts the power to determine the morality of both the decedent's dispositive scheme and survivors' claims. Proponents argue that this performs a vital social welfare function. Critics assert that such judicial discretion is a "terrible price" to pay for improved support of dependents in that it would introduce complexity and unpredictability, undermine estate planning, and hamper the orderly transfer of property rights.

━━■

Quicknotes

DECEDENT A person who is deceased.

━━■

In re Estate of Prestie

Decedent's wife (P) v. Decedent's son (D)

Nev. Sup. Ct., 138 P.3d 520 (2006).

NATURE OF CASE: Appeal from order adopting a probate commissioner's report and recommendation that decedent's will be revoked.

FACT SUMMARY: Maria (P), wife of W.R., who was deceased, contended that W.R.'s pour-over will, which he had made before remarrying her, should statutorily be revoked as to her because she married W.R. without entering into a marriage contract and because the will did not contain a provision providing for her or a provision expressing an intention to not provide for her. However, W.R., before remarrying Maria, had amended the accompanying inter vivos trust, which had named his son Scott (D) as beneficiary and trustee, to provide for Maria.

RULE OF LAW
An amendment to an inter vivos trust cannot rebut the presumption that a pour-over will is revoked as to an unintentionally omitted spouse.

FACTS: Maria (P) and W.R. were married, then divorced two years later, but remained friendly. Eventually, W.R. purchased a condominium. Then he simultaneously executed a pour-over will and an inter vivos trust. The pour-over will, devised W.R.'s entire estate to the trust. W.R.'s son, Scott (D), was named both the trustee and a beneficiary of the inter vivos trust. Neither the will nor the inter vivos trust provided for Maria (P). A few years later, Maria (P) moved in with W.R., who amended the inter vivos trust to grant Maria (P) a life estate in his condominium upon his death. A few weeks later, Maria (P) and W.R. were married for a second time. W.R. passed away approximately nine months later. Maria (P) eventually petitioned for a one-half intestate succession share of W.R.'s estate on the ground that W.R.'s will was revoked as to her by a statutory provision relating to the revocation of a will by marriage. A probate commissioner recommended that because W.R.'s will was executed before he remarried Maria (P) and because the amendment granting Maria (P) a life estate in the condominium was to the inter vivos trust, not to W.R.'s will, so that the will did not provide for her, the will be revoked as to her. The trial court subsequently adopted the commissioner's recommendation, and Scott (D) appealed. The state's highest court granted review.

ISSUE: Can an amendment to an inter vivos trust rebut the presumption that a pour-over will is revoked as to an unintentionally omitted spouse?

HOLDING AND DECISION: (Hardesty, J.) No. An amendment to an inter vivos trust cannot rebut the presumption that a pour-over will is revoked as to an unintentionally omitted spouse. The statute relating to revocation of a will by marriage provides that "If a person marries after making a will and the spouse survives the maker, the will is revoked as to the spouse, unless provision has been made for the spouse by marriage contract, or unless the spouse is provided for in the will, or in such a way mentioned therein as to show an intention not to make such provision. . . ." This statutory provision is unambiguous and the facts on their face satisfy its elements, so that a presumption of revocation is created. The trust amendment did not create a marriage contract and no other marriage contract provided for Maria (P). Moreover, W.R.'s will did not contain a provision providing for Maria (P) or a provision expressing an intent not to provide for her. The argument by Scott (D) that the inter vivos trust amendment bars Maria's (P) claim is rejected, since a fundamental rule of statutory construction is that the mention of one thing implies the exclusion of another. Applying this rule, it is clear that the revocation of a will under one chapter of the probate statute is unrelated to a trust proceeding governed by another chapter. Additionally, the trust section makes reference to other chapters, but makes no mention of the will chapter. Because the legislature made reference to other chapters, it can be inferred that it intentionally excluded mention of the will chapter. Affirmed.

ANALYSIS

The sole purpose of the revocation presumption statute is to guard against the unintentional disinheritance of the surviving spouse. Not all states take the approach used by the state (Nevada) here. Those states that reject the revocation presumption typically leave the elective share provisions as the principal protection for the surviving spouse. However, in many jurisdictions the elective share might limit the surviving spouse to one-third of the estate. The Uniform Probate Code in § 2-301 provides that a premarital will reflects the testator's intent to the extent that it provides for the testator's issue from previous relationships, but also provides a rebuttable presumption that this intent is negated upon remarriage.

Quicknotes

INTER VIVOS TRUST Property that is held by one person for the benefit of another and which is created by an instrument that takes effect during the life of the grantor.

Continued on next page.

LIFE ESTATE An interest in land measured by the life of the tenant or a third party.

POUR-OVER PROVISION A provision pursuant to a testamentary instrument, providing that the residuary estate be distributed to a different testamentary instrument, i.e., will to trust or trust to will.

STATUTORY CONSTRUCTION The examination and interpretation of statutes.

Gray v. Gray

Executor (P) v. Omitted descendant (D)

Ala. Sup. Ct., 947 So. 2d 1045 (2006).

NATURE OF CASE: Appeal from judgment that an omitted descendant is entitled to a share of decedent's estate.

FACT SUMMARY: The executor (P) of John Gray's (John's) estate, contended that Jack Gray (Jack) (D), John's son born after John's will was executed who was omitted from the will, was not entitled to a share of John's estate under the state's pretermitted child statute, even though John had divorced Jack's (D) mother before he died.

🏛 RULE OF LAW
Where a pretermitted child statute provides that an omitted child is not entitled to share in a testator parent's estate where at the time the will was executed the testator had one or more children and devised substantially all his estate to the other parent of the omitted child, the omitted child is not nonetheless entitled to share in the estate where the other children are from a prior marriage.

FACTS: John Gray (John) was married to Mary Gray (Mary) at the time he executed his last will. He had two children from a prior marriage; however, the will devised all of his estate to Mary and did not include his two children. Three years later, John and Mary had Jack Gray (Jack) (D). Five years thereafter, John and Mary divorced, and, as part of the divorce proceedings, certain of John's inheritances, assets and disbursements would be placed in trust for Jack (D). Under state law, even though John's will devised all of his estate to Mary, Mary would not inherit under John's will upon his death because of the divorce. John died five years later without having changed his will. The executor (P) of John's estate probated the will, and Jack (D) claimed that he was entitled to a share of John's estate under the state's pretermitted child statute, which provides that "If a testator fails to provide in his will for any of his children born or adopted after the execution of his will, the omitted child receives a share in the estate equal in value to that which he would have received if the testator had died intestate." The statute, however, has three exceptions. The executor (P) argued that two of these applied, namely that the pretermitted child is not entitled to a share of the estate because: "(2) When the will was executed the testator had one or more children and devised substantially all his estate to the other parent of the omitted child; or (3) The testator provided for the child by transfer outside the will and the intent that the transfer be in lieu of a testamentary provision be reasonably proven." Jack (D) argued that the first of these two exceptions was inapplica-

ble because it did not appear to contemplate a situation wherein the testator has children, divorces their mother, remarries, executes a will that makes no provision for any children whatsoever, and then has a child with that second wife. The probate court held for Jack (D), and the executor (P) appealed. The state's highest court granted review.

ISSUE: Where a pretermitted child statute provides that an omitted child is not entitled to share in a testator parent's estate where at the time the will was executed the testator had one or more children and devised substantially all his estate to the other parent of the omitted child, is the omitted child nonetheless entitled to share in the estate where the other children are from a prior marriage?

HOLDING AND DECISION: (See, J.) No. Where a pretermitted child statute provides that an omitted child is not entitled to share in a testator parent's estate where at the time the will was executed the testator had one or more children and devised substantially all his estate to the other parent of the omitted child, the omitted child is not nonetheless entitled to share in the estate where the other children are from a prior marriage. The statutory exception involved is neither ambiguous nor absurd, and therefore must be given effect as written. It does not, like the other exceptions, require a determination of intent. It states only two conditions for excluding an omitted child from an intestate share of the testator's estate: (1) the testator had one or more children at the time he executed his will, and (2) the testator's will devised substantially all of the testator's estate to the other parent of the omitted child. Because the statute is one of substance and is in derogation of the common law, it must be construed strictly. Jack's (D) argument, therefore, fails. The fact that John's other children were from a prior marriage is immaterial; the exception's two requirements are met: when John executed his will, he had two children by a prior marriage, and his will devised all of his estate to Jack's (D) mother Mary. If the legislature wishes to change the statute to apply to children in being at the time the will is executed, it may do so, but currently the statute unambiguously applies only to children born after the will's execution. Therefore, Jack (D) is not entitled to share in John's estate. Reversed and remanded.

▶ ANALYSIS

The majority asserts that the result reached under the exception at issue would not reach a level of absurdity requiring the court to conclude that the legislature meant

Continued on next page.

something other than what its words convey. For example, the legislature might well have assumed that in a case like this one it could anticipate that the child would be protected in the divorce proceeding, either directly or by a distribution of a share of the marital assets to the custodial parent. In this case, in fact, Jack (D) was provided for in the divorce proceeding by the creation of a trust. In addition, to adopt the dissent's construction, that the exception was intended to apply only to a child "then in being," would be to give to the statute a meaning opposite of what it said. While statutes in some jurisdictions are expressly made applicable to children alive when the will was executed as well as afterborn (or after-adopted) children, the statute at issue here by its terms was applicable only to afterborn/adopted children. Similarly, the Uniform Probate Code applies only to afterborn/adopted children.

■■■

Quicknotes

PRETERMITTED Omitted; usually refers to an heir who is unintentionally omitted from a testator's will.

■■■

In re Estate of Jackson

Decedent's son (P) v. Trustees of decedent's trust (D)

Okla. Sup. Ct., 194 P.3d 1269 (2008).

NATURE OF CASE: Plaintiff's appeal from lower court decision finding that assets of decedent's revocable inter vivos trust are not subject to the state's pretermitted heir statute.

FACT SUMMARY: Decedent Walter Jackson created a trust that named the Butlers (D) as trustees. Jackson did not leave a will. Upon Jackson's death, his son, Johnny Benjamin (P), argued that the state's pretermitted heir statute entitled him to the proceeds of the revocable trust.

> ## RULE OF LAW
> The pretermitted heir statute, providing for children unintentionally left out of a decedent's will, does not apply to a decedent's revocable inter vivos trust.

FACTS: Jackson died without leaving a will. During his life, he created a revocable inter vivos trust that named Robena Butler (D) and Harris Butler (D) as trustees. Upon his death, Benjamin (P), Jackson's son and sole surviving heir, petitioned the court for disgorgement of the trust assets. The state's pretermitted heir statute allows children unintentionally left out of a will to receive the same proceeds as those children named in the will. Benjamin (P) argued the state's pretermitted heir statute applied to the proceeds of a revocable trust just as it did to a will. The lower court found the statute did not encompass living trusts and denied Benjamin's (P) petition. After an intermediate appellate court affirmed, the Oklahoma Supreme Court granted Benjamin's petition for further appellate review.

ISSUE: Does the pretermitted heir statute, providing for children unintentionally left out of a decedent's will, apply to a decedent's revocable inter vivos trust?

HOLDING AND DECISION: (Taylor, J.) No. The pretermitted heir statute, providing for children unintentionally left out of a decedent's will, does not apply to a decedent's revocable inter vivos trust. The statute specifically refers only to circumstances where a decedent fails to name a child in his or her will. The statute makes no reference to a similar scenario involving a revocable living trust. Benjamin (P) argued the pretermitted heir statute is similar to statutes providing for disinherited spouses, known also as forced heir statutes or elective share statutes. Those statutes provide disinherited spouses with a right of election to a statutorily created minimum amount of the decedent's estate. Differences abound between the statutes. The pretermitted heir statute does not guarantee a child with a minimum amount of the decedent's estate. Also, unlike the forced heir statutes, a testator can disinherit a child if the will clearly expresses that intent. A testator can also leave one child a small amount, while that would not be allowed in the case of a spouse. Accordingly, Benjamin's (P) arguments that the pretermitted heir statute is similar to the forced heir statute are incorrect. The pretermitted heir statute does not reference revocable trusts. The statute also does not provide children with the same protection as the forced heir statute does for disinherited spouses. Affirmed.

▶ ANALYSIS

Most jurisdictions limit the coverage of pretermitted heir statutes to wills only. Some states have allowed them to cover revocable trusts as well where it is evident the testator left a child out of the trust unintentionally. Other states are removing references to wills and trusts and using the term "testamentary instrument." This will allow forced heir statutes and pretermitted heir statutes to reach a broader spectrum of testamentary documents.

Quicknotes

PRETERMITTED Omitted; usually refers to an heir who is unintentionally omitted from a testator's will.

TESTAMENTARY INSTRUMENT An instrument that takes effect upon the death of the maker.

Trusts: Fiduciary Administration

Quick Reference Rules of Law

Hartman v. Hartle

Daughter of testatrix (P) v. Executor (D)

N.J. Super. Ch. Div., 95 N.J. Eq. 123, 122 A. 615 (1923).

NATURE OF CASE: Bill in equity to set aside the sale of property by executors for fraud and illegality.

FACT SUMMARY: After an executor (D) indirectly sold property to his wife, who resold the property at a substantial profit, Hartman (P), testatrix's daughter, filed a complaint to set aside the original sale.

🏛 RULE OF LAW
A trustee breaches his duty of loyalty to the beneficiaries when he engages in self-dealing.

FACTS: Testatrix died leaving five children. She named her two sons-in-law (D) as executors. In her will, testatrix expressly directed the executors (D) to sell her real estate. The proceeds were to be divided equally among her children. However, part of the real estate was sold for $3,900 to Geick, a son of the testatrix. He bought it for his sister, Dieker, the wife of one of the executors (D). Dieker then resold the property for $5,500. Hartman (P), another of the testatrix's daughters, filed a complaint to set aside the first sale for fraud and illegality. She contended that the sale of the property by the executors (D) to Dieker, the wife of one of them, without previous authority from the court, was illegal and void.

ISSUE: Does a trustee breach his duty of loyalty to the beneficiaries when he engages in self-dealing?

HOLDING AND DECISION: (Foster, V.C.) Yes. A trustee breaches his duty of loyalty to the beneficiaries when he engages in self-dealing. It is the settled law of this state that a trustee cannot purchase from himself at his own sale and that his wife is under the same disability, unless leave to do so has been previously obtained under an order of the court. In view of the fact that the property is now owned by innocent purchasers, a resale cannot be ordered, but as an alternative, Dieker and the executors (D) will be held to pay one-fifth of their profit on the resale to Hartman (P). Decree so ordered.

▶ ANALYSIS

Once it is shown that a trustee has engaged in self-dealing, the no-further-inquiry rule is triggered; the trustee will be liable for any profit realized, without inquiry by the court as to the trustee's good faith or the transaction's reasonableness. The trustee may assert two defenses—either that the self-dealing was approved by the settlor, or was fully disclosed to the beneficiaries, who then gave their consent. The strict no-further-inquiry rule is justified by the fiduciary relationship between the trustee and the beneficiaries, which is held to a higher standard than arm's-length transactions.

■=■

Quicknotes

DUTY OF LOYALTY A director's duty to refrain from self-dealing or to take a position that is adverse to the corporation's best interests.

■=■

In re Gleeson's Will

Trustee of decedent's trust (P) v. Beneficiaries of the trust (D)

Ill. App. Ct., 124 N.E.2d 624 (1955).

NATURE OF CASE: Beneficiaries' appeal from lower court decision finding that the trustee did not deal with the trust in his individual capacity.

FACT SUMMARY: Mary Gleeson's will placed a 160-acre farm into a trust for the benefit of her three children. Con Colbrook (P) was the trustee. Prior to her death, Gleeson leased the farm to Colbrook (P). Upon her death, Colbrook (P) and his partner continued to lease the farm even though Colbrook (P) was the trustee of the trust property containing the 160-acre farm.

🏛 RULE OF LAW
A trustee cannot deal with the trust property in his individual capacity.

FACTS: Mary Gleeson's will placed a 160-acre farm into a trust for the benefit of her three children, Helen Black (D), Bernadine Gleeson (D), and Thomas Gleeson (D). Con Colbrook (P) was named trustee of the trust. Prior to her death, Gleeson leased the farm to Colbrook (P) and his business partner. Gleeson died fifteen days prior to the end of the lease. After the lease expired, Colbrook (P) held over as tenants under the lease for another year. It is undisputed Colbrook (P) and his partner made a profit during their time as tenants of the farm. After Gleeson's death, Colbrook (P) petitioned the court to be appointed as trustee of the trust. Gleeson's beneficiaries (D) objected on the ground that Colbrook (P) improperly dealt with himself while he was trustee of the trust property. The lower courts rejected the beneficiaries' (D) objections. The beneficiaries (D) appealed.

ISSUE: Can a trustee deal with the trust property in his individual capacity?

HOLDING AND DECISION: (Carroll, J.) No. A trustee cannot deal with the trust property in his individual capacity. Colbrook (P) argues that the particular circumstances of this case should allow for an exception. In particular, he argues that because Gleeson passed away fifteen days prior to the end of the lease, he did not have time to find a suitable tenant for the farm and such tenants are difficult to find. However, there is no evidence Colbrook (P) attempted to find a new tenant in the fifteen-day interval. In addition, Colbrook's (P) arguments that he transacted the lease in good faith and that he conferred openly with the trust beneficiaries (D) does not aid him. According to the settled principle, Colbrook (P) needed to decide whether to retain his tenancy or act as a trustee. It was improper for him to do both. Reversed and remanded.

▶ ANALYSIS

Typically, a trustee's simple good faith and openness about his or her dealings with trust property will not shield the trustee from liability. A trustee can only deal with trust property in his or her individual capacity if the settlor or the beneficiaries of the trust expressly authorize it or the trustee obtains judicial approval.

━■

Quicknotes

SETTLOR The grantor or donor of property that is to be held in trust for the benefit of another.

TRUSTEE A person who is entrusted to keep or administer property for the benefit of another.

━■

In re Rothko

Daughter of decedent (P) v. Executors of decedent's estate (D)

N.Y. Ct. App., 43 N.Y.2d 305, 372 N.E.2d 291, N.Y.S.2d 449 (1977).

NATURE OF CASE: Appeal from award of damages for breach of trust.

FACT SUMMARY: Kate Rothko (P), the decedent's daughter, contended that the three executors of the estate had violated their fiduciary duties by entering into contracts with businesses in which they had an interest and selling the decedent's paintings for less than their full value.

🏛 RULE OF LAW
A trustee must refrain from placing himself in a position where his personal interest or that of a third person does or may conflict with the interest of the beneficiaries.

FACTS: Mark Rothko, an abstract expressionist painter whose works through the years gained him an international reputation of greatness, died testate on February 25, 1970, leaving an estate consisting of 798 paintings of tremendous value. During a period of three weeks after the will was admitted to probate, the three executors, Reis (D), Stamos (D), and Levine (D), dealt with all 798 paintings. The executors agreed to sell to Marlborough A.G. (MAG), a Liechtenstein corporation, 100 of the paintings. The executors also consigned to Marlborough Gallery, Inc. (MNY) approximately 700 paintings. After Kate Rothko (P), the decedent's daughter, brought an action to remove the executors, it was established that Reis (D), in addition to being a coexecutor of the estate, was a director, secretary, and treasurer of MNY; that it was to the advantage of Stamos (D), as an aspiring artist, to curry favor with MNY; and that Levine (D), while not acting in self-interest or bad faith, nonetheless failed to exercise ordinary prudence in the performance of his fiduciary obligations since he was aware of the actual and potential conflicts of interests which existed. The trial court also held that the present value of the paintings was the proper measure of damages. All three executors and the two corporations then brought this appeal, contending, inter alia, that there was no breach of fiduciary duty since they had acted in good faith and the plan was fair and that the measure of damages should be based upon the value of the paintings at the time of sale.

ISSUE: Must a trustee refrain from placing himself in a position where his personal interest or that of a third person may or does conflict with the interest of the beneficiaries?

HOLDING AND DECISION: (Cooke, J.) Yes. While a trustee is administering the trust or estate, he must refrain from placing himself in a position where his personal interest or that of a third person does or may conflict with the interest of the beneficiaries. The duty of loyalty imposed on the fiduciary prevents him from accepting employment from a third party which is entering into a business transaction with the trust or estate. An executor who knows that his coexecutor is committing breaches of trust and not only fails to exert efforts directed toward prevention but accedes to them is legally accountable even though he was acting on the advice of counsel. If the trustee is authorized to sell trust property but in breach of trust he sells it for less than he should receive, he is liable for the value of the property at the time of the sale less the amount which he received. The trustee may be held liable for appreciation damages if it was his or her duty to retain the property upon the theory that the beneficiaries are entitled to be placed in the same position they would have been in had the breach not consisted of a sale of property that should have been retained. Here, there is no doubt that Reis (D) and Stamos (D) had a conflict of interest regarding MNY or that Levine (D) knew of such conflict and ignored it. Further, Rothko (P) is entitled to appreciation damages due to the wrongful acts of the executors. Affirmed.

▶ ANALYSIS

In addressing the issue of appreciation damages, Professor Scott states: "If the trustee is guilty of a breach of trust in selling trust property for an inadequate price, he is liable for the difference between the amount he should have received and the amount which he did receive. He is not liable, however, for any subsequent rise in value of the property sold." See 3 Scott, *Trust* (3d ed.) § 208.6, pp. 1689–1690.

Quicknotes

CONFLICT OF INTEREST Refers to ethical problems that arise, or may be anticipated to arise, between an attorney and his client, if the interests of the attorney, another client or a third party conflict with those of the present client.

DUTY OF LOYALTY A director's duty to refrain from self-dealing or taking a position that is adverse to the corporation's best interests.

Marsman v. Nasca

Wife of beneficiary (P) v. Trustee (D)

Mass. App. Ct., 30 Mass. App. 789, 573 N.E.2d 1025 (1991).

NATURE OF CASE: Appeal from judgment imposing constructive trust for breach of trust.

FACT SUMMARY: Because Farr (D), as trustee of Cappy Marsman's trust, did not inquire into Cappy's financial circumstances, Cappy was forced to give up the house he lived in as a means of solving his financial difficulties.

🏛 RULE OF LAW

Where a trust gives the trustee a discretionary power to pay amounts of the principal for the comfortable support and maintenance of a beneficiary, the trustee has a duty to inquire into the financial resources of that beneficiary so as to recognize his needs.

FACTS: Sara Marsman set up a trust that provided for her husband, Cappy, after her death. Farr (D), as trustee, had discretionary power to pay out amounts of the principal as he deemed advisable, but failed to adequately explain that power to Cappy. Because Cappy was denied access to the principal, financial difficulties caused him to transfer his house to Sara's daughter, Sally, and her husband, Marlette (D), reserving a life estate for himself. After Cappy's death, Marlette (D), now sole owner due to Sally's death, told Margaret (P), Cappy's second wife, to vacate the premises. Margaret (P) brought an action in the probate court, which held that Farr (D) had breached his duty to inquire into Cappy's finances. Marlette (D) was ordered to convey the house to Margaret (P), and Farr (D) was ordered to reimburse Marlette (D) for upkeep expenses. Marlette (D) and Farr (D) appealed.

ISSUE: Where a trust gives the trustee a discretionary power to pay amounts of the principal for the comfortable support and maintenance of a beneficiary, does the trustee have a duty to inquire into the financial resources of that beneficiary so as to recognize his needs?

HOLDING AND DECISION: (Dreben, J.) Yes. Where a trust gives the trustee a discretionary power to pay amounts of the principal for the comfortable support and maintenance of a beneficiary, the trustee has a duty to inquire into the financial resources of that beneficiary so as to recognize his needs. A life beneficiary is to be maintained in accordance with his normal standard of living. Had Farr (D) met his duties either of inquiry or of distribution under the trust, Cappy would not have lost his home. Sally and Marlette (D) cannot be charged as constructive trustees of the property, but the payments of principal that would have made it possible for Cappy to keep the house can be deemed to be a constructive trust in favor of his estate. Vacated and remanded for a determination of the amount to be paid Cappy's estate from the trust.

▶ ANALYSIS

Here, Farr (D) was directed by the trust agreement to pay Cappy enough for his "comfortable support," yet Farr (D) failed to do so. Prudence and reasonableness are the standard of conduct for trustees of a discretionary trust. However, a desire to save for a beneficiary's future medical needs does not warrant a persistent policy of miserliness toward those beneficiaries.

◼▬◼

Quicknotes

CONSTRUCTIVE TRUST A trust that arises by operation of law whereby the court imposes a trust upon property lawfully held by one party for the benefit of another, as a result of some wrongdoing by the party in possession so as to avoid unjust enrichment.

DISCRETIONARY TRUST A trust pursuant to which the trustee is authorized to make decisions regarding the investment of the trust funds and the distribution of such funds to beneficiaries.

EXCULPATORY CLAUSE A clause in a contract relieving one party from liability for certain unlawful conduct.

TENANCY BY THE ENTIRETY The ownership of property by a husband and wife whereby they hold undivided interests in the property with right of survivorship.

◼▬◼

In re Estate of Janes

Wife of testator (P) v. Trustee (D)

N.Y. Ct. App., 90 N.Y.2d 41, 681 N.E.2d 332, 659 N.Y.S.2d 165 (1997).

NATURE OF CASE: Appeal from award of damages for negligent retention of trust assets.

FACT SUMMARY: Mrs. Janes (P) argued that the trustee (D) appointed to oversee her husband's testamentary trusts violated his fiduciary duty to maintain a diversified portfolio of the trust's investments by retaining a majority of the assets in Kodak stock.

RULE OF LAW
A fiduciary, in executing his duties as trustee, is required to invest the assets of a trust as a prudent person would in the management of his own affairs.

FACTS: Rodney Janes, the testator, died in 1973, leaving an estate valued at $3.5 million. The estate held $2.5 million in stocks, 71 percent of which were shares in Eastman Kodak Company. Janes's will devised his estate to three trusts. The first trust was comprised of 50 percent of the estate, granting Mrs. Janes (P) the income for life and a general power of appointment as to the principal. Second, Janes created a charitable trust consisting of 25 percent of the assets of the estate. The rest of his assets were placed in a trust designating income to Mrs. Janes (P) for life and the remainder to the charitable trust. At the time of Janes's death, the Kodak stock was valued at $135 per share. By the end of 1973, however, the value of the shares had fallen to $109 per share. By 1978, the value of the stock had declined even further, to $40 per share. The surrogate court held that the estate's trustee (D) had violated its fiduciary duty by retaining the Kodak stock and employed a "lost profits" measure of damages. The appellate division affirmed, but modified the measure of damages used, concluding that the proper damages should be calculated as the difference between the stock's value at the time it should have been sold and its value when it was actually sold. Both parties appealed.

ISSUE: Does a trustee violate his fiduciary duty by failing to diversify the investment of trust assets?

HOLDING AND DECISION: (Levine, J.) Yes. A fiduciary, in executing his duties as trustee, is required to invest the assets of a trust as a prudent person would in the management of his own affairs. The trustee's predominate objectives must be the maintenance of the trust assets and the acquisition of a sufficient income. In determining whether the trustee has satisfied his duty to invest the trust assets prudently, the court must consider the attendant facts and circumstances. This requires the court to examine the trustee's thoughts and actions in respect to each investment of the trust property, at the moment the

act or omission occurred. While the court may not evaluate the trustee's decision based on the result of the investment, the court must necessarily consider the trustee's overall performance in managing the trust assets. The holding of a large percentage of the trust assets in one investment is prima facie evidence of imprudence. However, the individual investment must be examined in relation to several factors. These include the total value of the estate, relevant cost of living expenses, economic conditions, the beneficiaries' need, the asset's marketability, and potential tax liabilities. This requires the court to examine the individual investment in relation to the performance and circumstances of the trust as a whole. Here the trustee (D) failed to discharge his duties as would a prudent investor in the management of his own affairs. The appellate division was correct in setting damages as the amount of value lost to the trust by virtue of the improvident investment. This requires the court to determine the difference, between what the value of the stock was on the date that it should have been sold, and the value of the stock when it was in fact sold or at the date of the accounting. Applying this formula to the present case, the proper measure of damages is $4,065,029. Affirmed.

ANALYSIS

The determination of the date and value at which the investment should have been sold presents a difficult issue for resolution by the court. The court states that such action should be taken within a "reasonable" time period. The discernment of what constitutes a "reasonable" time necessarily depends upon the facts and circumstances of the individual case, and is determined consistent with the prudent investor standard.

■=■

Quicknotes

CHARITABLE TRUST A trust that is established for the benefit of a class of persons or for the public in general.

DUTY TO DIVERSIFY Duty of a trustee, in the administration of the trust, to diversify the investments made with the trust's funds or property.

POWER OF APPOINTMENT Power, created by another person in connection with a gratuitous transfer (often in trust) residing in a person (as trustee or otherwise), to affect the disposition or distribution of the property.

■=■

Wood v. U.S. Bank, N.A.

Trust beneficiary (P) v. Trustee's successor (D)

Ohio Ct. App., 828 N.E.2d 1072 (2005).

NATURE OF CASE: Appeal from verdict against plaintiff in action for trustee's failure to diversify trust assets.

FACT SUMMARY: Wood (P), a trust beneficiary, contended that Firstar (D), the trustee, violated its duty to diversify, even though the trust instrument permitted a trustee to retain its own stock (to avoid problems with the Rule of Undivided Loyalty).

🏛 RULE OF LAW
Even if a trust instrument allows the trustee to retain assets that would not normally be suitable, the trustee's duty to diversify remains, unless there are special circumstances or the trust instrument specifies otherwise.

FACTS: Wood (P) was a beneficiary of an $8 million trust her husband had created. Firstar (D) was the trustee. The trust instrument authorized Firstar (D) "to retain any securities in the same form as when received, including shares of a corporate Trustee . . . even though all of such securities are not of the class of investments a trustee may be permitted by law to make and to hold cash uninvested as they deem advisable or proper." This language permitted Firstar (D) to retain Firstar stock—which constituted 80 percent of the trust assets—in the trust. After her husband died, Wood (P) and her advisor requested that Firstar (D) sell some of the Firstar stock once the stock started increasing in value. Such an increase occurred after Firstar (D) merged with another bank, when the stock rose from $21 per share to $35 per share. Firstar (D) ignored these requests. Then the stock value plummeted, eventually reaching $16 per share. Around this time, Firstar (D) made the final distribution to the beneficiaries. Wood (P) brought suit, asserting that Firstar (D) had violated state law by failing to diversify the trust assets. According to expert testimony based on calculations using an average mutual fund as the basis for estimating value, Firstar's (D) failure to diversify, cost Wood (P) $771,099. Wood (P) claimed that, under state statute, based on the Uniform Prudent Investor Act (UPIA), Firstar (D) had a mandatory duty to diversify absent special circumstances, Firstar (D) had failed to show special circumstances that would have relaxed its mandatory duty to diversify that no such circumstances existed. She proposed jury instructions based on the UPIA, but the trial court rejected these and instead adopted Firstar's (D) instructions based on abuse-of-discretion and estoppel defenses. The jury returned a verdict for Firstar (D), and Wood (P) appealed. The state's intermediate appellate court granted review.

ISSUE: Even if a trust instrument allows the trustee to retain assets that would not normally be suitable, does the trustee's duty to diversify remain, unless there are special circumstances or the trust instrument specifies otherwise?

HOLDING AND DECISION: (Painter, J.) Yes. Even if a trust instrument allows the trustee to retain assets that would not normally be suitable, the trustee's duty to diversify remains, unless there are special circumstances or the trust instrument specifies otherwise. The UPIA codifies the common law rule that a trustee has the duty to diversify trust assets unless there are special circumstances where not diversifying better serves trust interests. This duty may be expanded, restricted, eliminated, or otherwise altered by the trust instrument. Here, Firstar (D) was given the authority to retain its own stock so it would not run afoul of the "The Rule of Undivided Loyalty," which requires a trustee's undivided loyalty to the beneficiaries and prohibits the trustee's ownership of its own stock, except where the settlor has given the trustee the power to retain the stock, as in this case. The only restriction to the exception is that the trustee "must not act in bad faith or abuse its discretion." The retention clause here, however, did not say anything about diversification, so that it did not affect Firstar's (D) duty to act prudently and to diversify. The language of a trust does not alter a trustee's duty to diversify unless the instrument creating the trust clearly indicates an intention to do so. Firstar's (D) failure to diversify, therefore, would have been excused only if it reasonably determined that there were special circumstances under which diversification would not be prudent. The issue of special circumstances, however, was never presented to the jury. Firstar (D) argues that it should not be liable to Wood (P) because it acted in reasonable reliance on the trust instrument. However, the Restatement (Third) of Trusts indicates that a general authorization in a trust instrument is insufficient to relieve a trustee of its duty to diversify. This is precisely what the retention language here was—a general authorization. The trust instrument did not expressly provide that the stock could be retained even if not prudent to do so, although it could have so provided. To abrogate the duty to diversify, the trust must contain specific language authorizing or directing the trustee to retain in a specific investment a larger percentage of the trust assets than would normally be prudent. The retention language did not go so far, as it merely authorized the trustee to retain its own stock. The instruction given to the jury indicated that a trustee has no

Continued on next page.

liability for retaining original investments provided there is no abuse of discretion—dishonesty or fraud—and the investments are retained in good faith. This instruction is rejected because it virtually assured a verdict for Firstar (D), as there were no allegations of dishonesty or fraud. Because of this erroneous instruction, the question of special circumstances was never placed before the jury. "Special circumstances" usually refers to holdings that are important to a family or a trust. Whether the Firstar stock was special to the family or trust is a question of fact that should have been considered by the jury. Wood (P) proposed the proper instruction under the UPIA: "A trustee must diversify the investments of a trust unless the trustee reasonably determines that, because of special circumstances, the purposes of the trust are better served without diversifying." Because if given this instruction, the jury could have gone the other way, a new trial must be ordered. Reversed and remanded.

▌ANALYSIS

Trustees should not be judged on hindsight, and a trustee who is authorized to retain assets but sells them is not liable merely because the securities later rise in value, or vice versa. Few would become trustees if they were liable every time they did not sell stock at the most propitious chance. This case was not, however, based on hindsight, but rather implicated Firstar's (D) duty to diversify, absent special circumstances; the trust would have benefited even more if Firstar (D) had simply performed its duty to diversify in the first place. As the Restatement (Third) of Trusts § 91, cmt. f (2007) explains: "[T]he fact that an investment is permitted does not relieve the trustee of the fundamental duty to act with prudence. The fiduciary must still exercise care, skill, and caution in making decisions to acquire or retain the investment."

━━━

Quicknotes

DUTY TO DIVERSIFY Duty of a trustee, in the administration of the trust, to diversify the investments made with the trust's funds or property.

FIDUCIARY DUTY A legal obligation to act for the benefit of another, including subordinating one's personal interests to that of the other person.

━━━

Howard v. Howard

Income beneficiary (P) v. Remainder beneficiary (D)

Or. Ct. App., 156 P.3d 89 (2007).

NATURE OF CASE: Appeal from court's instruction to trustee in action to interpret a trust's terms.

FACT SUMMARY: Marcene (P), the trust's income beneficiary, sought an interpretation of the trust's terms, and the trial court directed the trustee to not consider her personal income, assets, and financial posture in the administration of the trust. Coy (D), the trust's remainder beneficiary, contended that Leo, the settlor, had intended that Marcene's (P) financial situation be considered by the trustee and that the trial court had, therefore erred.

RULE OF LAW

Where a trust instrument expressly favors an income beneficiary over remainder beneficiaries and makes income payments mandatory, the income beneficiary's financial posture is not relevant to the administration of the trust.

FACTS: Leo and Marcene (P) were married, had significant assets of their own, and each had children from a prior marriage. Leo's trust instrument provided that after Leo's death, in the event that Marcene (P) survived Leo, his assets were to be divided into two trusts, a Family Trust and a Marital Trust. The trustee was to distribute a "nonmarital share"—the maximum amount that could pass free of the federal estate tax—to the Family Trust and the residue to the Marital Trust. The trust instrument provided that, during Marcene's (P) lifetime, the net income of both trusts had to be distributed to her, and no distributions of principal were to be made from either trust. On Marcene's (P) death, the residue of the Marital Trust was to be distributed to the Family Trust, which was to be divided among Leo's surviving children and the surviving issue of his children who predeceased Leo and Marcene (P). The trust instrument stated, "I intentionally make no provision herein for any of my stepchildren." The trust instrument provided for certain discretionary distributions, in which event the trustee could consider a beneficiary's other financial resources, and it also provided that distributions for Leo's and Marcene's (P) comfort and support took precedence over the remaindermen's rights. The trust instrument was drafted so it would expressly override state law, which otherwise would require that the trustee be neutral as between income beneficiaries and remainder beneficiaries. As drafted, it favored Marcene (P) as the income beneficiary, since Leo and Marcene (P) wanted first and foremost to provide for each other, with the remaindermen's needs being secondary. After Leo died, Marcene (P) and Coy (D), Leo's son and remainder bene-

ficiary, disputed how the trust should be administered, and Marcene (P) petitioned for its interpretation. The trial court determined that when the interests of Marcene (P) and the remainder beneficiaries conflicted, her interests would take precedence, and also determined that the growth of the corpus was not the trusts' primary object. Accordingly, the court directed the trustee to not consider Marcene's (P) personal income, assets, and financial posture in the administration of the trust. Coy (D) challenged this ruling as erroneous, and the state's intermediate appellate court granted review.

ISSUE: Where a trust instrument expressly favors an income beneficiary over remainder beneficiaries and makes income payments mandatory, is the income beneficiary's financial posture relevant to the administration of the trust?

HOLDING AND DECISION: (Ortega, J.) No. Where a trust instrument expressly favors an income beneficiary over remainder beneficiaries and makes income payments mandatory, the income beneficiary's financial posture is not relevant to the administration of the trust. Although a trustee owes a duty to remainder beneficiaries as well as to an income beneficiary, the trustee must carry out those duties in light of any preferences expressed in the trust instrument. Here, looking at the entire trust instrument, it is clear that Leo did not intend the trustee to consider Marcene's (P) other financial resources when administering the trusts' assets. The trust instrument requires the trustee to pay all the net trust income to Marcene (P), without any reference to her other resources or her needs. However, where certain distributions are discretionary, the trustee may consider other resources. Thus, it is clear that had Leo wished the trustee to consider Marcene's (P) other resources, he knew how to give such an instruction. Coy (D) contends, however, that if Marcene's (P) other resources are not considered, there is the potential for her to give gifts of the income to her children, or otherwise divert income, so as to circumvent Leo's desire not to provide for his stepchildren and to pass the remainder of his estate to his own children. To this, Marcene (P) argues that the trust instrument makes her "support, comfort, companionship, enjoyment and desires" a higher priority than the rights of the remainder beneficiaries, and that an investment strategy focused on preserving assets for distribution to the remainder beneficiaries would not comply with this intent. Marcene (P) is correct. The trust instrument states that Leo intended to make no provision for his

Continued on next page.

stepchildren, not that he intended to require consideration of Marcene's (P) other resources or to limit her income or ability to make gifts to her children. Thus, Leo's decision not to provide for his stepchildren circumscribed neither his direction of trust income to Marcene (P) nor his preference for her interests over those of the remainder beneficiaries. Therefore, the trial court did not err. Affirmed.

▶ ANALYSIS

Under many circumstances, the combination of traditional rules of principal-and-income accounting and the trustee's duty of impartiality constrained the ability of trustees to invest for suitable total return, as more recently required by the prudent investor rules of the Restatement (Third) of Trusts, as codified by the Uniform Prudent Investor Act (UPIA). To respond to this problem, 45 states and the District of Columbia have now (2009) adopted all or portions of the 1997 Uniform Principal and Income Act, with its adjustment power and stated goal of harmonizing principal-and-income accounting with the prudent investing rules. To serve essentially the same objective, 28 states now (2009) have some form of unitrust-conversion statute, usually as an alternative accompanying the adjustment power.

■═■

Quicknotes

INCOME BENEFICIARY A person who is the recipient of income generated by certain property.

REMAINDER BENEFICIARY A person who is to receive property that is held in trust after the termination of a preceding income interest.

■═■

In re Heller

[Parties not identified.]

N.Y. Ct. App., 849 N.E.2d 262 (2006).

NATURE OF CASE: Appeal by certified question from affirmance of denial of summary judgment for plaintiff in action to annul unitrust election and to revoke letters of trusteeship.

FACT SUMMARY: Bertha (P), a trust's income beneficiary, contended that the trustees (D), who were also remainder beneficiaries, could not, as a matter of law, elect the application of unitrust treatment to the trust, and that, in any event, retroactive unitrust treatment was prohibited.

RULE OF LAW

A trustee's status as a remainder beneficiary does not as a matter of law invalidate a unitrust election made by that trustee.

FACTS: Jacob created a testamentary trust for his wife, Bertha (P), and directed that she receive the greater of $40,000 or the total income of the trust. His two sons (D), who eventually became cotrustees, and his two daughters were named as the remainder beneficiaries. For many years after Jacob's death, Bertha (P) annually received around $190,000 from the trust. Then, in 2001, the state legislature enacted the Uniform Principal and Income Act (UPIA), which contained an optional unitrust provision. In 2003, the sons (D), as trustees, elected to have the unitrust provision apply retroactively to 2002, which resulted in Bertha's annual income being reduced to approximately $70,000. Bertha (P) (through her daughter, Davis (P), from an earlier marriage) brought suit and sought summary judgment on her motion seeking, among other things, an order annulling the unitrust election and revoking the letters of trusteeship issued to the sons (D). She also sought a determination that the election could not be made retroactive. The trial court denied the requested relief, and the state's intermediate appellate court granted review, affirming the denial of summary judgment. The court also granted leave to appeal and certified the following question to the state's highest court: "Was the opinion and order of [the intermediate appellate court] . . . properly made?" The state's highest court granted review and answered the certified question.

ISSUE: Does a trustee's status as a remainder beneficiary as a matter of law invalidate a unitrust election made by that trustee?

HOLDING AND DECISION: (Rosenblatt, J.) No. a trustee's status as a remainder beneficiary does not as a matter of law invalidate a unitrust election made by that trustee. The unitrust provision was enacted as part of legislation intended to facilitate compliance with the Prudent Investor Act of 1994, which encourages investing for total return on a portfolio. Under the prior iteration of this act, a trustee was required to balance the interests of the income beneficiary against those of the remainder beneficiary, and was constrained in making investments by the act's narrow definitions of income and principal that could result in sacrifices by either the income beneficiaries or the remainder beneficiaries. Under the current version of the act, the trustee is required to pursue an overall investment strategy that will maximize returns for all beneficiaries. A trustee investing for a portfolio's total return under the Prudent Investor Act may now adjust principal and income to compensate for the effects of the investment decisions on distribution to income beneficiaries. Alternatively, the optional unitrust provision permits trustees to calculate income according to a fixed formula. A trustee thus may achieve impartial treatment of income and remainder beneficiaries by electing unitrust status with the result that the income increases in proportion to the value of the principal. If a trust's assets are primarily interests in non-appreciating investments producing high yields for income beneficiaries, a unitrust election may initially result in a substantial decrease in the distribution to any income beneficiary, at least until the portfolio is diversified—which is the scenario presented here. Contrary to Bertha's (P) assertion, the legislation does not impede unitrust election by an interested trustee; such an election is not inconsistent, per se, with common-law limitations on the conduct of fiduciaries; and the statute permits trustees to select retroactive application. The legislature prohibited trustees from adjusting principal and income if they were a remainderman, but did not include such a prohibition with the unitrust election. Instead, the legislature created a presumption in favor of unitrust application. For these reasons, the legislature did not mean to prohibit trustees who have a beneficial interest from electing unitrust treatment. Also, under common law, while a trustee is prohibited from self-dealing, the trustee in some instances, such as in this case, owes a fiduciary duty to both the income beneficiaries and remainder beneficiaries. That these beneficiaries' interests happen to align with those of the trustee does not relieve the trustee of their duties to all beneficiaries, and, therefore, electing unitrust treatment does not violate the common law. Because a unitrust election from which a trustee benefits will be scrutinized by the courts with special care, in determining whether application of the unitrust provision is appropriate, it remains for the trial court to review the

Continued on next page.

process and assure the fairness of the trustees' election, by applying relevant factors. Such application presents questions of fact precluding summary judgment. The certified question is answered in the affirmative. Affirmed.

▶ ANALYSIS

With a unitrust, the percentage of the total return to be paid to the income beneficiary is predetermined, although need not be fixed. In states that provide for an optional unitrust, the payout percentage is usually set by statute, typically between 3 to 5 percent, and it is applied to a rolling average value over the prior few years. In this case, for example, an income beneficiary receives an annual income distribution of "four percent of the net fair market values of the assets held in the trust on the first business day of the current valuation year" for the first three years of unitrust treatment. This is true regardless of the actual income earned by the trust. Starting in the fourth year, the value of the trust assets is determined by calculating the average of three figures: the net fair market value on the first business day of the current valuation year and the net fair market values on the first business days of the prior two valuation years. Income generated in excess of this amount is applied to principal.

■━■

Quicknotes

INCOME BENEFICIARY A person who is the recipient of income generated by certain property.

REMAINDER BENEFICIARY A person who is to receive property that is held in trust after the termination of a preceding income interest.

■━■

Allard v. Pacific National Bank

Beneficiaries (P) v. Trustee bank (D)

Wash. Sup. Ct., 663 P.2d 104 (1983).

NATURE OF CASE: Appeal of denial of challenge to trustee's disposition of trust property.

FACT SUMMARY: Pacific National Bank (D), trustee, sold certain trust property without informing the beneficiaries or trying to sell on the open market.

🏛 RULE OF LAW
A trustee, when disposing of important trust property, should inform the beneficiaries and attempt to obtain the highest possible price.

FACTS: Pacific National Bank (D) was a trustee of a trust. The only significant trust asset was a parcel of developed real estate. The lessee of the property, which had a purchase right of first refusal, offered to purchase the property. After some negotiations, a sale was consummated. The beneficiaries were not informed of this until after the sale. The beneficiaries brought an action for breach of fiduciary duty, contending that the property should have been offered in the open market. The trial court held in favor of the Bank (D), and the beneficiaries appealed.

ISSUE: When disposing of important trust property, should a trustee inform the beneficiaries and attempt to obtain the highest possible price?

HOLDING AND DECISION: (Dolliver, J.) Yes. A trustee, when disposing of important trust property, should inform the beneficiaries and attempt to obtain the highest possible price. A trustee owes the beneficiaries the highest degree of loyalty and good faith. Inherent in this is that beneficiaries be appraised of important trust asset transactions. Even where, as here, consent of the beneficiaries is unnecessary for a trustee to dispose of trust assets, the beneficiaries have a right to know of pending property dispositions. For instance, they may wish to purchase the property themselves. Also, attempting to obtain the highest possible price is incumbent upon the trustee. Here, since the Bank (D) never tried to sell on the open market, it cannot be known if the highest price was obtained. Reversed and remanded.

▌ ANALYSIS

A subissue in this case involved the expected standard of care of the Bank (D). The court noted that some commentators have contended that a professional trustee should be held to a higher standard than a nonprofessional one. The court did not rule on this, however, because the trust instrument itself delineated the proper standard of care.

Quicknotes

BREACH OF FIDUCIARY DUTY The failure of a fiduciary to observe the standard of care exercised by professionals of similar education and experience.

Fletcher v. Fletcher

Beneficiary (P) v. Trustee (D)

Va. Sup. Ct., 480 S.E.2d 488 (1997).

NATURE OF CASE: Appeal from decision mandating opening of trust documents.

FACT SUMMARY: James Fletcher (P), the beneficiary of a trust, sought to compel Henry Fletcher (D) and the other trustees to reveal the entire contents of the trust document.

RULE OF LAW

Trustees have a duty to provide complete and accurate information as to the nature and amount of the trust property to the beneficiary of the trust.

FACTS: Elinor Fletcher executed a trust that upon her death provided for the establishment of three trusts benefiting James (P), Andrew, and Emily Fletcher. Henry Fletcher (D) and a bank were made trustees and given the discretion to pay income and principal to provide medical care to the beneficiaries. After Elinor died and the trust came into effect, James (P) filed suit against the trustees (D) requesting all the details about the trust. The trustees (D) provided only certain pages of the trust documents and claimed that Elinor wanted the terms to be kept confidential. The trustees (D) sought to dismiss the action on the basis that it did not state a claim. However, the trial court ruled that James (P) was entitled to see all the provisions of the trust agreement. The trustees (D) appealed.

ISSUE: Do trustees have a duty to provide complete and accurate information as to the nature and amount of the trust property to the beneficiary of the trust?

HOLDING AND DECISION: (Compton, J.) Yes. Trustees have a duty to provide complete and accurate information as to the nature and amount of the trust property to the beneficiary of the trust. The beneficiary is the equitable owner of trust property. The trustee is the mere representative whose function is to attend to the safety of the trust property. This arrangement does not imply that the beneficiary is to be kept ignorant of the nature and details of the trust and its administration. Therefore, trustees have a duty to provide beneficiaries with this information at reasonable times. Although the terms of the trust may regulate the amount of information the trustee must give, the beneficiary is always entitled to such information as is reasonably necessary to enable enforcement of rights under the trust. In the present case, without access to the trust agreement, James (P) has no basis upon which to scrutinize whether the trustees (D) are discharging their duty impartially and with reasonable care. Accordingly, the trustees (D) must disclose the information. Affirmed.

ANALYSIS

The court noted that the trustees (D) claimed Elinor orally indicated a desire for confidentiality. However, there was no evidence submitted on this matter at the trial level to properly judge this claim. While the trustees (D) could still try to demonstrate this, the decision was fairly clear in indicating that James (P), as beneficiary, had broad rights to the information he was seeking.

Quicknotes

DUTY TO DISCLOSE The duty owed by a fiduciary to reveal those facts that have a material effect on the interests of the party that must be informed.

TRUSTEE A person who is entrusted to keep or administer property for the benefit of another.

National Academy of Sciences v. Cambridge Trust Co.

Remainderman (P) v. Bank (D)

Mass. Sup. Jud. Ct., 346 N.E.2d 879 (1976).

NATURE OF CASE: Appeal from a petition seeking revocation of seven decrees allowing the trustee's accounting.

FACT SUMMARY: The National Academy of Sciences (P), a remainderman under a trust, brought an action seeking revocation of seven court decrees allowing accounts of the Cambridge Trust Company (D), the trustee.

 RULE OF LAW
Where the subject matter is one of fact in respect to which a person can have precise and accurate knowledge and he speaks as of his own knowledge and has no such knowledge, his affirmation constitutes constructive or technical fraud.

FACTS: The will of Troland left all of his real and personal property to be held in trust by the Cambridge Trust Company (the bank) (D), with the net income to be paid to his wife, provided she did not remarry. On his wife's remarriage or death, the bank (D) was to transfer the trust and trusteeship to the National Academy of Sciences (P). The bank (D) paid income from the trust to the widow until her death in 1967. In 1945, the widow remarried without the bank's (D) knowledge. Thereafter, the academy (P) brought an action seeking revocation of the bank's (D) account. The judge revoked the accounting and ordered restoration to the trusts of those amounts erroneously delivered to the decedent's widow. The appellate court affirmed, and the bank (D) appealed.

ISSUE: Where the subject matter is one of fact in respect to which a person can have knowledge and he speaks as of his own knowledge and has no such knowledge, does his affirmation constitute fraud?

HOLDING AND DECISION: (Reardon, J.) Yes. The principle is well settled that if a person makes a representation of fact as of his own knowledge and such representation is not true as to a subject matter susceptible of knowledge, if the party to whom it is made relies and acts upon it as true and sustains damage by it, it is fraud, for which the party making it is responsible. In this case, the marital status of Mrs. Troland/Flynn was a fact susceptible of precise knowledge. The bank (D) made representations concerning this fact of its own knowledge when it had no such knowledge, and the academy (P) to whom the representations were made relied on them to its detriment. The bank (D) exerted no effort at all to ascertain if Mrs. Troland had remarried even to the extent of annually requesting a statement or certificate from her to that effect. Affirmed.

▶ ANALYSIS

In order to avoid expensive accountings, provisions are often inserted in a trust instrument providing that judicial accountings should be dispensed with and accounts rendered periodically to the adult income beneficiaries of the trust. In the case of testamentary trusts, a few courts have indicated that a testator will not be permitted to dispense with statutorily required accountings. (Bogert & Bogert, *Trusts & Trustees*, § 973, 2d ed. 1962). In the case of inter vivos trusts, which are not placed under judicial supervision by statutes, it would appear that a "no judicial accounting" provision does not contravene public policy.

Quicknotes

CONSTRUCTIVE FRAUD Breach of a duty at law or in equity that tends to deceive another to whom the duty is owed, resulting in damages.

FIDUCIARY DUTY A legal obligation to act for the benefit of another, including subordinating one's personal interests to that of the other person.

Trusts: Alienation and Modification

Quick Reference Rules of Law

Scheffel v. Krueger

Creditor (P) v. Trust beneficiary (D)

N.H. Sup. Ct., 782 A.2d 410 (2001).

NATURE OF CASE: Appeal of dismissal of trustee process action.

FACT SUMMARY: Scheffel (P) was awarded a judgment against Krueger (D) and attempted to reach trust assets of which Krueger (D) was the beneficiary.

🏛 RULE OF LAW
Spendthrift trust assets are not reachable by tort creditors even when the beneficiary's conduct constitutes a criminal act, unless the beneficiary is also the settlor or the assets were fraudulently transferred to the trust.

FACTS: Scheffel (P) was awarded damages in a tort action against Krueger (D) for his sexual assault of her minor child and subsequent broadcast of the act over the Internet. Scheffel (P) sought an attachment of Krueger's (D) beneficial interest in the Kyle Krueger Irrevocable Trust (Trust). The Trust was established by Krueger's (D) grandmother, and its terms direct the trustee to pay all of the net income from the trust to Krueger (D) at least quarterly, or more frequently if he requests. The trustee is also authorized to pay any of the principal to Krueger (D) if in the trustee's sole discretion the funds are necessary for the maintenance, support, and education of Krueger (D). Krueger (D) cannot touch the principal until 2016 and is prohibited from making any voluntary or involuntary transfers of his interest in the Trust. The Trust specifically provides that the Trust proceeds cannot be assigned or given to creditors or reached by any legal or equitable process in satisfaction of any debt or liability prior to its receipt by Krueger (D). Scheffel (P) filed a trustee process action against Citizens Bank NH (D), the trustee defendant. Citizens (D) argued that the spendthrift provision barred the claim and moved to release the attachment and dismiss the claim. The Superior Court ruled that under RSA 564:23 (1997) the spendthrift provision is enforceable and dismissed Scheffel's (P) trustee process action. Scheffel (P) appealed.

ISSUE: Did the legislature intend RSA 564:23 to shield trust assets from tort creditors, especially when the beneficiary's conduct constituted a criminal act?

HOLDING AND DECISION: (Duggan, J.) Yes. The legislature did intend RSA 564:23 to shield trust assets from tort creditors, even when the beneficiary's conduct constitutes a criminal act, unless the exceptions apply. According to RSA 564:23, a spendthrift trust, is enforceable unless the beneficiary is also the settlor or the assets were fraudulently transferred to the trust. In the present case,

neither of these exceptions applies. Moreover, the Trust instrument is a valid spendthrift trust because it contains a provision which does not allow the beneficiary to transfer his right to future payments, and a creditor shall not be able to subject the beneficiary's interest to the payment of its claim. Furthermore, the statute plainly states that a creditor of a beneficiary shall not be able to subject the beneficiary's interest to the payment of its claim. Therefore, the legislature did not intend that a tort creditor should be exempted from a spendthrift provision. Since the legislature did make two other exemptions, we must presume that no others were intended. In addition, no rule of public policy is available to overcome the statutory rule. The legislature has enacted a statute repudiating the public policy exception sought by Scheffel (P) and the court cannot question the wisdom of the statute. Lastly, the Trust's purpose, to provide for Krueger's support, maintenance, and education, may still be fulfilled while Krueger (D) is incarcerated and after he is released, therefore the Trust should not be terminated. Affirmed.

▶ ANALYSIS

This case is a prime example of how a spendthrift trust can be used not only as an estate-planning tool, but can also protect beneficiaries from creditors. In *Wilcox v. Gentry*, 867 P.2d 281 (Kan. 1994), the judgment creditors were able to garnish the payments from the trust because the trust was a discretionary trust with no spendthrift clause. Unlike in New Hampshire, where the present case occurred, in certain jurisdictions spendthrift trusts cannot protect beneficiaries from creditors in some situations. For example, in *Bacardi v. White*, 463 So. 2d 218 (Fla. 1985), disbursements from a spendthrift trust could be garnished to enforce judgments for alimony.

■=■

Quicknotes

SPENDTHRIFT TRUST A trust formed for the beneficiary's support, but with restrictions imposed so as to safeguard against the beneficiary's abuse.

■=■

Federal Trade Commission v. Affordable Media, LLC

Government agency (P) v. Telemarketing business (D)

179 F.3d 1228 (9th Cir. 1999).

NATURE OF CASE: Appeal of finding of civil contempt for failure to repatriate funds.

FACT SUMMARY: The Andersons (D), a married couple on trial for their part in a fraudulent telemarketing scheme, had established an irrevocable trust under the jurisdiction of the Cook Islands. When ordered by the court to repatriate the funds in the trust, the Andersons (D) asserted that under the terms of the trust, they were unable to comply. The court found them in civil contempt.

🏛 **RULE OF LAW**
A party who is a protector for an offshore trust of which he is a beneficiary cannot assert an impossibility defense with regard to his ability to repatriate the trust's assets.

FACTS: The Andersons (D) organized a telemarketing scheme in which they sold investors the rights to profits from products sold on late-night television. The products included such questionable items as a water-filled dumbbell and a talking pet tag. The Andersons (D) appeared to be perpetrating a Ponzi scheme in which earlier investors are paid by later investors' investments until there are no more investors. The Federal Trade Commission (FTC) (P), upon hearing about the Andersons' (D) business practices, filed a complaint with the United States District Court for the District of Nevada, charging the Andersons (D) with violating the Federal Trade Commission Act and the Telemarketing Sales Rule. Upon a motion filed by the FTC (P), the court issued an ex parte temporary restraining order against the Andersons (D). Subsequent to two days of hearings, the court entered a preliminary injunction, incorporating the provisions of the temporary restraining order. The temporary restraining order and the preliminary injunction required the Andersons (D) to repatriate whatever assets were being held for their benefit outside the country. Earlier, the Andersons (D) had created an irrevocable trust under the jurisdiction of the Cook Islands. Under the terms of the trust, the Andersons (D) were named co-trustees along with AsiaCiti Trust Limited (AsiaCiti), a company licensed under the laws of the Cook Islands to conduct trustee services. Further, the provisions of the trust stated that under "an event of duress," AsiaCiti could remove the Andersons (D) as co-trustees. The Andersons (D) were also protectors of the trust. When the Andersons (D) notified AsiaCiti that they were under court order to repatriate the funds in the trust, AsiaCiti informed them that the temporary restraining order was an "event of duress." Hence, they were told, they were being removed as co-trustees. Consequently, the Andersons (D)

would not have access to the funds to repatriate them. The district court found the Andersons (D) in civil contempt because they had not repatriated the trust's assets, nor had they provided an accounting of the trust's assets. The court continued the hearing several times to allow the Andersons (D) to purge themselves of their contempt. The Andersons (D) indicated that it was impossible for them to comply with the court's order because they did not have control of the trust. Ultimately, the court ordered them taken into custody. The Andersons (D) appealed the issuance of the preliminary injunction and the court's finding them in contempt.

ISSUE: May a party who is a protector of an offshore trust of which he is a beneficiary assert an impossibility defense with regard to repatriating the trust's assets?

HOLDING AND DECISION: (Wiggins, J.) No. A party who is a protector of an offshore trust of which he is a beneficiary may not assert an impossibility defense with regard to repatriating the trust's assets. Here, the Andersons (D) had created an offshore trust to put the trust's assets beyond the jurisdiction of the United States. However, the Andersons (D) retained control over the trust's assets by naming themselves protectors. The Andersons' (D) powers as protectors are not solely negative ones. They have affirmative powers to appoint new trustees. Hence, the anti-duress provisions are subject to the Andersons (D) as protectors. Therefore, the Andersons (D) could force a foreign trustee to repatriate the assets. Therefore, they cannot avail themselves of the impossibility defense. Affirmed.

▶ **ANALYSIS**

Some offshore trusts provide protectors with only negative powers. Such protectors might have the power only to veto trustee decisions. Other protectors' powers are not subject to anti-duress provisions. Since the Andersons could appoint new trustees, they had the power to appoint ones who would comply with the court order and repatriate the trust's funds.

■■■

Quicknotes

IRREVOCABLE TRUST A trust that is not capable of being revoked after it is established.

REPATRIATION The return of an individual or property to the state from which it originated.

■■■

In re Estate of Brown

Beneficiary (P) v. Court (D)

Vt. Sup. Ct., 148 Vt. 94, 528 A.2d 752 (1987).

NATURE OF CASE: Appeal from judgment terminating trust.

FACT SUMMARY: The lifetime beneficiaries (P) of Brown's trust petitioned the court (D) to terminate the trust.

RULE OF LAW
An active trust may not be terminated, even with the consent of all the beneficiaries, if a material purpose of the settlor remains to be accomplished.

FACTS: Andrew Brown died, passing his entire estate into a trust. The trust income and principal were to be used to provide an education for the children of his nephew, Woolson Brown. After that purpose was accomplished, the trust income and principal were to be used for the care and maintenance of Woolson and his wife so that they could live in the style to which they were accustomed. At their death, the remainder was to pass to Woolson's children. The trustee complied with the terms of the trust by using the proceeds for the education of Woolson's children and applying the proceeds to benefit Woolson and his wife after the education purpose was completed. Woolson and his wife petitioned the probate court for termination of the trust, arguing that the sole remaining purpose of the trust was to maintain their lifestyle and that the distribution of the assets was necessary to accomplish this purpose. The remaindermen, Woolson's children, filed consents to the proposed termination. The probate court denied Woolson's petition to terminate, and Woolson appealed. The superior court reversed, concluding that the only material trust purpose, the education of the children, had been accomplished. The trustee appealed.

ISSUE: May an active trust be terminated, even with the consent of all the beneficiaries, if a material purpose of the settlor remains to be accomplished?

HOLDING AND DECISION: (Gibson, J.) No. An active trust may not be terminated, even with the consent of all the beneficiaries, if a material purpose of the settlor remains to be accomplished. Here, the termination cannot be compelled because a material purpose remains to be accomplished. The trust instrument had two purposes. First, it provided for the education of Woolson's children. It is clear that the educational purpose of the trust was achieved. The second purpose was the assurance of lifelong income for the beneficiaries through the discretion of the trustee. The trustee has to use all the income and such part of the principal as is necessary for this purpose. This purpose would be defeated if termination of the trust were allowed. Reversed.

ANALYSIS

Some courts will allow the termination of a testamentary trust by a compromise agreement between the beneficiaries and heirs entered into soon after the testator's death. In one case, the court allowed such a compromise regardless of whether a material purpose of the trust was defeated by the trust's termination (*Budin v. Levy*, 343 Mass. 644, 180 N.E. 2d 74 (1982)).

Quicknotes

LIFE-INCOME BENEFICIARY A person who is the recipient of income generated by certain property for the duration of the person's life, the remainder of which is to pass on to another individual upon the income beneficiary's death.

REMAINDERMAN A person, who has an interest in property to commence upon the termination of a present possessory interest.

RESIDUARY BENEFICIARIES Person specified pursuant to will to receive the portion of the estate remaining following distribution of the assets and the payment of costs.

SPENDTHRIFT TRUST A trust formed for the beneficiary's support, but with restrictions imposed so as to safeguard against the beneficiary's abuse.

SUPPORT TRUST A trust pursuant to which the trustee is authorized only to distribute such funds as are required for the support of the beneficiary.

In re Riddell

[Parties not identified.]

Wash. Ct. App., 157 P.3d 888 (2007).

NATURE OF CASE: Appeal from denial of motion by trustee to create a special needs trust.

FACT SUMMARY: Ralph Riddell (Ralph), the trustee of a consolidated trust, contended that the trust should be modified to a special needs trust for his daughter, Nancy, who suffered from schizophrenia affective disorder and bipolar disorder, since that would preserve the settlor's (his parents') intent that Nancy attain a level of responsibility, stability, and maturity to handle the trust funds before receiving the distribution, and that due to Nancy's mental illness, allowing a distribution to her would defeat the settlors' intent and the trust's purpose.

RULE OF LAW
Equitable deviation may be used to modify a trust's administrative or distributive provision or to permit the trustee to deviate from such a provision, where circumstances not anticipated by the settlor have changed and the modification or deviation will further the primary purposes of the trust and is consistent with law or policy.

FACTS: Ralph Riddell's (Ralph's) parents established trusts for the benefit of Ralph, his wife, and Ralph's children, i.e., the settlors' grandchildren. The trusts provided that upon the death of Ralph and his wife, the grandchildren would receive the trust benefits until age 35, when the trusts would terminate and the trustee would distribute the principal to the grandchildren. Ralph's daughter, Nancy, who was over 35 and suffered from schizophrenia affective disorder and bipolar disorder, was not expected to live independently for the remainder of her life. Therefore, Ralph sought to create a "special needs" trust on her behalf, instead of distributing to her the trust principal, which was around $667,500. He filed a petition asking the trial court to consolidate the trusts and to modify the consolidated trust to create a "special needs" trust on Nancy's behalf, instead of distributing the trust principal to her. He argued that a special needs trust was necessary because, upon distribution, Nancy's trust funds would either be seized by the State to pay her extraordinary medical bills or Nancy would manage the funds poorly due to her mental illness and lack of judgment. He argued that the modification would preserve and properly manage Nancy's funds for her benefit. The trial court granted the motion to consolidate the trusts, but denied the motion to modify. It stated that it did not have the power to modify the trust unless unanticipated events existed that were unknown to the settlor that would result in defeating the trust's purpose. The trial court found that the trust's purpose was "to

provide for the education, support, maintenance, and medical care of the beneficiaries" and that a modification would only "permit[ ] the family to immunize itself financially from reimbursing the State for costs of [Nancy's medical] care." It stated that it would not allow a modification "merely because a change would be more advantageous to the beneficiaries." The trial court denied a motion by Ralph for reconsideration, and the state's intermediate appellate court granted review.

ISSUE: May equitable deviation be used to modify a trust's administrative or distributive provision, or to permit the trustee to deviate from such a provision, where circumstances not anticipated by the settlor have changed and the modification or deviation will further the primary purposes of the trust and is consistent with law or policy?

HOLDING AND DECISION: (Penoyar, J.) Yes. Equitable deviation may be used to modify a trust's administrative or distributive provision or to permit the trustee to deviate from such a provision, where circumstances not anticipated by the settlor have changed and the modification or deviation will further the primary purposes of the trust and is consistent with law or policy. Under state law, equitable deviation may be used to modify a trust's administrative or distributive provision, or to permit the trustee to deviate from such a provision, provided two prongs are satisfied: (1) changed circumstances not anticipated by the settlor and (2) the modification or deviation will further the purposes of the trust. This test adopts the Restatement (Third) of Trusts, which requires a lower threshold finding than the older Restatement and gives courts broader discretion in permitting deviation of a trust. A determination relating to the second prong is subjective and attempts to determine the settlor's primary purpose in establishing the trust. The reason to modify is to give effect to the settlor's intent, had the circumstances in question been anticipated. Here, there is no dispute that the circumstances had changed. The trial court found that the "stated" purpose of the trust was to provide for the beneficiaries' education, support, maintenance, and medical care. Thus, it found that the primary purpose was to provide for Nancy during her lifetime. Because the trust was to terminate at age 35, it was also the settlors' intent that Nancy has the money to dispose of as she saw fit, which would include any estate planning that she might choose to do. Thus, the changed circumstances have intervened to frustrate the settlors' intent, since Nancy is unable to manage the funds or to pass them to her children, and since there is a great likelihood that the funds will be lost to

Continued on next page.

the State for her medical care. It is clear that the settlors would have wanted a different result. In 1993, Congress provided for special needs trusts intended to care for the needs of persons with disabilities and preserve government benefits eligibility, while allowing families to provide for the supplemental needs of a disabled person that government assistance does not provide. The trial court in its ruling determined that the trust should not be modified to permit the family to shield itself from "reimbursing the State" for the costs of Nancy's medical care due to her disability. However, given that Congress permitted the creation of special needs trusts in order to allow disabled persons to continue to receive governmental assistance for their medical care, the trial court should not have considered any loss to the State in determining whether an equitable deviation was allowed since the law invites, rather than discourages, the creation of special needs trusts in just this sort of situation. Under 42 U.S.C. § 1396p(d)(4)(A), although the State receives all remaining trust amounts upon trust termination for medical assistance paid on behalf of the disabled beneficiary, the State is not entitled to receive payback upon termination of a third party special needs trust for medical assistance provided for the disabled beneficiary. Here, the trust was established and funded by the grandparents for the beneficiary Nancy; it is a third party special needs trust. The trust is not subject to State assistance payback and is not required to have a payback provision. On remand, the trial court should order such equitable deviation as is consistent with the settlors' intent in light of the changed circumstances. Reversed and remanded.

▶ ANALYSIS

The Restatement (Third) of Trusts not only provides for equitable deviation, as in this case, but also provides for nonjudicial combination and division of trusts, and, similarly, for the termination of a trust if it is no longer economically viable.

■══■

Quicknotes

EQUITABLE DEVIATION DOCTRINE Allows for deviation from trust terms if the purposes of the trust would be defeated under the attendant circumstances.

■══■

Ladysmith Rescue Squad, Inc. v. Newlin

Trust beneficiary (P) v. Trust beneficiary (D)

Va. Sup. Ct., 694 S.E.2d 604 (2010).

NATURE OF CASE: Appeal from lower court decision approving a division of trust assets to allow some of the beneficiaries to receive immediately the full proceeds of the trust.

FACT SUMMARY: Miller Crosby's will placed five million dollars into a trust for the benefit of four individuals. The individuals received interest from the trust during their lifetimes. After the death of the four individuals, the remainder of the trust proceeds would go to two charitable trusts for the Upper Caroline Volunteer Fire Department and the Ladysmith Volunteer Rescue Squad. The two surviving individuals sought to terminate the trust and receive the full proceeds of the trust assets immediately.

🏛 RULE OF LAW
Under the Uniform Trust Code, a court has the authority to modify or terminate a trust only when circumstances arise that were not anticipated by the settlor and when such modification or termination will further the purposes of the trust.

FACTS: Miller Crosby's will placed five million dollars into a trust for the benefit of four individuals. Crosby died in 2004. As of 2009, two of the individuals remained alive, Gloria Essaye (P) and William Orrock (P). The trust provided them with interest from the trust during the course of their lives. Spendthrift clauses in the will insulated the beneficiaries' interest in the trust from creditors and prevented the beneficiaries from encumbering the trust assets before they received any funds from the trust. After the death of Essaye (P) and Orrock (P), the remaining funds would go to two charitable trusts for the Upper Caroline Volunteer Fire Department and the Ladysmith Volunteer Rescue Squad (D). Essaye (P), Orrock (P), the Upper Caroline Volunteer Fire Department (P), and the trustees of the trust petitioned the court to: (1) divide the testamentary trust into two equal trusts to be called the Upper Caroline Trust and the Ladysmith Trust; and (2) to then terminate the Upper Caroline Trust. Under the proposed arrangement, Essaye (P) and Orrock (P) would receive trust proceeds based on their life expectancies. The Upper Caroline Trust would then receive the remainder of that particular trust. Ladysmith Volunteer Rescue Squad (D) objected on the grounds the motions completely frustrated Crosby's intent to place the money in trust for certain beneficiaries during their lifetimes. The lower court granted the motions. Ladysmith (D) appealed.

ISSUE: Under the Uniform Trust Code, does a court have the authority to modify or terminate a trust only when circumstances arise that were not anticipated by the settlor and when such modification or termination will further the purposes of the trust?

HOLDING AND DECISION: (Russell, J.) Yes. Under the Uniform Trust Code, a court has the authority to modify or terminate a trust only when circumstances arise that were not anticipated by the settlor and when such modification or termination will further the purposes of the trust. When faced with petitions to modify or terminate a trust, the testator's or settlor's intention should prevail over the desires of the beneficiaries. No provision of the Uniform Trust Code allows beneficiaries of a trust to modify a trust merely to receive their trust proceeds quicker. Here, there is no evidence the trust has been mismanaged, has become uneconomical, or that its goals have become unattainable. The burden is on the beneficiaries to prove that circumstances have arisen that were unforeseen by the settlor. The beneficiaries have not made any such showing. Under Crosby's testamentary scheme, Essaye (P) and Orrock (P) were to receive interest from the trust during their lifetimes. The charitable trusts would only be created after their deaths. The lower court's approval of the motions completely frustrated Crosby's intentions. The case is remanded with an order that the lower court deny both motions. Reversed and remanded.

▶ ANALYSIS

Beneficiaries of a trust face a heavy burden when attempting to modify or terminate a trust. This is particularly true when it is evident the beneficiaries seek to receive the full proceeds of the trust immediately rather than continue the testator's plan for disbursement of the proceeds. Also, in many states, the state Attorney General has some level of jurisdiction over charitable trusts and will often join a pending case if it appears the purposes of a charitable trust may be frustrated.

Quicknotes

CHARITABLE TRUST A trust that is established for charitable purposes.

SPENDTHRIFT PROVISION A provision in a trust providing for the beneficiary's support, but with restrictions imposed so as to safeguard against the beneficiary's alienation of his interest therein.

Davis v. U.S. Bank National Association

Trust beneficiary (P) v. Trustee (D)

Mo. Ct. App., 243 S.W.3d 425 (2007).

NATURE OF CASE: Appeal from summary judgment for plaintiff in action seeking the replacement of a trustee and removal of trust assets.

FACT SUMMARY: Davis (P), the income beneficiary of his grandfather's Trust, petitioned under the state's Uniform Trust Code (UTC), in his name and those of his children ("Son" and "Daughter"), the residual beneficiaries, to have the current trustee (Trustee) (D) removed and replaced by U.S. Trust Company of Delaware (UST), and to have the Trust assets moved to UST. The Trustee (D) contended that Davis's (P) failure to join all of the remainder beneficiaries of the trust as parties to his lawsuit deprived the court of subject matter jurisdiction; that Davis (P) could not virtually represent Son and Daughter because their interests inherently conflicted; and that Davis (P) failed to show that removal of the Trustee (D) would best serve all the beneficiaries' interests.

> ## 🏛 RULE OF LAW
> (1) Under UTC § 706(b)(4), all remainder beneficiaries of a trust do not have to be joined in a petition to remove a trustee for the court to have subject matter jurisdiction.
> (2) Under UTC § 303(6), a parent may represent a minor child in seeking to remove a trustee where there is no inherent conflict of interest between the parent and child as to such removal, and their interests are substantially identical.
> (3) Under UTC § 706(b)(4), a trustee may be removed where the qualified beneficiaries seeking such removal have presented factually supported evidence that such removal will inure to the beneficiaries' benefit, and where the trust does not prohibit such removal.

FACTS: Davis's (P) grandfather established a Trust under which Davis (P), as the income beneficiary of the Trust, was entitled to receive the entire net income of the Trust for life. Upon his death, the principal of the Trust was to be divided among his then living children in equal shares and distributed to each child. Davis (P) had two children ("Son" and "Daughter"). The Trust also provided that if Davis (P) had no surviving children upon his death, Davis's (P) share would pass to various remainder beneficiaries. For many years, the Trustee (D) was located in Missouri, whereas Davis (P) was a resident of Pennsylvania. Eventually, Davis (P) petitioned under the state's Uniform Trust Code (UTC), in his name and those of Son and

Daughter, to have the current Trustee (D) removed and replaced by U.S. Trust Company of Delaware (UST), and to have the Trust assets moved to UST. As part of his petition, Davis (P) presented evidence that: UST's fees would be over $10,000 less per year and UST would permit an independent investment adviser; there would be no state income tax on trust income; he was a 30-minute car drive away from UST; and the proposed investment advisor had a complete understanding of Davis (P) and his family's unique personal financial situation and how the Trust coordinated with his family's financial objectives. The trial court granted summary judgment to Davis (P), and the Trustee (D) appealed, claiming that summary judgment should not have been granted because a conflict of interest existed between Davis (P) and Son and Daughter, so that Davis (P) could not represent the interests of Son and Daughter; Davis (P) had failed to name necessary and indispensable parties to the lawsuit; Davis (P) had failed to show removal of the Trustee (D) would best serve the interests of the beneficiaries; removal of the Trustee (D) would be inconsistent with a material purpose of the Trust; and discovery was needed. The state's intermediate appellate court granted review.

ISSUE:

(1) Under UTC § 706(b)(4), must all remainder beneficiaries of a trust be joined in a petition to remove a trustee for the court to have subject matter jurisdiction?

(2) Under UTC § 303(6), may a parent represent a minor child in seeking to remove a trustee where there is no inherent conflict of interest between the parent and child as to such removal, and their interests are substantially identical?

(3) Under UTC § 706(b)(4), may a trustee be removed where the qualified beneficiaries seeking such removal have presented factually supported evidence that such removal will inure to the beneficiaries' benefit, and where the trust does not prohibit such removal?

HOLDING AND DECISION: (Sullivan, J.)

(1) No. Under UTC § 706(b)(4), all remainder beneficiaries of a trust do not have to be joined in a petition to remove a trustee for the court to have subject matter jurisdiction. Instead, UTC § 706(b)(4) provides that only "qualified" beneficiaries must be joined. A qualified beneficiary means a beneficiary who, on the date the beneficiary's qualification is determined is a permissible distributee. Here, Son and Daughter were the permissible distributees at the time of the filing of the suit, and, as such, Davis (P) and Son and Daughter are all of

Continued on next page.

the qualified beneficiaries of the Trust. The remote remainder beneficiaries of the Trust are not qualified beneficiaries. Accordingly, all of the qualified beneficiaries were before the court, which, therefore, had subject matter jurisdiction. Affirmed as to this issue.

(2) Yes. Under UTC § 303(6), a parent may represent a minor child in seeking to remove a trustee where there is no inherent conflict of interest between the parent and child as to such removal, and their interests are substantially identical. Here, Davis (P) and Son and Daughter have substantially identical interests which are not in conflict with regard to removing the Trustee (D) and implementing UST as Trustee. Even if there is a conflict of interest between Davis (P) and his children as to some issues unrelated to trustee removal (the Trustee (D) asserts there is an inherent conflict of interest between income beneficiaries and residual beneficiaries) the conflict must be "with respect to a particular question or dispute." As such, whether there is a conflict of interest must be determined on a case-by-case basis. There is no such conflict here as relates to the removal of Trustee (D). Therefore, Davis (P) could virtually represent his children in seeking such removal. Affirmed as to this issue.

(3) Yes. Under UTC § 706(b)(4), a trustee may be removed where the qualified beneficiaries seeking such removal have presented factually supported evidence that such removal will inure to the beneficiaries' benefit, and where the trust does not prohibit such removal. Here, Davis (P) presented evidence that UST's annual fees would be close to 24 percent lower than those being charged by Trustee (D), and Trustee (D) did not dispute this figure, but merely called it speculative and hearsay. Under the UTC, the petitioner only has to show that the change in trustee will somehow inure to his and the other beneficiaries' benefit—and Davis (P) has done that. Trustee (D) also claims that the change in trustee is inconsistent with the material purpose of the Trust as the Trust clearly did not contemplate the change, but does contemplate keeping the same Trustee in the same state. This argument is speculative and without any evidentiary support. It is also irrelevant, because the UTC provides for the change of trustee as long as the terms of the Trust do not prohibit it. Here, the terms of the Trust do not include such a prohibition. Accordingly, there are no further factual disputes, so that discovery is not needed. Affirmed as to this issue.

▶ ANALYSIS

UTC § 706 changes traditional trust law by permitting a "no-fault" change of trustee where the beneficiaries request such a change and can, as in this case, show that some benefit will inure to the beneficiaries as a result. Under traditional law, the beneficiaries did not have the right to request such a change. Nonetheless, the UTC § 706 may be overridden by contradictory terms in the trust instrument.

━■━

Quicknotes

JURISDICTION The authority of a court to hear and declare judgment in respect to a particular matter.

REMAINDER BENEFICIARY A person who is to receive property that is held in trust after the termination of a preceding income interest.

━■━

CHAPTER 11

Trusts: Charitable Purposes, Cy Pres, and Supervision

Quick Reference Rules of Law

Shenandoah Valley National Bank v. Taylor

Trustee (D) v. Heir-at-law (P)

Va. Sup. Ct. App., 192 Va. 135, 63 S.E.2d 786 (1951).

NATURE OF CASE: Suit challenging validity of a testamentary trust.

FACT SUMMARY: A testator created a perpetual trust, the income of which was to be paid in equal shares to each student in a particular grade school just before Christmas and Easter. Although the payments were purportedly for educational purposes, an heir challenged the validity of the trust.

🏛 RULE OF LAW
For a charitable trust to be valid, it must provide relief for the poor or needy or otherwise benefit or advance the social interest of the community.

FACTS: The terms of the testator's will left the bulk of his $86,000 estate to the Shenandoah Valley National Bank (D), as trustee, to administer as a perpetual trust. The trust funds were to be invested and the income was to be paid to all first-, second-, and third-grade students in a particular local grade school. The payments were to be made in equal shares to each student directly and were to be distributed just before the Christmas and Easter vacations. The trust directed that the money so distributed was to be used by each student for the furtherance of his or her education. Although the testator had no children or other close relatives, Taylor (P), a distant relative and heir, brought suit challenging the validity of the trust as not being charitable and therefore violative of the rule against perpetuities.

ISSUE: For a charitable trust to be valid, must it provide relief for the poor or needy or otherwise benefit or advance the social interest of the community?

HOLDING AND DECISION: (Miller, J.) Yes. For a charitable trust to be valid, it must provide relief for the poor or needy or otherwise benefit or advance the social interest of the community. There is a fundamental difference between a trust that is charitable and one that is benevolent. A benevolent trust, while it may be praiseworthy, is a private enterprise and is subject to the rule against perpetuities. A charitable trust is public and is not subject to the rule. For a perpetual charitable trust to be valid, it must provide relief to the poor or needy or otherwise benefit or advance the social interest of the community. The most common examples of such interests include the relief of poverty, the advancement of education, the advancement of religion, the promotion of health, and governmental or municipal purposes. The keystone is the accomplishment of a purpose which is beneficial to the community. While the testator's scheme would surely delight the recipients, there is no way that the stated purpose

of educational advancement can be assured. The timing of the payments and the ages of the children practically assure the opposite. This trust cannot be classified as charitable, and as it violates the rule against perpetuities, it must fail. Affirmed.

▶ ANALYSIS

A perpetual charitable trust may validly be directed toward a small ascertainable group so long as the recipients are qualified as to actual need. Such provisions as providing for the support of needy widows and children of the deceased ministers of a particular church have been upheld, for example. Where no need test is applied, the group benefited must be needy by definition, such as young seamstresses (upheld at a time before minimum wage laws). Generally, the larger the class is, the less strict the application of the needs test.

Quicknotes

CHARITABLE TRUST A trust that is established for the benefit of a class of persons or for the public in general.

PERPETUAL TRUST A trust which is to continue for as long as its purpose is necessary.

RULE AGAINST PERPETUITIES The doctrine that a future interest that is incapable of vesting within twenty-one years of lives in being at the time it is created is immediately void.

TESTAMENTARY TRUST A trust, created by will and effective only after the grantor's death, since the assets that comprise the corpus of the trust are assumed to vest at that time.

In re Neher's Will

[Parties not identified.]

N.Y. Ct. App., 279 N.Y. 370, 18 N.E.2d 625 (1939).

NATURE OF CASE: Appeal from the denial of a petition for a decree to construe and reform a charitable gift.

FACT SUMMARY: When Red Hook Village (P) found it did not have the resources to establish and maintain a hospital on property willed to the village (P) by Ella Neher, the village (P) petitioned the court for permission to establish an administration building designated as the "Herbert Neher Memorial Hall."

🏛 RULE OF LAW
Where a will gives real property for a general charitable purpose, the gift may be reformed cy pres when compliance with a particular purpose grafted onto the general purpose is impracticable.

FACTS: Ella Neher's will gave her home in Red Hook Village (P) to the village (P) to be used as a memorial to the memory of her husband. She further directed that the property be used as a hospital to be known as the "Herbert Neher Memorial Hospital." The village (P) accepted the gift, but later discovered that it was without the resources necessary to establish and maintain a hospital on the property. Furthermore, a modern hospital in a neighboring village adequately served the needs of both communities. Instead, the village (P) petitioned the court for leave to erect and maintain a building for the administration purposes of the village (P), to be designated as the "Herbert Neher Memorial Hall." The court denied the petition. The appellate division affirmed. The village (P) appealed.

ISSUE: Where a will gives real property for a general charitable purpose, may the gift be reformed cy pres when compliance with a particular purpose grafted onto the general purpose is impracticable?

HOLDING AND DECISION: (Loughran, J.) Yes. Where a will gives real property for a general charitable purpose, the gift may be reformed cy pres when compliance with a particular purpose grafted onto the general purpose is impracticable. When taken as a whole the true construction of the paragraph outlining the gift in Neher's will is that the paramount intention was to give the property for a general charitable purpose rather than a particular charitable purpose. Neher's gift to the village (P) did not specify what sort of medical or surgical care should be provided. The direction grafted on to the general gift, that the property be used for a hospital, may be ignored where, as here, the village (P) finds compliance with that direction impracticable due to a lack of resources. Reversed and remanded.

▶ ANALYSIS

Application of the doctrine of cy pres allows a charitable trust to continue rather than fail. The doctrine's application occurs where the court can discern a primary general charitable intent and where the altered charitable purpose falls within the general charitable intent of the settlor. Such reformation allows the donor's general intent to be carried out even where changes unforeseen by the settlor eliminate the need for the gift's original intended use.

Quicknotes

CHARITABLE TRUST A trust that is established for the benefit of a class of persons or for the public in general.

DOCTRINE OF CY PRES Equitable doctrine applied in order to give effect to an instrument, which would be unlawful if enforced strictly, as close to the drafter's intent as possible without violating the law.

Smithers v. St. Luke's-Roosevelt Hospital Center

Estate's administratrix (P) v. Charitable donee (D)

N.Y. App. Div., 723 N.Y.S.2d 426 (2001).

NATURE OF CASE: Appeal from dismissal for lack of standing to enforce terms of a charitable gift.

FACT SUMMARY: Smithers (P), administratrix for her husband's estate, brought suit to enforce the terms of a charitable gift made by her deceased husband to St. Luke's Roosevelt Hospital Center (the "Hospital") (D). The gift was restricted for the purpose of establishing an alcoholism center and maintaining it in its own building.

RULE OF LAW

The estate of a donor of a charitable gift has standing to sue the donee to enforce the terms of the gift.

FACTS: Mr. Smithers made a $10 million gift to St. Luke's Roosevelt Hospital Center (the "Hospital") (D), which was dedicated for the purpose of establishing an alcoholism rehabilitation center. One of the conditions of the gift was that the center be housed in its own building, separate from the Hospital (D). Years of investigation by the state Attorney General (D) revealed that the Hospital (D) had misappropriated funds from the charitable fund to fund other hospital projects. The Attorney General (D) entered into an agreement with the Hospital (D), whereby the Hospital (D) agreed to not use gift funds for any purpose other than to benefit the center and to return to the gift fund proceeds from any sale of the building in which the center was housed. Smithers (P), administratrix for Mr. Smithers' estate, filed a claim against both the Hospital (D) and Attorney General (D) to enforce the terms of her deceased husband's gift. She sought an accounting of the funds of the gift, and also sought an injunction preventing the Hospital (D) from selling the building in which the rehabilitation center was housed, or, alternatively, preventing disbursement of the funds from the sale. The Hospital (D) and Attorney General (D) moved to dismiss, and the trial court granted the defendants' motions. The appellate division granted review.

ISSUE: Does the estate of a donor of a charitable gift have standing to sue the donee to enforce the terms of the gift?

HOLDING AND DECISION: (Ellerin, J.) Yes. The estate of a donor of a charitable gift has standing to sue the donee to enforce the terms of the gift. Standing to enforce the terms of charitable gifts is not exclusive to the Attorney General (D). Here, Smithers (P) is bringing her suit as administratrix of her husband's estate, not on her own behalf or on behalf of the Center's beneficiaries.

Therefore, the general rule barring beneficiaries from suing charitable corporations has no application here. The donor of a charitable gift is in a better position than the Attorney General (D) to be vigilant and, if he or she is so inclined, to enforce his or her own intent. Mr. Smithers was the founding donor of the Smithers Center, which he established to carry out his vision of "first class alcoholism treatment and training." In his agreement with the Hospital (D) he reserved to himself the right to veto the Hospital's (D) project plans and staff appointments for the Smithers Center. He and Smithers (P) remained actively involved in the affairs of the Smithers Center until his death, and she thereafter. During his lifetime, when Mr. Smithers found that his intent was not carried out by the Hospital (D), he decided not to donate the balance of the gift. It was only when the Hospital (D) expressly agreed to the various restrictions imposed by Mr. Smithers that he completed the gift. The Hospital's (D) subsequent unauthorized deviation from the terms of the completed gift commenced during Smithers's lifetime and was discovered shortly after he died. To hold that, in her capacity as her late husband's representative, Smithers (P) has no standing to institute an action to enforce the terms of the gift is to contravene the well-settled principle that a donor's expressed intent is entitled to protection and the long-standing recognition under state law of standing for a donor such as Mr. Smithers. There is thus a need for co-existent standing for the Attorney General (D) and the donor; the Attorney General's (D) interest in enforcing gift terms is not necessarily congruent with that of the donor. Therefore, the distinct but related interests of the donor and the Attorney General (D) are best served by continuing to accord standing to donors to enforce the terms of their own gifts concurrent with the Attorney General's (D) standing to enforce such gifts on behalf of the beneficiaries thereof. Reversed on the standing issue.

DISSENT: (Friedman, J.) When a charitable gift is made, without any provision for a reversion of the gift to the donor or his heirs, the interest of the donor and his heirs is permanently excluded. Accordingly, in the absence of a right of reverter, the right to seek enforcement of the terms of a charitable gift is restricted to the Attorney General (D). This general rule is consistent with the common-law rule, and with the approach found in the Restatement (Second) of Trusts. Such a rule is necessary to avoid "vexatious litigation" by parties who do not have a tangible stake in the outcome of the litigation. It is uncontroverted that the estate was not the donor of the gift. Thus

Continued on next page.

even if pure donor standing were recognized, (as the majority concludes) this could not be a basis for granting standing to Mr. Smithers's estate. To the extent that Mr. Smithers may have had standing based upon his right to exercise discretionary control over the gift, i.e., via the right to appoint key staffing positions, that right was personal to him, abated upon his death, and did not devolve to his estate.

▶ ANALYSIS

The approach taken by the court in this case finds support in the Uniform Trust Code, which provides that "[t]he settlor of a charitable trust, among others, may maintain a proceeding to enforce the trust." Of course, this can be interpreted as granting only a personal right in the donor, not one that survives the donor's death.

■═■

Quicknotes

CHARITABLE TRUST A trust that is established for charitable purposes.

DONEE A person to whom a gift is made.

DONOR A person who gives real or personal property or value.

■═■

Quick Reference Rules of Law

Irwin Union Bank & Trust Co. v. Long

Bank (D) v. Ex-wife of trustee (P)

Ind. Ct. App., 160 Ind. App. 509, 312 N.E.2d 908 (1974).

NATURE OF CASE: Appeal from order allowing execution on a portion of a trust corpus.

FACT SUMMARY: The trial court ordered that four percent of the trust corpus of a trust held as trustee by Irwin Union Bank and Trust (D) was subject to execution in favor of his ex-wife (P).

🏛 RULE OF LAW
A power of appointment that is unexercised may not be reached by a creditor of the trustee.

FACTS: Philip Long was made the beneficiary of a trust by his mother and was granted a right of appointment of four percent of the trust corpus. Long was subsequently sued by his wife, Victoria Long (P), for divorce, and a judgment in the amount of $15,000 was entered in favor of Victoria (P). Victoria (P) then filed an action to execute upon 4 percent of the trust corpus in which she contended that, because Philip had a right of appointment with regard to this percentage of the trust, it could be reached by his creditors. The trial court, over the objections of the trustee, Irwin Union Bank and Trust Co. (D), that an unexercised right of appointment cannot be reached by creditors, issued the writ of execution. Union Bank (D) appealed.

ISSUE: May an unexercised right of appointment be reached by creditors of the trust's beneficiary?

HOLDING AND DECISION: (Lowdermilk, J.) No. An unexercised right of appointment may not be reached by creditors of the beneficiary. In the absence of a statute, the unexercised general right of appointment cannot be reached by creditors, as to hold to the contrary would allow creditors to force the exercise of said power upon the beneficiary. If the beneficiary chooses not to exercise the power, creditors cannot force him to do so. Where the power is a special power, the appointee derives no benefit therefrom, and, therefore, it cannot be reached by his creditors. As a result, the trial court erred in granting the writ of execution. Reversed and remanded.

▶ ANALYSIS

The principal case (*Gilman v. Bell*, 99 Ill. 144 [1881]) is cited and followed by the Restatement (Second) Property donative transfers. The basis upon which this case is determined is that a right of appointment is not property. Because the beneficiary does not derive any benefit from it, it cannot be attached by his creditors. The power of appointment is personal to the beneficiary and therefore cannot be alienated. As a result, it lacks a fundamental element of the concept of property and therefore cannot be attached.

Quicknotes

POWER OF APPOINTMENT Power, created by another person in connection with a gratuitous transfer (often in trust) residing in a person (as trustee or otherwise), to affect the disposition or distribution of the property.

TRUST CORPUS The aggregate body of assets placed into a trust.

Beals v. State Street Bank & Trust Co.

[Parties not identified.]

Mass. Sup. Jud. Ct., 367 Mass. 318, 326 N.E.2d 896 (1975).

NATURE OF CASE: Petition for instructions on distribution of a portion of a trust.

FACT SUMMARY: In an action seeking instructions on how a portion of a trust should be distributed, State Street Bank, as trustee, sought to determine if a power of appointment could be considered to have been exercised by a general residuary clause in a will.

⬛ RULE OF LAW
The fact that there has been a prior partial release of a general power does not obviate the application of that rule of construction which presumes that a general residuary clause in a will exercises a general power of appointment.

FACTS: As trustee, State Street Bank & Trust Co. sought instructions on how a portion of a trust should be distributed. The central question was whether Isabella had, by means of the general residuary clause in her will, exercised the power of appointment she had been given by the trust. While she had been given a general power of appointment, Isabella had subsequently partially released her general power of appointment. She released it "to the extent that such power empowers me to appoint to any one other than one or more of the . . . descendants [surviving me] of Arthur Hunnewell."

ISSUE: Does the fact that there has been a prior partial release of a general power obviate the application of that rule of construction which presumes that a general residuary clause in a will exercises a general power of appointment?

HOLDING AND DECISION: (Wilkins, J.) No. The fact that there has been a prior partial release of a general power of appointment does not obviate the application of that rule of construction which presumes that a general residuary clause in a will exercises a general power of appointment. That same rule has not been extended to special powers. In this case, the power initially given to Isabella was a power of general appointment that she reduced to what was effectively a special power by her own actions, which themselves amounted to treating the property as her own. Thus, the rule applicable to special powers is not on point, and it must be considered that Isabella exercised her power of appointment by means of the general residuary clause in her will.

▶ ANALYSIS

A majority of jurisdictions take the approach adopted in the following provision of the Uniform Probate Code (§ 2-610): "A general residuary clause in a will, or a will making general disposition of all of the testator's property, does not exercise a power of appointment held by the testator unless specific reference is made to the power or there is some other indication of intention to include the property subject to the power." Since this case was heard, Massachusetts has adopted the Uniform Probate Code.

◼▬◼

Quicknotes

POWER OF APPOINTMENT Power, created by another person in connection with a gratuitous transfer (often in trust) residing in a person (as trustee or otherwise), to affect the disposition or distribution of the property.

RESIDUARY CLAUSE (OF WILL) A clause contained in a will disposing of the assets remaining following distribution of the estate.

◼▬◼

Timmons v. Ingrahm

Decedent's adopted children (P) v. Decedent's wife (D)

Fla. Dist. Ct. App., 36 So. 3d 861 (2010).

NATURE OF CASE: Appeal from lower court decision allowing decedent's wife to modify a family trust to effectively disinherit the decedent's adopted children.

FACT SUMMARY: Frank Timmons Sr.'s will created two trusts, a Marital Trust for the benefit of his wife, Myrtle Ingrahm (D), and a Family Trust created for Timmons Sr.'s two adopted children (P) and the four children of Ingrahm (D) from a prior marriage. Ingrahm (D) petitioned the court to remove the adopted children (P) from the Family Trust.

🏛 RULE OF LAW

A technical legal term used in a testamentary instrument should be accorded its usual legal definition unless it is clear the testator employed the term in a different sense.

FACTS: Frank Timmons Sr.'s will created two trusts, a Marital Trust for the benefit of his wife, Myrtle Ingrahm (D), and a Family Trust created for Timmons Sr.'s two adopted children (P) and the four children of Ingrahm (D) from a prior marriage. Timmons Sr.'s adopted children, Frank Timmons Jr. (P) and Jacquelyn Forman (P), were his children from a prior marriage. Ingrahm (D) did not adopt them as her own children. Similarly, Ingrahm's (D) four children were from her prior marriage. Timmons Sr. did not adopt them when he married Ingrahm (D). Ingrahm (D) served as trustee of both trusts. The trusts provided that Ingrahm (D) was the sole income beneficiary of both trusts during her lifetime. Upon her death, the remaining proceeds of the Marital Trust would pour over into the Family Trust. The trust assets would be divided in equal shares among his children then living. The will specifically defined "children" as Timmons Sr.'s adopted children and the four children of Ingrahm (D). After Timmons Sr.'s death, Ingrahm (P) sought to use the limited power of appointment in the Family Trust to remove Frank Timmons Jr. (P) and Jacquelyn Forman (P) as beneficiaries. The relevant provision in the Family Trust stated that Ingrahm (D) had a limited power to deliver any or all of the trust principle to any of "my then living lineal descendants." Ingrahm (D) executed a brief document entitled Exercise of Limited Power of Appointment which expressly removed Frank Timmons Jr. (P) and Jacquelyn Forman (P) from the Family Trust. Frank Timmons Jr. (D) and Jacquelyn Forman (D) brought this action against Ingrahm (D) for breach of a fiduciary duty and for an accounting. Specifically, their argument was that because the limited power of appointment referred to Timmons Sr.'s "lineal" descendants, the power could only be exercised in favor of them and not her four children. The lower court granted summary judgment to Ingrahm (D). Frank Timmons Jr. (D) and Jacquelyn Forman (D) appealed.

ISSUE: Should a technical legal term used in a testamentary instrument be accorded its usual legal definition unless it is clear the testator employed the term in a different sense?

HOLDING AND DECISION: (Evander, J.) Yes. A technical legal term used in a testamentary instrument should be accorded its usual legal definition unless it is clear the testator employed the term in a different sense. Lineal descendant is defined to mean any person in any generational level down an individual's descending line. Adopted children are included in the definition. Ingrahm (D) argues that because Timmons Sr.'s will defines children to include her four children, the term "lineal" descendant in the Family Trust encompasses her four children. The argument is flawed. While Timmons Sr.'s will provided a different definition of the term "children" to specifically include his wife's four children, the Family Trust did not redefine the legal definition of lineal descendant. In addition, there is no language in the will providing Ingrahm (D) with the power to disinherit Timmons Sr.'s children. Accordingly, there is no evidence that Timmons Sr. intended to expand the definition of lineal descendant beyond its customary usage. Accordingly, Ingrahm (D) had no power to use her limited power of appointment for the benefit of her children. Reversed.

▎ANALYSIS

The guiding principle for the interpretation of testamentary instruments is to ascertain the intent of the testator. A second principle is that a court should not rewrite a will or a trust unless there is clear evidence there was a mistake. Here, to find in favor of Timmons Sr.'s adopted children, the court relied on the legal hook that Timmons Sr. did not redefine lineal descendants to include the children of his wife. Practically speaking, the court also relied on Timmons Sr.'s intent that his children should not be disinherited by his wife after his death.

■=■

Quicknotes

TESTAMENTARY INSTRUMENT An instrument that takes effect upon the death of the maker.

■=■

Brown v. Miller

Decedent's estate (D) v. Decedent's son (P)

Fla. Dist. Ct. App., 2 So. 3d 321 (2008).

NATURE OF CASE: Appeal from lower court decision invalidating decedent's transfer of seven million dollars from a trust created by his wife into a trust for his exclusive benefit.

FACT SUMMARY: Elinor Miller created several trusts during her lifetime including a trust called Trust A-2. Her trust document allowed her husband, Bill Miller, as primary beneficiary, to remove amounts of principal from Trust A-2 "from time to time" during his lifetime for his benefit. Before his death in 2004, Bill Miller transferred the balance of over seven million dollars from Trust A-2 to the newly created Bill Miller Trust.

🏛 RULE OF LAW
A trust provision granting a beneficiary the right to request payment from the trustee of additional amounts of trust principle from time to time grants the beneficiary unrestricted power to use some or all of the trust proceeds for his or her benefit.

FACTS: Elinor Miller created several trusts during her lifetime including a trust called Trust A-2. Her trust document allowed her husband, Bill Miller, as primary beneficiary, to remove amounts of principal from Trust A-2 "from time to time" during his lifetime for his benefit. Elinor's trust stated that upon Bill Miller's death, the remainder of the A-2 trust, not appointed or used by Bill Miller, would be held in trust for Thomas Miller III (P), Elinor and Bill's son. Before his death in 2004, Bill Miller transferred $420,000 from Trust A-2 to the newly created Bill Miller Trust. He then transferred the remaining balance of seven million dollars from Trust A-2 to the Bill Miller Trust. After Bill's death, Thomas Miller III (P) petitioned the court to invalidate Bill Miller's transfers from Trust A-2 on the grounds they were inconsistent with the trust language in Elinor's original trust document. The lower court agreed and granted him partial summary judgment. Bill Miller's estate (D) appealed.

ISSUE: Does a trust provision granting a beneficiary the right to request payment from the trustee of additional amounts of trust principle from time to time grant the beneficiary unrestricted power to use some or all of the trust proceeds for his or her benefit?

HOLDING AND DECISION: (Evander, J.) Yes. A trust provision granting a beneficiary the right to request payment from the trustee of additional amounts of trust principle from time to time grants the beneficiary unrestricted power to use some or all of the trust proceeds for his or her benefit. Thomas Miller III (P) argues that the language permitting Bill Miller to request additional trust proceeds "from time to time" does not mean he could remove the trust proceeds "in one fell swoop." First, the parties agree the elder Miller made two different transfers, as opposed to one. Second, many other courts have found that the language, "from time to time," does not serve as a limitation on the beneficiary's right to receive any or all of the trust proceeds. Elinor's trust manifested her clear intent that Bill Miller be able to receive any or all of the Trust A-2 proceeds at any time. In addition, Thomas Miller III (P) argues Elinor's trust only allowed her husband to receive trust proceeds, and not a separate trust entity created by her husband. The argument is flawed. The Bill Miller Trust was revocable by Bill Miller during his lifetime. He therefore effectively controlled the trust assets. Accordingly, a donation from Trust A-2 to the Bill Miller Trust was a donation to Bill Miller himself. Because Elinor's trust document clearly gave Bill Miller the authority to remove trust proceeds, the lower court erred in granting partial summary judgment to Thomas Miller III (P). Reversed.

▶ ANALYSIS

Most jurisdictions agree that the language "from time to time" provides beneficiaries with the authority to remove any and all trust proceeds in any manner. As with all trusts, the intent of the testator is paramount. Here, Elinor's trust also stated that Thomas Miller III (P) would only receive trust funds that were not expended or appointed by Bill Miller during his lifetime.

■=■

Quicknotes

PARTIAL SUMMARY JUDGMENT Judgment rendered by a court in response to a motion by one of the parties, claiming that the lack of a question of material fact in respect to one of the issues warrants disposition of that issue without going to the jury.

REVOCABLE TRUST A trust where trustor reserves the right to revoke the trust.

■=■

Loring v. Marshall

[Parties not identified.]

Mass. Sup. Jud. Ct., 396 Mass. 166, 484 N.E.2d 1315 (1985).

NATURE OF CASE: Declaratory judgment action seeking determination of proper testamentary beneficiary.

FACT SUMMARY: Morse, beneficiary with power of appointment under Hovey's will, declined to appoint his portion of the proceeds to all potential appointees.

> **RULE OF LAW**
> When a beneficiary with powers of appointment appoints his portion of will proceeds to less than the full class of potential appointees, the non-appointed class members will take the beneficiary's share if the appointees are deceased.

FACTS: Hovey's will made Morse a beneficiary thereof. The will, by its terms, gave Morse the power to appoint the proceeds of the testamentary trust created by the will to his wife and issue. Morse, in his will, left only a nominal legacy to his son and appointed his trust proceeds to his wife. Following the wife's death, both Morse's son and the trust's remaindermen made claim to the trust principal.

ISSUE: When a beneficiary with powers of appointment appoints his portion of will proceeds to less than the full class of potential appointees, will the nonappointed class members take the beneficiary's share if the appointees are deceased?

HOLDING AND DECISION: (Wilkins, J.) Yes. When a beneficiary with powers of appointment appoints his portion of will proceeds to less than the full class of potential appointees, the nonappointed class members will take the beneficiary's share if the appointees are deceased. If a will does not contain a provision creating a gift in default of appointment, it is presumed that a testator wished testamentary proceeds to remain within the class of beneficiaries and their potential appointees. If the beneficiaries and actual appointees no longer live, then the law presumes that the testator intended the proceeds to pass to the remaining potential appointees. Here, Morse's son is a living potential appointee, and, therefore, the proceeds are properly his. The cause is remitted to the trial court for a determination of executor and counsel fees.

ANALYSIS

The position taken by the court here appears to be the majority rule. It can be found in the Restatement, (Second) of Property, Donative Transfers § 24.2. Essentially, the rule implies a donative intent on the part of the testator to the entire class of named potential appointees. This presumption can be rebutted, if the will so provides.

Quicknotes

INCOME BENEFICIARY A person who is the recipient of income generated by certain property.

POWER OF APPOINTMENT Power, created by another person in connection with a gratuitous transfer (often in trust) residing in a person (as trustee or otherwise), to affect the disposition or distribution of the property.

REMAINDERMAN A person, who has an interest in property to commence upon the termination of a present possessory interest.

CHAPTER 13

Trusts: Construction and Future Interests

Quick Reference Rules of Law

In re Estate of Gilbert

Executor (P) v. Beneficiary (D)

N.Y. Surrog. Ct., 156 Misc. 2d 379, 592 N.Y.S.2d 224 (1992).

NATURE OF CASE: Motion to declare trust beneficiary's renunciation void.

FACT SUMMARY: When Lester (D), who was a beneficiary of discretionary trusts under his father's will, renounced his interest in the estate, the executor (P) moved to declare the renunciation premature and therefore invalid.

> ### 🏛 RULE OF LAW
> A beneficiary of a discretionary trust may renounce his interest in the disposition.

FACTS: Decedent was survived by a wife and four children. By will, he created two sets of discretionary trusts for the benefit of his children. One son, Lester (D), who had taken a vow of poverty, renounced his share of the estate. Lester (D) was a discretionary income beneficiary of two testamentary trusts. The executor (P) filed a motion to declare Lester's (D) renunciation void. The executor (P) argued that Lester (D) possessed no current property interest to renounce and that a renunciation could be made only after the trustees exercised their discretion to distribute income or principal.

ISSUE: May a beneficiary of a discretionary trust renounce his interest in the disposition?

HOLDING AND DECISION: (Roth, S.) Yes. A beneficiary of a discretionary trust may renounce his interest in the disposition. Renunciations are governed by statute. A statutory renunciation need not relate to specific property. Instead, the statute merely requires the disclaimant to renounce his or her interest in a trust. Therefore, a beneficiary of a discretionary trust may renounce his interest in the disposition. Assuming, arguendo, that in order to be effective the renounced interest must be in the nature of property, Lester's (D) renunciation would still be valid. Courts have recognized the right of a trust beneficiary to compel a distribution of funds where trustees abuse their discretion in refusing to make distributions. Therefore, a beneficiary who has the right to compel trustees to distribute trust property under certain circumstances arguably has a current interest that could be deemed property for the purpose of an effective renunciation. Motion denied.

▶ ANALYSIS

As important as the attempt to effectuate the intent of the testator is, an individual cannot be compelled to accept an inheritance against his will. Furthermore, once an individual has disclaimed or renounced his interest in an estate, most states by statute presume the individual to have predeceased the testator. This is preferable to attempting to litigate the testator's intent had he known the individual would renounce.

■=■

Quicknotes

CONTINGENT REMAINDER A remainder limited to a person not in being, not certain or ascertained, or so limited to a certain person that his right to the state depends upon some contingent event in the future.

DISCRETIONARY TRUST A trust pursuant to which the trustee is authorized to make decisions regarding the investment of the trust funds and the distribution of such funds to beneficiaries.

GUARDIAN AD LITEM Person designated by the court to represent an infant or ward in a particular legal proceeding.

RENUNCIATION The abandonment of a right or interest.

■=■

Tait v. Community First Trust Co.

Children of deceased trust beneficiaries (P) v. Trustee (P)

Ark Sup. Ct., ___ S.W. 3d ___, 2012 Ark 455.

NATURE OF CASE: Appeal from lower court decision finding that the interests of deceased trust beneficiaries lapsed when they predeceased the settlor of the trust.

FACT SUMMARY: William Fowler and Annie Fowler created the Fowler Family Trust. The trust stated that after their deaths, the remaining trust property would pass to various children and stepchildren. Three of the named beneficiaries died before William Fowler, having survived his wife, passed away in 2011. The descendants of the deceased beneficiaries claimed they had a vested right to a portion of the trust proceeds.

RULE OF LAW
The interest of a beneficiary of an inter vivos trust vests at the time the settlor creates the trust, and that interest does not lapse when the beneficiary predeceases the settlor.

FACTS: William Fowler and Annie Fowler created the Fowler Family Trust. The trust stated that after their deaths, the remaining trust property would pass to various children and stepchildren. Annie Fowler died in 1999. Three of the named beneficiaries then died before William Fowler passed away in 2011. The descendants of the deceased beneficiaries, Debbie Tait (D), Kerry Jones (D), Leanna Lackey (D) and Lesia Winters (D), claimed the interest in the trust survived the death of their parents and should pass on to them as descendants. The trustee of the trust, Community First Trust Co. (P), petitioned the court to construe the trust. It argued the interests of the deceased beneficiaries lapsed because they predeceased William Fowler. The lower court agreed with Community First Trust (P). Tait (D) and the children of the other deceased beneficiaries appealed.

ISSUE: Does the interest of a beneficiary of an inter vivos trust vest at the time the settlor creates the trust, and does that interest not lapse when the beneficiary predeceases the settlor?

HOLDING AND DECISION: (Goodson, J.) Yes. The interest of a beneficiary of an inter vivos trust vests at the time the settlor creates the trust, and that interest does not lapse when the beneficiary predeceases the settlor. A contrary line of cases has held that the interest of a trust beneficiary does not vest until the death of the settlor of the trust; accordingly, if a beneficiary predeceases the settlor of the trust, the beneficiary's interest lapses. The modern rule is that the interest vests at the time the trust is created, even though it is subject to the settlor's power to revoke or modify the trust document during the settlor's lifetime. Stated otherwise, a delay in enjoyment of the trust proceeds does not imply that the beneficiary must survive the settlor. Accordingly, the lower court's order finding that the beneficiaries' interest in the trust lapsed when they predeceased William Fowler was in error. Because the court finds that the interest does not lapse, the court does not need to consider Tait's (D) alternative argument that the state's anti-lapse statute applies to revocable trusts as it does to wills. Reversed.

⏵ ANALYSIS

The rule followed in most states is that a beneficiary need not survive the settlor for his or her interest to pass on to the descendants unless the trust document expressly states that the beneficiary must survive in order for the future interest to vest.

Quicknotes

INTER VIVOS TRUST Property that is held by one person for the benefit of another and which is created by an instrument that takes effect during the life of the grantor.

VESTED INTEREST A present right to property, although the right to the possession of such property may not be enjoyed until a future date.

Clobberie's Case

[Parties not identified.]

Ch., 86 Eng. Rep. 476, 2 Ventris 342 (1677).

NATURE OF CASE: Suit seeking an order construing a bequest.

FACT SUMMARY: Money was bequeathed to a woman at her age of twenty-one years or day of marriage, to be paid with interest. The woman died without marrying or attaining the age of twenty-one.

RULE OF LAW
If a bequest is "to be paid" at the happening of a certain event, the money passes to the estate of the beneficiary even if he dies before the contingency occurs.

FACTS: Money was bequeathed to a certain woman at her age of twenty-one years or day of marriage, to be paid to her with interest. She died prior to marrying or attaining the age of twenty-one. It was argued that the bequest, instead of lapsing, should pass to the executor of her estate.

ISSUE: If a bequest is "to be paid" at the occurrence of a stated event, but the beneficiary dies before the contingency occurs, does the bequest pass to his estate?

HOLDING AND DECISION: (Lord Finch, Ch.) Yes. If a bequest is "to be paid" at the happening of a certain event, the money passes to the estate of the beneficiary even if he dies before the contingency occurs. In this case, money was bequeathed to the woman at her age of twenty-one years or her wedding day and was to be paid with interest. Thus, upon her death, the money passed to the executor of her estate. If the money had merely been bequeathed at the occurrence of a stated event, the death of the beneficiary prior to its occurrence would have resulted in the loss of the money. But, where the money is "to be paid" at the occurrence of the designated event, it shall pass to the beneficiary's executors despite his failure to survive until the event takes place. Therefore, the bequest to the woman in this case passes to her executor.

ANALYSIS

The rule in *Clobberie's Case* has long perplexed the student of future interests in property. The rule causes significantly different consequences to ensue, from the minutest differences, in language. The rule in *Clobberie's Case* is still applied by some courts, although it has been repeatedly modified and updated. Perhaps no case of comparable succinctness has enjoyed notoriety equivalent to that earned by *Clobberie's Case*.

Quicknotes

BEQUEST A transfer of property that is accomplished by means of a testamentary instrument.

Dewire v. Haveles

[Parties not identified.]

Mass. Sup. Jud. Ct., 404 Mass. 274, 534 N.E.2d 782 (1989).

NATURE OF CASE: Action to declare rights in a residuary trust.

FACT SUMMARY: Haveles contended the testator failed to manifest a contrary intent in his will that a right of survivorship should apply to a gift to the grandchildren; therefore, Dewire was not entitled to share in her father's legacy.

🏛 RULE OF LAW
Members of a class pursuant to a class gift are joint tenants with rights of survivorship unless a contrary intent is expressed in the will.

FACTS: Thomas Dewire died, leaving a widow, a son named Thomas Jr., and three grandchildren. He placed his estate in a residuary trust, the income payable to his widow for life and on her death to his son, his widow, and Thomas Jr.'s children. After the testator's death, Thomas Jr. had three more children by a second wife and then died. He was survived by six children, including Thomas III, who served as trustee until his death. Thomas III left one child, Jennifer. Upon Thomas III's death, an action was brought to determine the rights of the remaining grandchildren in the estate. Haveles contended that Jennifer, the issue of Thomas III, could not take a share of the grandchildren's gift, as a class gift had been created for the grandchildren with a right of survivorship. Jennifer contended that a contrary intent was manifested in the original will to supersede the joint tenancy, and, therefore, she was entitled to her father's share.

ISSUE: Does a class gift create a joint tenancy with right of survivorship in the absence of contrary intent expressed in the will?

HOLDING AND DECISION: (Wilkins, J.) Yes. A class gift creates a joint tenancy with right of survivorship unless a contrary intent is expressed in the will. Because the testator must have intended for the income of the trust to be paid out during the term of its existence, the only logical recipients of that income would be the issue, by right of representation, of deceased grandchildren, the same group of people who would take the trust assets upon termination of the trust. As a result, a contrary intent to the right of survivorship was expressed in the will, and, therefore, Jennifer was entitled to her father's share of the estate.

▌ ANALYSIS

The court as a side issue indicated that this will violated the rule against perpetuities. This most confusing and ancient rule has been the source of many will invalidations.

However, the will in this case survived under the general policy that upholds the balance of a will when one part is invalid. Had a joint tenancy been recognized in this case, Thomas III's share would have passed to his remaining cousins rather than passing on to his daughter.

■■■

Quicknotes

CLASS GIFT A gift to a group of unspecified persons whose number, identity, and share of the gift will be determined sometime in the future.

JOINT TENANCY An interest in property whereby a single interest is owned by two or more persons and created by a single instrument; joint tenants possess equal interests in the use of the entire property, and the last survivor is entitled to absolute ownership.

RIGHT OF SURVIVORSHIP Between two or more persons, such as in a joint tenancy relationship, the right to the property of a deceased passes to the survivor.

RULE AGAINST PERPETUITIES The doctrine that a future interest that is incapable of vesting within twenty-one years of lives in being at the time it is created is immediately void.

■■■

Estate of Woodworth

[Parties not identified.]

Cal. Ct. App., 22 Cal. Rptr. 2d 676 (1993).

NATURE OF CASE: Appeal from an order rejecting a claim to the remainder of a testamentary trust.

FACT SUMMARY: Because the trustee was uncertain as to whether the heirs at law of the ancestor named to take the remainder of the Woodworth trust should be determined at the date of the named ancestor's death or at the date of the life tenant's death, the trustee petitioned the court for that determination.

🏛 RULE OF LAW
The identity of heirs entitled to trust assets must be determined at the date of death of the named ancestor who predeceased the life tenant, not at the date of death of the life tenant.

FACTS: Woodworth's will distributed a portion of his estate outright to his wife, Mamie Barlow Woodworth, with the balance to be administered as a testamentary trust with Mamie as the life tenant. Upon her death, any remainder of the trust estate was to go to Woodworth's sister, Elizabeth Plass, or to her heirs-at-law, if she no longer survived. Elizabeth died before Mamie but was survived by her husband, Ray Plass, a niece, and a nephew. Ray also died before Mamie, leaving the residue of his estate to the Regents of the University of California. At Mamie's death, the trustee petitioned the probate court as to the date for determining who would receive the distribution of the trust estate. Concluding that the heirs must be determined as of the date of death of the life tenant, Mamie, the court ordered the assets distributed to Elizabeth's niece and nephew. The regents appealed.

ISSUE: Must the identity of heirs entitled to trust assets be determined at the date of death of the named ancestor who predeceased the life tenant, not at the date of death of the life tenant?

HOLDING AND DECISION: (DiBiaso, J.) Yes. The identity of heirs entitled to trust assets must be determined at the date of death of the named ancestor who predeceased the life tenant, not at the date of death of the life tenant. Nothing in the language of the other provisions of the decree of distribution revealed Woodworth's intent or desire. The general rule favoring early vesting was well-established long before Woodworth died. Nothing in the decree forecloses the possibility that Woodworth took into account the fact that Raymond Plass might succeed to a portion of the trust remainder. Moreover, the fact that the university, an entity, is not a relative of Elizabeth Plass or one of her heirs at law is not material. In addition, the language of the decree does not contain any expression of

futurity in the description of the ancestor's heirs. Therefore, the regents have a claim to the assets of the trust. Reversed.

▶ ANALYSIS

In the absence of any firm indication of testamentary intent, the rules of construction must be implemented in order to ensure uniformity and predictability in the law. This is preferable to carrying out a court's ad hoc sense of what is, with perfect hindsight, acceptable in a particular set of circumstances. Here, at the time of Elizabeth Plass's death, her "heir-at-law" was her husband, Ray.

■■■

Quicknotes

DEFEASIBLE FEE SIMPLE ESTATE A fee-simple interest in land that is subject to being terminated upon the happening of a future event.

LIFE ESTATE An interest in land, measured by the life of the tenant or a third party.

LIFE TENANT An individual whose estate in real property is measured either by his own life or by that of another.

REMAINDER An interest in land that remains after the termination of the immediately preceding estate.

TESTAMENTARY TRUST A trust created by will and effective only after the grantor's death, since the assets that comprise the corpus of the trust are assumed to vest at that time.

■■■

Wealth Transfer Taxation

Quick Reference Rules of Law

Estate of Holtz v. Commissioner

Trustee (P) v. Commissioner (D)

U.S.T.C., 38 T.C. 37 (1962).

NATURE OF CASE: Appeal from imposition of gift tax.

FACT SUMMARY: Holtz's estate (P) disputed a determination by the Commissioner (D) that taxable gifts resulted from transfers to a trust that he established.

RULE OF LAW
If a trustee is free to exercise his unfettered discretion and there is nothing to impel or compel him to invade the corpus, the settlor retains a mere expectancy that does not make the gift of corpus incomplete, thus indicating that the settlor has abandoned dominion and control over the property.

FACTS: Holtz transferred funds to a trust by deed of trust in 1953, wherein Holtz was the settlor and the Land Title Bank and Trust Company was the trustee (P). The trust instrument provided that during the lifetime of the settlor the income should be paid to him and as much principal as the trustee (P) "may from time to time think is desirable for the welfare, comfort and support of the Settlor, or for his hospitalization or other emergency needs." At the settlor's death, the income of the trust would go to his wife if she survived him, as well as any of the principal that she might need in accordance with the trustee's (P) discretion. The trust was to terminate at the death of the survivor of the settlor and his wife, and the remaining principal was payable to the survivor's estate. Holtz transferred property worth $384,117 to the trust in 1953, and in 1955, he transferred an additional $50,000 in cash. The Commissioner (D) subsequently determined that as a result of these transfers, Holtz made taxable gifts that were subject to the appropriate gift tax. Holtz's estate (P) contested and claimed that the transfers were not completed gifts and not subject to a gift tax.

ISSUE: If a trustee is free to exercise his unfettered discretion and there is nothing to impel or compel him to invade the corpus, does the settlor retain a mere expectancy that does not make the gift of corpus incomplete?

HOLDING AND DECISION: (Drennan, J.) Yes. The rule generally is that if the trustee is free to exercise his unfettered discretion and there is nothing to impel or compel him to invade the corpus, the settlor retains a mere expectancy which establishes a completed gift to the corpus. However, where, as here, the trustee's (P) discretion is governed by some external standard that a court may apply in compelling compliance with the conditions of the trust agreement and the trustee's (P) power to invade is unlimited, then the gift of corpus in unlimited. Since the

trustee (P) had the unfettered power to use all of the corpus for the benefit of the settlor, it was entirely possible that the entire corpus might be distributed to the settlor during his lifetime with the result that no one other than the settlor would receive any portion thereof. As long as that possibility was present pursuant to the terms of the trust agreement, then the settlor had not abandoned sufficient control and dominion over the property to make the gift complete. Reversed.

ANALYSIS

The donor has the primary liability for paying the gift tax, and if the donor does not pay, then the donee is liable for the unpaid gift tax. The executor or administrator of a decedent's estate has personal liability for payment of the estate tax but is limited only for reimbursement out of the decedent's estate. Persons in possession of the decedent's property are liable for the tax due if there is no administration of the estate.

■■■

Quicknotes

CORPUS The principal property comprising a trust, not including interest or income.

GIFT TAX A tax levied on the transfer of property that is made as a gift.

SETTLOR The grantor or donor of property that is to be held in trust for the benefit of another.

■■■

Estate of Cristofani v. Commissioner

Trustee (P) v. Tax commissioner (D)

U.S.T.C., 97 T.C. 74 (1991).

NATURE OF CASE: Appeal from a disallowance of an annual gift exclusion.

FACT SUMMARY: After establishing an irrevocable trust for her two children and five grandchildren, Maria Cristofani claimed two $70,000 annual transfers to the trust qualified as annual exclusions under federal tax law.

RULE OF LAW
When a trust instrument gives a beneficiary the legal power to demand immediate possession of corpus, that power constitutes a present interest in property sufficient to qualify for gift tax exclusion.

FACTS: Decedent Maria Cristofani established an irrevocable trust for her two children and five grandchildren. The parents were named as trustees (P) for the children's trust. All seven beneficiaries of the trust had the right to withdraw an annual amount not to exceed the amount specified for the federal gift tax exclusion, that is, up to $10,000. There was no agreement or understanding between Maria, the trustees (P), and the beneficiaries that the grandchildren would not immediately exercise their withdrawal rights. Thus, Maria did not report two $70,000 transfers to the trust, claiming them as seven annual exclusions for each of the applicable periods. The Commissioner (D) allowed the annual exclusions with respect to Maria's two children, but disallowed the exclusions for the five grandchildren after determining that they were not transfers of present interests in property. Maria's estate (P) appealed.

ISSUE: When a trust instrument gives a beneficiary the legal power to demand immediate possession of corpus, does that power constitute a present interest in property?

HOLDING AND DECISION: (Ruwe, J.) Yes. When a trust instrument gives a beneficiary the legal power to demand immediate possession of corpus, that power constitutes a present interest in property sufficient to qualify for gift tax exclusion. The likelihood that a beneficiary will actually receive present enjoyment of the property is not the test for determining whether a present interest has been received. In this case, each grandchild possessed the legal right to withdraw trust corpus, and the trustees would be unable to legally resist a grandchild's withdrawal demand. Moreover, based upon the provisions of the children's trust, Cristofani intended to benefit her grandchildren, contrary to the contention of the Commissioner (D). Although the grandchildren never exercised their respective withdrawal rights, this does not vitiate the fact that they had the legal right to do so. Accordingly, the exclusions are allowed. Reversed.

▶ ANALYSIS

The court here relied on *Crummey v. Commissioner*, 397 F.2d 82 (9th Cir. 1968), which originally granted the gift tax shelter to beneficiaries with withdrawal powers. This case is important because it extends the annual exclusion to so-called *Crummey* power holders who are only contingent beneficiaries, like Maria's grandchildren. It is a victory for taxpayers because it supports an increased number of $10,000 tax-free gifts available to trustors.

Quicknotes

CORPUS The principal property comprising a trust, not including interest or income.

DONEE A person to whom a gift is made.

DURABLE POWER OF ATTORNEY A written document pursuant to which one party confers the authority to act as an agent on his behalf to another party and which is to become effective if the grantor should later become incapacitated.

FUTURE INTEREST An interest in property, the right to possession or enjoyment of which is to take place at some time in the future.

GIFT TAX A tax levied on the transfer of property that is made as a gift.

REMAINDER INTEREST An interest in land that remains after the termination of the immediately preceding estate.

Estate of Maxwell v. Commissioner

Estate (P) v. Tax commissioner (D)

3 F.3d 591 (2d Cir. 1993).

NATURE OF CASE: Appeal from assessment of estate tax deficiency.

FACT SUMMARY: When decedent transferred property to her son and his wife at the end of her life with the intention of remaining in possession so that he would not have to pay off a mortgage note executed in her favor, the Commissioner of the IRS (D) assessed a deficiency against her estate (P) when it reported only the unpaid balance on the note rather than the fair market value of the residence, which was twice as much.

> ## 🏛 RULE OF LAW
> The value of property disposed of during a decedent's lifetime shall be included in the gross estate where she has retained possession or enjoyment of it until her death and the transfer was not a bona fide sale for adequate and full consideration.

FACTS: Decedent, an eighty-two-year-old suffering from cancer, conveyed her personal residence of twenty-seven years to her son and only heir and his wife, the Maxwells, for $270,000. Decedent forgave $20,000 of the purchase price at the time of the transfer, and a note for $250,000 was executed in her favor. Simultaneously, the home was leased back to her for five years. Two days later, decedent executed a will with a provision forgiving the balance owing on the note at her death. After the transfer, she continued to live alone in the house until her death two years later. During that time, the rent payments by decedent functionally canceled out interest payments on the note paid by the Maxwells, and she forgave $20,000 on the note each year. Less than two months after her death, the house was sold for $550,000. On the decedent's estate tax return, the estate (P) reported only the $210,000 remaining on the debt. The IRS Commissioner (D) found that the transaction was a transfer with retained life estate and assessed an estate tax deficiency to adjust for the difference between the reported $210,000 and the fair market value of $550,000. The estate (P) appealed to the Tax Court. At oral argument, the estate (P) admitted that there was an intention among the parties the mortgage note not be paid. The Tax Court affirmed the Commissioner's (D) ruling, and the estate (P) appealed.

ISSUE: Shall the value of property disposed of during a decedent's lifetime be included in the gross estate where she has retained possession or enjoyment of the property until her death and the transfer was not a bona fide sale for adequate and full consideration?

HOLDING AND DECISION: (Lasker, J.) Yes. The value of property disposed of during a decedent's lifetime shall be included in the gross estate where she has retained possession or enjoyment of it until her death, unless the transfer was a bona fide sale for adequate and full consideration. Possession or enjoyment of property is retained by the transferor when there is an express or implied understanding to that effect among the parties at the time of the transfer. The burden is on the decedent's estate to disprove the existence of any adverse implied agreement or understanding. The estate (P) has not met its burden in this case. Similarly, intent is a relevant inquiry in determining whether a transaction is bona fide. Where, as here, there is an implied agreement between the parties that the grantee would never be called upon to make any payments to the grantor, the note given by the grantee has no value at all. Therefore, the conveyance to the Maxwells was not a bona fide sale for an adequate and full consideration. Affirmed.

▶ ANALYSIS

The case above involved the application of § 2036(a) of the Internal Revenue Code. Section 2036(a) provides: "The value of the gross estate shall include the value of all property to the extent of any interest therein of which the decedent has at any time made a transfer (except in case of a bona fide sale for an adequate and full consideration in money or money's worth), by trust or otherwise, under which he has retained for his life or for any period which does not in fact end before his death—(1) The possession or enjoyment of, or the right to the income from, the property, or (2) The right, either alone or in conjunction with any person, to designate the persons who shall possess or enjoy the property or the income therefrom."

Quicknotes

BONA FIDE In good faith.

DECEDENT A person who is deceased.

CONSIDERATION Value given by one party in exchange for performance or a promise to perform by another party.

LIFE ESTATE An interest in land measured by the life of the tenant or a third party.

Old Colony Trust Co. v. United States

Estate administrator (D) v. Federal government (P)

423 F.2d 601 (1st Cir. 1970).

NATURE OF CASE: Appeal from finding of estate tax deficiency.

FACT SUMMARY: Old Colony (D), the administrator of the estate of the unnamed decedent, contended that the estate should not include a trust established by the settlor which gave the trustee power to stop payments to the settlor's son at any time.

RULE OF LAW

The corpus of a trust included in an estate will not be fixed solely because the settlor named himself as trustee.

FACTS: The decedent, unnamed in the case, established an inter vivos trust prior to his death in which the initial life beneficiary of the trust was the settlor's adult son. Eighty percent of the income was normally to be payable to him and the balance added to the principal. Article 4 of the trust agreement permitted the trustees to increase the percentage of income payable to the son beyond the 80 percent "in their absolute discretion . . . when in their opinion such increase is needed in case of sickness, or desirable in view of changed circumstances." In addition, under Article 4 the trustees were given the discretion to cease paying income to the son and add it all to principal "during such period as the Trustees may decide that the stoppage of such payments is for his best interests." Article 7 gave the trustees broad administrative and management powers over the trust corpus. After the death of the settlor, who also had acted as the sole trustee of the trust, the Government (P) sought to include the corpus of the trust in the estate of the settlor, contending that the settlor had possessed the ownership of the corpus because he could designate the persons who could enjoy its income and that until the date of his death he had an absolute right to alter, amend, or terminate the trust. After the trial court ruled for the Government (P), the executor of the estate (D) appealed.

ISSUE: Will the corpus of a trust included in an estate not be taxed solely because the settlor named himself as trustee?

HOLDING AND DECISION: (Aldrich, J.) Yes. A settlor will not find the corpus of the trust included in his estate merely because he named himself a trustee. He must have reserved a power to himself that is inconsistent with the full termination of ownership. Trustee powers given for the administration or management of the trust must be equitably exercised for the benefit of the trust as a whole. It is difficult to see how a power can be subject to control by the probate court and exercisable only in what the trustee fairly concludes is in the interests of the trust and its beneficiaries as a whole and at the same time is an ownership power. However, under Article 4 of the trust, the trustees could increase the life tenant's income "in case of sickness, or . . . in view of changed circumstances." Alternatively, they could reduce it "for his best interests." Additional payments to a beneficiary, whenever in his best interests is a broad standard, showing the plain indicia of ownership. With the present settlor-trustee free to determine the standard himself, a finding of ownership was warranted. To put it another way, the cost of holding onto the strings may prove to be a rope burn. Affirmed.

ANALYSIS

In this case, the court held that the mere grant of administrative control to the trustees did not equate to indicia of ownership. In its decision, the court held that no aggregation of purely administrative powers can meet the government's amorphous test of "sufficient dominion and control" so as to be equated with ownership. The court also noted that trustee powers were not to be construed more broadly for tax purposes than a probate court would construe them for administrative purposes.

■■■■

Quicknotes

INTER VIVOS TRUST Property that is held by one person for the benefit of another and which is created by an instrument that takes effect during the life of the grantor.

TRUST CORPUS The aggregate body of assets placed into a trust.

■■■■

Estate of Vissering v. Commissioner

Trustees (P) v. Tax commissioner (D)

990 F.2d 578 (10th Cir. 1993).

NATURE OF CASE: Appeal from a judgment including the assets of a trust in the gross estate of a cotrustee.

FACT SUMMARY: Because the tax court determined that Vissering, at the time of his death, held a general power of appointment over the assets of a trust of which he was a cotrustee, the court included the assets of the trust in Vissering's gross estate (P) for federal estate tax purposes.

🏛 RULE OF LAW
A power vested in a trustee to invade the principal of the trust for his own benefit is sufficient to find the decedent trustee to have a general power of appointment, unless the power is limited by an ascertainable standard related to health, education, support, or maintenance.

FACTS: Vissering and a bank were cotrustees (P) of a trust created by his mother. The trust agreement authorized the trustees (P) to pay over, use, or expend, for the direct or indirect benefit of any of the beneficiaries, whatever amount or amounts of the principal of the trust as may, in the discretion of the trustees (P), be required for the continued comfort, support, maintenance, or education of said beneficiary. The tax court found that Vissering held a general power of appointment at the time of his death, and therefore the assets of the trust were to be included in his gross estate for federal estate tax purposes. The estate (P) appealed.

ISSUE: Is a power vested in a trustee to invade the principal of the trust for his own benefit sufficient to find the decedent trustee to have a general power of appointment, unless the power is limited by an ascertainable standard related to health, education, support, or maintenance?

HOLDING AND DECISION: (Logan, C.J.) Yes. A power vested in a trustee to invade the principal of the trust for his own benefit is sufficient to find the decedent trustee to have a general power of appointment, unless the power is limited by an ascertainable standard related to health, education, support, or maintenance. A trust document permitting invasion of principal for comfort, without further qualifying language, creates a general power of appointment. However, there is modifying language in the trust at issue. "Comfort," in context, does not permit an unlimited power of invasion. Moreover, invasion of the corpus is permitted only to the extent "required," not to the extent "determined" or "desired." Thus, the tax court

erred in finding that Vissering had a general power of appointment includable in his estate (P). Reversed and remanded.

▶ ANALYSIS

The court of appeals undertook a de novo review. Since the trust was created in Florida, specifying that Florida law controlled, the court of appeals looked to what it believed the Florida courts would hold. The estate (P) argued unsuccessfully that Vissering (P) was not a trustee at the time of death since he had been judged incapacitated by a New Mexico court.

■=■

Quicknotes

CONTINGENT BENEFICIARY A third party who is the recipient of the benefit of a transaction undertaken by another, the receipt of which is based on the uncertain happening of another event.

POWER OF APPOINTMENT Power, created by another person in connection with a gratuitous transfer (often in trust) residing in a person (as trustee or otherwise), to affect the disposition or distribution of the property.

REMAINDER BENEFICIARY A person who is to receive property that is held in trust after the termination of a preceding income interest.

■=■

Estate of Rapp v. Commissioner

Estate (P) v. Internal Revenue Service (D)

140 F.3d 1211 (9th Cir.1998).

NATURE OF CASE: Appeal from tax court ruling.

FACT SUMMARY: A California probate court reformed Rapp's will so that part of the estate (P) was tax exempt, but the Internal Revenue Service (IRS) (D) applied its own analysis.

> ## 🏛 RULE OF LAW
> Federal tax courts are not bound by state probate rulings with regard to estate tax determinations.

FACTS: Bert Rapp died in 1988, survived by a wife and two children. His will left half his property to a trust, but the will did not create a qualified terminable interest property (QTIP) trust, which would have allowed Mrs. Rapp to deduct the trust property from the estate (P) for purposes of taxes. However, a California probate court reformed the will to create a QTIP trust. When the estate (P) filed a federal tax statement and claimed a QTIP trust deduction, the IRS sent a notice of deficiency. In the subsequent federal tax court proceeding, the court reviewed California law and determined that the reformation of the will was improper because there was no evidence to suggest that Rapp had really intended to create a QTIP trust. The tax court ruled for the IRS (D) and the estate (P) appealed.

ISSUE: Are federal tax courts bound by state probate rulings with regard to estate tax determinations?

HOLDING AND DECISION: (Fletcher, J.) No. Federal tax courts are not bound by state probate rulings with regard to estate tax determinations. Generally, the value of property passed directly from a testator to a surviving spouse is deducted before computing federal estate taxes. However, if the interest passing consists only of a life estate or terminable interest, the value is not deducted. One exception to this is if the terminable interest qualifies as a QTIP, in which case the surviving spouse can elect the marital deduction. In California, probate courts have the authority to modify or reform trusts under the appropriate circumstances. However, federal tax courts are not bound by res judicata and collateral estoppel from making their own determination on the validity of related deductions unless the state's highest court has definitively ruled on the case. In the present case, Rapp's estate (P) initiated the request to reform the will and trust directly for the purposes of affecting federal estate tax liability. The tax court was not bound by the state probate decision and properly applied the law itself, finding that the probate court holding was contrary to the state law. Accordingly, while the estate (P) is still entitled to the reformation of the trust, it is not entitled to receive the federal tax benefits of a QTIP trust. Affirmed.

▶ ANALYSIS

The estate (P) claimed that not allowing the QTIP deduction would create a split among circuit courts with regard to the measuring date of a QTIP. But the court insisted that it was dealing with only the narrow issue of whether the tax court was bound by the state probate decision. Since it wasn't, and ruled that there never was a QTIP trust, the measuring date issue never arose here.

Quicknotes

PROBATE The administration of a decedent's estate.

REFORMATION A correction of a written instrument ordered by a court to cause it to reflect the true intentions of the parties.

Common Latin Words and Phrases Encountered in the Law

A FORTIORI: Because one fact exists or has been proven, therefore a second fact that is related to the first fact must also exist.

A PRIORI: From the cause to the effect. A term of logic used to denote that when one generally accepted truth is shown to be a cause, another particular effect must necessarily follow.

AB INITIO: From the beginning; a condition which has existed throughout, as in a marriage which was void ab initio.

ACTUS REUS: The wrongful act; in criminal law, such action sufficient to trigger criminal liability.

AD VALOREM: According to value; an ad valorem tax is imposed upon an item located within the taxing jurisdiction calculated by the value of such item.

AMICUS CURIAE: Friend of the court. Its most common usage takes the form of an amicus curiae brief, filed by a person who is not a party to an action but is nonetheless allowed to offer an argument supporting his legal interests.

ARGUENDO: In arguing. A statement, possibly hypothetical, made for the purpose of argument, is one made arguendo.

BILL QUIA TIMET: A bill to quiet title (establish ownership) to real property.

BONA FIDE: True, honest, or genuine. May refer to a person's legal position based on good faith or lacking notice of fraud (such as a bona fide purchaser for value) or to the authenticity of a particular document (such as a bona fide last will and testament).

CAUSA MORTIS: With approaching death in mind. A gift causa mortis is a gift given by a party who feels certain that death is imminent.

CAVEAT EMPTOR: Let the buyer beware. This maxim is reflected in the rule of law that a buyer purchases at his own risk because it is his responsibility to examine, judge, test, and otherwise inspect what he is buying.

CERTIORARI: A writ of review. Petitions for review of a case by the United States Supreme Court are most often done by means of a writ of certiorari.

CONTRA: On the other hand. Opposite. Contrary to.

CORAM NOBIS: Before us; writs of error directed to the court that originally rendered the judgment.

CORAM VOBIS: Before you; writs of error directed by an appellate court to a lower court to correct a factual error.

CORPUS DELICTI: The body of the crime; the requisite elements of a crime amounting to objective proof that a crime has been committed.

CUM TESTAMENTO ANNEXO, ADMINISTRATOR (ADMINISTRATOR C.T.A.): With will annexed; an administrator c.t.a. settles an estate pursuant to a will in which he is not appointed.

DE BONIS NON, ADMINISTRATOR (ADMINISTRATOR D.B.N.): Of goods not administered; an administrator d.b.n. settles a partially settled estate.

DE FACTO: In fact; in reality; actually. Existing in fact but not officially approved or engendered.

DE JURE: By right; lawful. Describes a condition that is legitimate "as a matter of law," in contrast to the term "de facto," which connotes something existing in fact but not legally sanctioned or authorized. For example, de facto segregation refers to segregation brought about by housing patterns, etc., whereas de jure segregation refers to segregation created by law.

DE MINIMIS: Of minimal importance; insignificant; a trifle; not worth bothering about.

DE NOVO: Anew; a second time; afresh. A trial de novo is a new trial held at the appellate level as if the case originated there and the trial at a lower level had not taken place.

DICTA: Generally used as an abbreviated form of obiter dicta, a term describing those portions of a judicial opinion incidental or not necessary to resolution of the specific question before the court. Such nonessential statements and remarks are not considered to be binding precedent.

DUCES TECUM: Refers to a particular type of writ or subpoena requesting a party or organization to produce certain documents in their possession.

EN BANC: Full bench. Where a court sits with all justices present rather than the usual quorum.

EX PARTE: For one side or one party only. An ex parte proceeding is one undertaken for the benefit of only one party, without notice to, or an appearance by, an adverse party.

EX POST FACTO: After the fact. An ex post facto law is a law that retroactively changes the consequences of a prior act.

EX REL.: Abbreviated form of the term "ex relatione," meaning upon relation or information. When the state brings an action in which it has no interest against an individual at the instigation of one who has a private interest in the matter.

FORUM NON CONVENIENS: Inconvenient forum. Although a court may have jurisdiction over the case, the action should be tried in a more conveniently located court, one to which parties and witnesses may more easily travel, for example.

GUARDIAN AD LITEM: A guardian of an infant as to litigation, appointed to represent the infant and pursue his/her rights.

HABEAS CORPUS: You have the body. The modern writ of habeas corpus is a writ directing that a person (body) being detained (such as a prisoner) be brought before the court so that the legality of his detention can be judicially ascertained.

IN CAMERA: In private, in chambers. When a hearing is held before a judge in his chambers or when all spectators are excluded from the courtroom.

IN FORMA PAUPERIS: In the manner of a pauper. A party who proceeds in forma pauperis because of his poverty is one who is allowed to bring suit without liability for costs.

INFRA: Below, under. A word referring the reader to a later part of a book. (The opposite of supra.)

IN LOCO PARENTIS: In the place of a parent.

IN PARI DELICTO: Equally wrong; a court of equity will not grant requested relief to an applicant who is in pari delicto, or as much at fault in the transactions giving rise to the controversy as is the opponent of the applicant.

IN PARI MATERIA: On like subject matter or upon the same matter. Statutes relating to the same person or things are said to be in pari materia. It is a general rule of statutory construction that such statutes should be construed together, i.e., looked at as if they together constituted one law.

IN PERSONAM: Against the person. Jurisdiction over the person of an individual.

IN RE: In the matter of. Used to designate a proceeding involving an estate or other property.

IN REM: A term that signifies an action against the res, or thing. An action in rem is basically one that is taken directly against property, as distinguished from an action in personam, i.e., against the person.

INTER ALIA: Among other things. Used to show that the whole of a statement, pleading, list, statute, etc., has not been set forth in its entirety.

INTER PARTES: Between the parties. May refer to contracts, conveyances or other transactions having legal significance.

INTER VIVOS: Between the living. An inter vivos gift is a gift made by a living grantor, as distinguished from bequests contained in a will, which pass upon the death of the testator.

IPSO FACTO: By the mere fact itself.

JUS: Law or the entire body of law.

LEX LOCI: The law of the place; the notion that the rights of parties to a legal proceeding are governed by the law of the place where those rights arose.

MALUM IN SE: Evil or wrong in and of itself; inherently wrong. This term describes an act that is wrong by its very nature, as opposed to one which would not be wrong but for the fact that there is a specific legal prohibition against it (malum prohibitum).

MALUM PROHIBITUM: Wrong because prohibited, but not inherently evil. Used to describe something that is wrong because it is expressly forbidden by law but that is not in and of itself evil, e.g., speeding.

MANDAMUS: We command. A writ directing an official to take a certain action.

MENS REA: A guilty mind; a criminal intent. A term used to signify the mental state that accompanies a crime or other prohibited act. Some crimes require only a general mens rea (general intent to do the prohibited act), but others, like assault with intent to murder, require the existence of a specific mens rea.

MODUS OPERANDI: Method of operating; generally refers to the manner or style of a criminal in committing crimes, admissible in appropriate cases as evidence of the identity of a defendant.

NEXUS: A connection to.

NISI PRIUS: A court of first impression. A nisi prius court is one where issues of fact are tried before a judge or jury.

N.O.V. (NON OBSTANTE VEREDICTO): Notwithstanding the verdict. A judgment n.o.v. is a judgment given in favor of one party despite the fact that a verdict was returned in favor of the other party, the justification being that the verdict either had no reasonable support in fact or was contrary to law.

NUNC PRO TUNC: Now for then. This phrase refers to actions that may be taken and will then have full retroactive effect.

PENDENTE LITE: Pending the suit; pending litigation under way.

PER CAPITA: By head; beneficiaries of an estate, if they take in equal shares, take per capita.

PER CURIAM: By the court; signifies an opinion ostensibly written "by the whole court" and with no identified author.

PER SE: By itself, in itself; inherently.

PER STIRPES: By representation. Used primarily in the law of wills to describe the method of distribution where a person, generally because of death, is unable to take that which is left to him by the will of another, and therefore his heirs divide such property between them rather than take under the will individually.

PRIMA FACIE: On its face, at first sight. A prima facie case is one that is sufficient on its face, meaning that the evidence supporting it is adequate to establish the case until contradicted or overcome by other evidence.

PRO TANTO: For so much; as far as it goes. Often used in eminent domain cases when a property owner receives partial payment for his land without prejudice to his right to bring suit for the full amount he claims his land to be worth.

QUANTUM MERUIT: As much as he deserves. Refers to recovery based on the doctrine of unjust enrichment in those cases in which a party has rendered valuable services or furnished materials that were accepted and enjoyed by another under circumstances that would reasonably notify the recipient that the rendering party expected to be paid. In essence, the law implies a contract to pay the reasonable value of the services or materials furnished.

QUASI: Almost like; as if; nearly. This term is essentially used to signify that one subject or thing is almost analogous to another but that material differences between them do exist. For example, a quasi-criminal proceeding is one that is not strictly criminal but shares enough of the same characteristics to require some of the same safeguards (e.g., procedural due process must be followed in a parole hearing).

QUID PRO QUO: Something for something. In contract law, the consideration, something of value, passed between the parties to render the contract binding.

RES GESTAE: Things done; in evidence law, this principle justifies the admission of a statement that would otherwise be hearsay when it is made so closely to the event in question as to be said to be a part of it, or with such spontaneity as not to have the possibility of falsehood.

RES IPSA LOQUITUR: The thing speaks for itself. This doctrine gives rise to a rebuttable presumption of negligence when the instrumentality causing the injury was within the exclusive control of the defendant, and the injury was one that does not normally occur unless a person has been negligent.

RES JUDICATA: A matter adjudged. Doctrine which provides that once a court of competent jurisdiction has rendered a final judgment or decree on the merits, that judgment or decree is conclusive upon the parties to the case and prevents them from engaging in any other litigation on the points and issues determined therein.

RESPONDEAT SUPERIOR: Let the master reply. This doctrine holds the master liable for the wrongful acts of his servant (or the principal for his agent) in those cases in which the servant (or agent) was acting within the scope of his authority at the time of the injury.

STARE DECISIS: To stand by or adhere to that which has been decided. The common law doctrine of stare decisis attempts to give security and certainty to the law by following the policy that once a principle of law as applicable to a certain set of facts has been set forth in a decision, it forms a precedent which will subsequently be followed, even though a different decision might be made were it the first time the question had arisen. Of course, stare decisis is not an inviolable principle and is departed from in instances where there is good cause (e.g., considerations of public policy led the Supreme Court to disregard prior decisions sanctioning segregation).

SUPRA: Above. A word referring a reader to an earlier part of a book.

ULTRA VIRES: Beyond the power. This phrase is most commonly used to refer to actions taken by a corporation that are beyond the power or legal authority of the corporation.

Addendum of French Derivatives

IN PAIS: Not pursuant to legal proceedings.

CHATTEL: Tangible personal property.

CY PRES: Doctrine permitting courts to apply trust funds to purposes not expressed in the trust but necessary to carry out the settlor's intent.

PER AUTRE VIE: For another's life; during another's life. In property law, an estate may be granted that will terminate upon the death of someone other than the grantee.

PROFIT A PRENDRE: A license to remove minerals or other produce from land.

VOIR DIRE: Process of questioning jurors as to their predispositions about the case or parties to a proceeding in order to identify those jurors displaying bias or prejudice.

Casenote® Legal Briefs